i found it
on the internet

i found it on the internet

coming of age online

second edition

FRANCES JACOBSON HARRIS

AMERICAN LIBRARY ASSOCIATION
Chicago 2011

FRANCES JACOBSON HARRIS is the librarian at University Laboratory High School, University of Illinois at Urbana-Champaign, and is professor of library administration, University Library. She team-teaches a required computer literacy course sequence for eighth- and ninth-grade students that includes information-literacy and Internet-ethics components. Harris is the author of many articles and presents frequently on topics related to young adults, Internet ethics, and digital information. She earned her master's degree in library and information science at the University of Denver.

Printed in the United States of America

15 14 13 12 11   5 4 3 2 1

While extensive effort has gone into ensuring the reliability of the information in this book, the publisher makes no warranty, express or implied, with respect to the material contained herein.

ISBN-13: 978-0-8389-1066-5

Library of Congress Cataloging-in-Publication Data
Harris, Frances Jacobson.
 I found it on the Internet : coming of age online / Frances Jacobson Harris. -- 2nd ed.
     p. cm.
 Includes bibliographical references and index.
 ISBN 978-0-8389-1066-5 (alk. paper)
 1. Libraries and teenagers. 2. Internet and teenagers. 3. Internet in school libraries. 4. Internet--Social aspects. 5. Internet--Moral and ethical aspects. 6. Information retrieval. 7. Information literacy--Study and teaching. 8. Libraries and the Internet. 9. Information technology--Social aspects. I. Title.
 Z718.5.H38 2011
 025.04--dc22   2010013644

Book cover and text design in Andika Basic and Charis SIL by Karen Sheets de Gracia.
Cover illustration ©Piko72/Shutterstock, Inc.

⊚ This paper meets the requirements of ANSI/NISO Z39.48-1992 (Permanence of Paper).

ALA Editions also publishes its books in a variety of electronic formats. For more information, visit the ALA Store at www.alastore.ala.org and select eEditions.

CONTENTS

PREFACE

Back in the fall of 1987, during my first week on the job at the University of Illinois at Urbana-Champaign's University Laboratory High School, two boys climbed out of a library window onto our aged second-floor balcony and proceeded to bombard the students below with water from their high-powered squirt guns. At that time the library had one computer, which we booted up from a cassette tape player. It connected us to a regional union catalog that students searched using a command line interface to find books in our library. Today, our students are just as likely to bombard one another with barbed digital missives as they are with water. In the library, they now have access to multiple full-service computer workstations, all with high-speed Internet access and links to a wide variety of user-friendly catalogs and databases. Clearly, many things are different now than they were in 1987 (or 1967 or 1947, for that matter). Our tools and systems have changed dramatically. But other things are not so different. The teenagers who use the tools and systems are still teenagers.

As a school librarian for more than twenty years and an academic librarian for eight years prior to that, I have seen many exciting developments in information and communication technologies. I have also seen how teenagers alter their modus operandi as a result of growing up with ever-evolving new technologies. The first edition of this book, published just a few years ago, makes no mention of the social media technologies that permeate today's digital world. Unfortunately, the popular press focuses a good deal of attention on problems that arise from teens' use of social media, including their eagerness to expose their personal lives online and the ease with which they can access and share all manner of digital content. But the attention paid to these high-profile issues misses the point by oversimplifying the complex issues that are involved. In my experience, teens' personal, social, and intellectual development is now inextricably tied to developments in the wider worlds of communication and information technologies. We cannot stop or even slow down these changes. Instead, it is essential to acknowledge their impact and try to understand the ways in which the full range of youth experience is affected by them.

I have also come to believe that the impact of digital technologies is more complex than the pervasive focus on generational differences would imply. It is no longer terribly helpful to reduce our analyses of technology integration to differences in how technology is used by adults, teens, or Generations A, B, and C. Teens are not equally adept at (or even interested in) all forms of new technology. Socioeconomic and cultural factors also influence levels of engagement. Perhaps one generalization that *can* be made is that age does drive expectations and assumptions about technology. For this generation and the generations to come, digital connectivity is part of the landscape of life. By virtue of its very ubiquity, technology itself has ceased to be the important factor. Instead, it is the activity—what young people are *doing* with the technology—that defines the experience. Rather than speaking in terms of generational differences, it makes more sense to look at teens' activities and relationships, with an eye toward how technology might influence or shape those.

For these reasons, I prefer to think of young people's use of technology and media in ecological terms because the activities and their tools are so interconnected. Findings from the large-scale ethnographic project Kids' Informal Learning with Digital Media, funded by the John D. and Catherine T. MacArthur Foundation, reveal that young people's use of digital media is both friendship-driven and interest-driven (Ito et al. 2010). Teens' levels of engagement are defined along a continuum of practice that ranges from "hanging out," to "messing around," to the more invested "geeking out," depending on individual interest in a given media activity. The researchers found this construct to be more meaningful than trying to categorize their subjects' activity using quantitative variables like media type, frequency of media use, or demographic categories such as gender, age, or socioeconomic status. By focusing on personal relationships and levels of investment, the findings are more reflective of technical, social, and cultural patterns. Findings also acknowledge ways in which "different youth at different times possess varying levels of technology and media-related expertise, interest, and motivation" (Ito et al. 2010, 36). In other words, the researchers recognize teens as differentiated individuals with personal agency. As someone who works with teens on a daily basis, I find this perspective from the academy refreshing.

How do libraries and librarians fit into this picture? As institutions, libraries have not stood still in response to the technology tidal wave. The library used to mean "The Library"—a physical structure, a place to store books, a destination that enabled a specified set of activities (reading, research) and required certain behaviors (quiet, respect). Almost all the information within it had been vetted and selected. Teaching library use was a matter of explaining the organization of resources and the various search protocols and rules. Now, in an information world that seems anarchic, the instructional work of a librarian is part Sherlock Holmes and part Indiana Jones. Where we used to point out the differences between magazines and journals, we must now also teach that there is a difference between fraudulence and honesty, between mindless ranting and erudite punditry. Only then can we begin to talk about such traditional nuances as the differences between self-publishing, editorial review, and peer review.

Librarians are also becoming ethicists, counselors, and activity coordinators. The increased confluence of information and communication technologies has permanently altered the nature of a career once focused primarily on information organization and retrieval activities. Teens use the technologies as much for personal development as for the purposes intended by their inventors. As youth librarians, we need to understand that supporting such exploration is part of our jobs. We are in a unique position to heed the negative ways teens choose to use the technology at their disposal as well as the unpleasant experiences they may endure at the hands of others who wield that technology. It is no longer sufficient to teach our well-worn lessons on intellectual property rights and plagiarism. Now we must also educate students to protect themselves online as well as to become responsible users of information and communication technologies.

This book examines the significance of coming of age in a world in which access to online information and communication tools is a fact of everyday life. I explore the impact of this phenomenon and what it means to librarians and teachers, addressing thorny underlying issues in ways that I hope will help us think not only about *what* we do but also *why* we do it and where we want to go next. How can we situate libraries as active partners in this developing ecosystem? We have already come a long way. Our professional literature is replete with how-to manuals for teaching with technology and running technology-based libraries. But we still must come to terms with the way kids perceive the world as a result of growing up with digital technology. By listening to teens and learning from their perspectives, we stand a much better chance of embedding core library services and systems into their digital-media ecologies. In turn, one of the most important things we can do as professionals is to continue modeling and teaching what we know. As librarians and educators, we are in a position to provide the kind of direction and structure that teenagers need to navigate some pretty murky waters. We will succeed by working *with* teens rather than *for* them (or even despite them), as partners and collaborators in retooling and invigorating our vision of library services for the future.

ACKNOWLEDGMENTS

There are many people to thank when it comes to the preparation of a book. I cannot begin to name all those who have had a hand in helping me with this endeavor. So let me just say thank you, in the loudest possible voice, to the individuals who have been so generous with their time and thoughts. I would like to deliver particular words of thanks to the following folks:

The students of University Laboratory High School, without whom there would be no book. Thank you for your insights, your generous responses to my questions, your insatiable curiosity, and your never-ending ability to make me laugh. I have learned more from you than I can say.

The teachers at Uni High, for their collaboration and for allowing me to play with their classes. Special thanks to ultra–good sports Billy Vaughn, Steve Rayburn, Janet Morford, and Suzanne Linder.

The staff at my library—Runelle Shriver and graduate assistants Corinne Hatcher, Jenny Snow, Natalie Sapkarov, and Julia Burns—for supporting our students, teachers, and me as I slogged through the second edition of this book.

My personal learning network for all the tweeting, blogging, networking, and continuous support that I cannot imagine doing without. You know who you are!

My sons, Daniel and Simon, now well into adulthood, for sharing their hindsight (and present sight), putting up with my stories, and giving me their moral support.

My husband, Mitch, my dance partner for life.

PART ONE

today's landscape

1
teenagers and the library

Teenagers and libraries. These are two words that are not often used in the same sentence, least of all by teens. Libraries are not cool places. Only losers hang out in them. The people who work there are unfriendly and unhelpful. Libraries do not have enough technology. They need to provide better books and magazines. Libraries have too many restrictive rules and fees. Libraries are more like morgues than like places you want to be.

How did we come to deserve such a bad rap? We pride ourselves on our collections, carefully assembled to support curricular and independent learning needs. We buy popular fiction, subscribe to trendy magazines, and organize activities to encourage reading and to support the social and emotional needs of our users. We make interlibrary loan services available and work with our counterparts in other types of libraries—school, public, and academic—to enlarge the information world for teens. Unfortunately, though, we have not always been completely successful in our delivery of these services.

Despite professional guides and standards and our good intentions, libraries do not have a great track record when it comes to welcoming teenagers. Mary K. Chelton (1999) found that school librarians actually spend a relatively small proportion of their time on information service encounters. Instead, "service" often signifies rote activities—such as helping with equipment—that have nothing to do with real human interaction and can be performed by staff with less education and training. Most distressing, the substance of most student-library staff interactions is enforcement related, being "directed toward traffic control, compliance with the district-mandated pass system, and conformance with behavioral rules" (106). Chelton concludes that teens remember more about how they were treated in the library than they do about the specific outcome of the visit.

Teenagers have long been marginalized in the public library setting as well, relegated to a "problem patron" category all their own (Chelton 2001, 2002). Yes, teenagers arrive in hordes when school is dismissed, appearing to use the library only as a place to socialize until dinnertime. During those few hours, many of them create havoc with the equipment and disturb "legitimate" library patrons. In one controversial case, New Jersey's Maplewood Memorial Library closed its two buildings on weekdays from 2:45 p.m. to 5 p.m. after failing to find a way to manage the daily influx of rowdy middle schoolers (Kelley 2007). Chelton reminds us that adolescence is a distinct developmental stage of life, characterized by social learning. A teenager's "work" is to challenge authority, to find a balance between what one is told to do and what one wants to do, and above all to learn how to be a communicator in order to build social relationships and feelings of belonging (Grinter and Palen 2002). Library staff, however, often seem to expect learning in the library to be a solitary pursuit. Interactivity should occur only with library resources or staff. Chelton argues that this prevailing attitude "flies in the face of one of the most important maturation processes of adolescence, namely, social competence" (2002, 27). Her view is reflected in the widely cited Search Institute's list of "40 Developmental Assets for Adolescents," which includes interpersonal and cultural competence and confirms the importance of community involvement in the raising of a child (Search Institute, 1997, 2007).

Teenagers have personal as well as academic needs that ought to be met by library services. Up to 60 percent of a typical midsized public library's users are under the age of eighteen (Walter 2003). The teenagers among these young users are in the library to do homework and research but also to check out CDs, to read magazines, and to see and be seen. Librarians do not need to compromise their professional standards or personal values to accommodate teenagers. Teens are better served when librarians simply employ the same courtesies that they would use when working with adults. For example, Chelton (1999) witnessed school library staff asking students questions like "What do you need?" Although there is nothing technically wrong with this question, as phrased it rings out like a challenge. The emphasis is on the "you," on the inherent other-ness of the new arrival. Chelton suggests simple adjustments in tone and language to indicate respect and caring, such as asking "Hello, how can I help?" The emphasis is then on the "I," the implication being that the institution and the staff exist to serve the new arrival. Besides alterations in verbal tone, there are nonverbal ways to indicate welcoming and to instill a sense of belonging. Libraries can create social spaces for teens. They can purchase overstuffed chairs as easily as straight-backed ones. The collection can be built to reflect teen interests. Library staff can even reach beyond their personal expertise to create a welcoming environment. The Queens Library in New York City chose to use its financial resources to hire youth counselors rather than security guards (Shell 2008; O'Connor 2008). The counselors' job is to create programming and engage teenagers when they are in the library. Instead of receiving regular visits from the police to break up fights, library staff has seen circulation skyrocket.

Failure to follow through with appropriate service to teenagers is only part of the story. Even without the sting of insensitive or inadequate treatment, teens are still unlikely to want to spend much time in libraries. Loertscher and Woolls (2002) ask some tough questions in their overview of the research on teenage users of libraries. What do we know about when and why teens use libraries? Do teens regard libraries as an essential service in their lives? Do teens feel that the library, even a "perfect" one, is important to them? Loertscher and Woolls speculate that the paucity of research on this topic is because scholars already know what they would discover, what the library's ratings would be. "Even if we limited our questioning to 'things in school that help me succeed,' would the school or public library rank in the top five?" (31). The authors are doubtful.

Libraries are places that can easily induce feelings of inadequacy in adults as well as teenagers. One is supposed to know how to use libraries, supposed to hunger for the knowledge all those books represent. The teenagers who do not go to the library on a regular basis may avoid it because of the "supposed-to" factor as well as the hostile reception they have received in the past. Any efforts to make amends have met with less than outright success, in part because teens' primary experience with libraries is in the context of schooling, of information needs that are imposed by others.

THE IMPOSED QUERY

Melissa Gross (2006) has developed an intriguing line of research on the "imposed query," information seeking that is externally imposed rather than self-generated. The imposed query, in and of itself, is not a bad thing. We often very much want to find the thing we have been asked to find. But for a young person, the imposed query is often linked with unhappy circumstances—homework, a difficult teacher, a weekend with no free time. And it follows that libraries are often associated with the unpleasantness of imposed queries. Libraries become places to look for information other people want you to find, not for information that you yourself find intrinsically compelling or valuable.

Interestingly, Gross found that younger children ask a preponderance of self-generated questions in the school library, but that older children (upper-level elementary) primarily ask imposed questions. Again, our good intentions as educators seem to go awry. If imposed queries rule the day, what has happened to the notion that true education begins with the curiosity of the learner? The importance of inquiry-based learning was first articulated by John Dewey (1902, 1915), and its value continues to be widely recognized and discussed (Stripling 2003; Aulls and Shore 2008). But in practice, we seem to be actually killing the instinct to satisfy natural curiosity in the library. Extrapolating from Gross's research, one can assume that the imposed query phenomenon continues to escalate through the teenage years. So even in the best, most teenager-friendly library, teens are bound to approach the library with caution, even attitude.

EVERYDAY LIFE INFORMATION SEEKING

What about the everyday "stuff" that people need to find out? The self-generated query? Contemporary researchers now study "everyday life information seeking" (ELIS), a relatively new branch of information studies (Savolainen 1995; Spink and Cole 2001). There is a difference in how people go about meeting everyday life information needs and how they approach information needs that are associated with occupational or school-related contexts.

> In occupational or school information seeking, the user is seeking information in a controlled environment with a definite end product that has some sort of paradigmatic quality to it. ELIS, on the other hand, is fluid, depending on the motivation, education, and other characteristics of the multitude of ordinary people seeking information for a multitude of aspects of everyday life. (Spink and Cole 2001, 301)

Can library information systems cope with the unpredictable demands of everyday life information needs? It is easy to make the case that there has always been a disconnect in how library users, teenagers included, have viewed "library" information as opposed to "real" information, the kind of information that is necessary for managing one's everyday life. For example, I think it is unlikely that my mother would call the library for help with a recipe, even though the library's shelves are stocked with cookbooks. She would call a friend first. And the typical teenager working on a car is much more inclined to seek information from a friend, a relative, the local garage, or Google before checking the auto mechanics collection at the library. When information needs are more deeply personal, such as when lesbian and gay teenagers first begin the process of self-recognition, libraries are not likely to be on the radar. In these cases, questioning teens turn to sources like online message boards and chat rooms, the "queer" section of the local bookstore, and positive stories about gay public figures (Mehra and Braquet 2007).

It is true that the library is full of people using cookbooks, auto mechanics guides, and even books about the coming-out experience. The two information realms are not mutually exclusive. But they tend to be used in different ways. My mother might go to the library in advance of an event to browse cookbooks and get ideas for recipes. But in the heat of battle, when a vital ingredient is missing or the cake is not rising the way it should, other information resources may be more appropriate. For many sound reasons, teenagers and adults have always used and will continue to use informal, nonlibrary information networks for immediate, everyday life information needs.

FORMAL VERSUS INFORMAL INFORMATION SYSTEMS

I have discussed two basic motivations for seeking information: the imposed query and everyday life information seeking. Such divergent needs require different types of information-retrieval environments: formal systems and informal systems. Formal information systems are intended for the finite, definable scope of occupational and school information seeking. Library catalogs, databases, and their companions are examples of formal information systems. By contrast, informal information systems are generally context-specific, varying widely in appearance and manifestation. The local barber shop may host an informal information system, as does the bulletin board in the college student union. Today's world offers online versions of these informal information systems, packaged with liberal doses of advice and opinion. For example, Amazon helps users find books (and other products) but also provides user-generated book reviews. Such networks generally have formal attributes (e.g., search functions and topical hierarchies), but they respond to everyday life, context-dependent information problems.

Brenda Dervin (1976) identifies several false assumptions that information professionals hold about user information needs. One of these assumptions is that information is acquired only through formal information systems. In fact, people generally report that their use of formal systems is low. Even highly educated individuals rely heavily on interpersonal sources like friends and colleagues. Dervin disagrees with our professional habit of labeling this behavior a symptom of the "law of least effort" in the acquisition of information. Instead, she points to another faulty assumption—that "objective" information is the only valuable information. Users need information that is both objective (i.e., factual, datalike) as well as interpretive, contextual, and subjective, such as the information provided by so many of today's web-based services. Angie's List (www.angieslist.com), which provides consumer reviews of contractors, and "recommender" communities like eOpinions.com are examples of thriving information resources that provide other than "objective" information. In sum, to satisfy both types of information needs, we require both formal and informal information systems and services.

Formal Information Systems

Formal information systems are developed to be consulted and queried in purposeful ways, meaning that users must have some idea of what they need to know. This last phrase sounds facile, but anyone who has worked with teenagers (or other information seekers, for that matter) has learned that this knowledge of the destination cannot be assumed. Formal systems are designed in top-down fashion by experts who use highly defined rules for classification and retrieval. The rules may or may not be fully understood by users but are the key to successful information retrieval. Users must take some responsibility for learning an information system's attributes, adapting their queries to match the system's functionality. Formal systems, though ordered and generally intended for universal access, are not perfect. Their boundaries and characteristics often elude users, who then have difficulty translating their information needs into forms that can be processed by the system.

We are surrounded by formal information-retrieval systems in modern society, not just in the library. The yellow pages of the telephone book are organized by topic and provide cross-references that guide users to system-defined categories. Users must be able to navigate the alphabet, follow hierarchical subdivisions, and produce alternative terminology when cross-references are not adequately supplied. Hospital directories are fairly simple formal systems, typically listing doctors and departments by specialty and possibly offering an alphabetical name index. Still, the consumer looking for an ear, nose, and throat specialist may need to know to consult the directory under "otolaryngology."

Informal Information Systems

Informal information-retrieval systems generally evolve from the bottom up rather than the top down, emerging directly from the community of users. The local barbershop clique forms over time, relying on the participants themselves to be information providers. In such cases, users do not search so much as they share. When consulting informal sources of information, users (wittingly or unwittingly) acquire auxiliary information. The teenager who visits a local mechanic for advice also discovers what the garage smells like and which tools the mechanic actually uses on the job. My mother, in consulting a friend, finds out how a finished dish should feel to the touch and what happens if one ingredient is substituted for another. The young lesbian hears the confidence in the voice of an "out" teacher at her school's Gay-Straight Alliance meeting. Informal information seeking also encompasses habits of information consumption, such as reading a daily newspaper or having the radio playing while going about one's household chores.

In the informal environment, information often comes to the user rather than the other way around. When we open the daily paper, read the day's dose of blogs, or check our Twitter feed, following various links embedded in the entries (and then hyperlinking in serendipitous ways from those), we are not so much looking for specific information as we are letting information come to us. We then filter this information through the perspective of our current needs and interests, some of which may not have even reached our consciousness. Finally, formal information systems can be used as informal systems. People search library catalogs, but they also browse the shelves and select materials they might not otherwise have thought to look for.

Teenagers: Formal or Informal?

Where do teenagers fit into this formal-informal information-systems picture? Most research on adolescent information seeking has been applied to the imposed query environment, whether the object of that searching has been traditional formal information systems or newer, electronic systems (Neuman 2003). Although it continues to be important to understand teens' information use in the context of formal learning, there is little research that describes teenagers' self-directed information needs (Walter 2003). We do not know much about what teens search for and why, although some researchers have looked at specific topics of teen interest like health and sexuality (Burek Pierce 2007; Mehra and Braquet 2007). It certainly appears that formal information systems are losing out with the teen audience. Teens generally use them only when required to, in the context of the imposed query. At the same time, it is not entirely apparent that teenagers differentiate clearly between informal and formal information environments.

Dresang (1999) opines that "researchers have not been accustomed to studying competent youth in serious yet informal information-seeking situations, largely because such situations have rarely existed" (1124). Her view is that we need a new paradigm for studying teenagers' productive informal information-seeking behavior in today's nonhierarchical, matrixlike information environment. Some are responding to this challenge by developing models for studying teen information behavior (Fisher et al. 2007; Hughes-Hassell and Agosto 2007). Although it seems self-evident that teenagers overwhelmingly favor informal systems, how they use those systems may be much more purposeful than has previously been understood.

THE LIBRARY VERSUS THE INTERNET

Because of its association with formal school learning, the library is typically regarded as a land of formal information seeking. True, people go to the public library to find a good book to read, keep up with financial news, work on their résumés, or use the copier machine. But when it comes to finding Information-with-a-capital-*I* for imposed query situations, the library is what comes to mind. However, the times are changing. For everyday life information needs, and increasingly for imposed query information needs, many people—adults, teenagers, and children—are going elsewhere. And where is that elsewhere? These days, elsewhere seems to be the Internet, which has become both a boon to library service and a source of competition.

Is the Internet part of the formal information world or the informal information world? People tend to think of the Internet as an informal information system, perhaps because intermediaries (e.g., the library and librarians) are not required, so individuals are in control of their own search processes. But the reality is more complex than that. The Internet is a multifaceted global information system made up of interconnected local, national, and international computer networks and their associated services. Each service has a different technical structure and functional application, which gives it formal or informal information-retrieval attributes. The World Wide Web ("the Web") is but one of those Internet services, albeit the most ubiquitous one. Therefore, when people refer to "the Internet," they often mean "the Web." The Web itself is home to formal and informal information systems, as will be discussed in the next chapter.

The Internet is generally an excellent vehicle for everyday life information seeking. Its content and access tools are fluid, ever-expanding, and infinitely variable. Inquirers can use the Internet to quickly find answers to highly specific, arcane, or personal questions. The library, on the other hand, has highly structured information systems, which make it seem plodding and inflexible. On the surface, the library primarily provides an information function, while the Internet does many things. The Internet is both the end and the means because of its nature as a system of systems, an überproductivity tool that allows consumers to manage their banking, catalog and store their personal photos, and shop without ever leaving home. The Internet has extraordinary value as a communications tool. E-mail, still the "killer app" of the Internet, remains its most-used online tool (Pew Internet and American Life Project 2009). Searching for information is the first runner-up to e-mail, followed by activities ranging from checking the weather to making travel reservations.

In the Internet environment, communication and information-retrieval functions are increasingly indistinct. Students e-mail documents to themselves, taking notes in one window while reading source material in another, instant messaging all the while. Consider the plethora of "Ask an Expert" services that are available online, which personalize high-quality content using communication channels. There is no library counterpart except for chat reference service, which came along relatively late in online communication history.

The Internet is an open medium. It enables content producers as well as individuals to publish information without the services of intermediaries. In the read/write Web 2.0 environment, no editors, publishers, vendors, or catalogers are required to vet the information, reshape it, or contextualize it. Clearly, the Internet has profoundly changed the shape of the information landscape. Users flock to it because of its multiple attributes and its one-stop-shopping reputation. In an imaginary popularity contest, the Internet would certainly beat out the library, even in cases when the Internet may not be the most appropriate destination. But the competition is an artificial one because, for many reasons that will be addressed in this book, the two choices are not truly opposing ones. In fact, one is often a vehicle for the other, with the lines so blurred that users are not even aware of the true origin of the information they are accessing. At the same time, it cannot be denied that the Internet "side" is winning the teenage market. Let's take a look at how that battle is going.

Teenagers and the Internet

How do teenagers use the Internet as an information resource? Among the most prolific and reliable sources of information on how Americans use the Internet are the reports and presentations produced by the Pew Internet and American Life Project (www.pewinternet.org). Pew researchers report that though teens use the Internet for research, they are more likely than their older counterparts to seek entertainment through online videos, games, and virtual worlds; to download music; to read and write blogs; and to use social networking sites to stay in touch with friends (Jones and Fox 2009). Unfortunately, the Pew project has not really taken a hard look at how online teens use the Internet to do research for school since 2001, when data revealed a usage rate of 94 percent for this purpose (Lenhart, Rainie, and Lewis 2001). Of the teens surveyed, 71 percent report relying mostly on the Internet for their most recent big school project, 24 percent rely mostly on the library, and 4 percent use both equally. Reasons cited for online use were the Internet's ease, speed, and accessibility. Teens also use the Internet for conducting research on personal interests, from fashion and music news to more sensitive topics that call for privacy while searching. The Pew report on college students (Jones 2002) shows an even greater disparity between Internet and library use, with 73 percent using the Internet more than the library for research and only 9 percent reporting that they use the library more than the Internet.

For the conclusions reached as well as the questions *not* investigated, the Pew project's various reports are potentially frustrating for librarians. For example, in the report on teenagers, the teens do not seem to have been asked *which* Internet resources they were using for school research. Were they perhaps sometimes using subscription databases, which are web-delivered resources provided by the library? Students seldom differentiate among Internet resources to such a fine degree, especially when access is transparent and they can connect remotely.

The Pew report on college students (Jones 2002) is more explicit than the report on teens about the use of specific resources. However, the report is potentially more damaging to librarian egos. The researchers found that though academic resources are offered online, most students either do not know how to find them or have not been shown how to. The students are much more likely to go to commercial search engines to type in their research queries, using library computers primarily for web surfing, checking e-mail, and instant messaging. The study notes that "college students seem to rely on information seeking habits formed prior to arriving at college" (13), a finding that has interesting implications for school librarians. Yet the profession must be doing something right. The young adults of Generation Y (ages eighteen to approximately thirty) are the most likely to say they will use libraries in the future when they encounter information problems, with 40 percent saying they would do so compared with 20 percent of those above age thirty (Estabrook, Witt, and Rainie 2007).

A False Choice

At first glance, it looks like libraries are losing on two fronts. We are losing our traditional customers, the ones who would come in to use the formal information systems for which we have been the gatekeepers. And we are losing, or lost long ago, those who are engaged in everyday life information seeking. In this book I try to present the case that the situation is not nearly so simplistic. We are not facing an either-the-library-or-the-Internet dichotomy, a future in which the choices belong to either the Luddites or the technonerds. The Internet is now in the library, and the library is in the Internet. The card catalog, *Readers' Guide,* and their descendants have migrated to a web environment. Librarians have dumped their vertical files in favor of links on their web pages. Reference sources are available both online and in print form.

The art of searching for information is evolving as well. Most users have not really grasped the distinction between the *visible* Web (searchable by standard web search engines) and the *invisible* Web (resources that are hidden behind subscription databases or other secondary search interfaces). They are more likely to search the invisible Web while in the library, where licensing agreements are transparent and skilled staff are present to assist. At the same time, everyday life information seeking is becoming more purposeful now that the Internet has made a body of "published" everyday life information available and search engines have provided a means of searching it. The Pew reports have documented levels and types of searching activity—the what—but have not really plumbed the why and the how. It is up to information scientists to follow up. Some trends, though, are clear. For teenagers, the really essential difference between the notions of "Internet" (visible or invisible) and "library" is the Internet's unique ability to facilitate communication and connection to others. For teenagers, information is nothing without communication, interactivity, and the opportunity for direct engagement with content.

INFORMATION AND COMMUNICATION TECHNOLOGY (ICT)

If communication is so important, how does it fit in with "information," as libraries know and provide it? "Information" has a different meaning for information professionals than it has for information consumers, particularly teenagers. Dervin (1976) spoke of this difference in terms of the "functional units" of information systems. For the library, the functional unit might be a book or a document or a website. For the individual, the functional unit is generally a communication transaction, or, as Dervin puts it, "responses, instructions, reinforcements, solutions, answers, ideas, companionships, assistances wherever and however they may be found" (331). In other words, librarians conceptualize their services differently than their customers do. From the user's perspective, communication properties are key to successful information-seeking experiences. Without them, information remains inert, devoid of usefulness.

Dervin developed this line of thought in the 1970s, long before the Internet as we know it was even imagined. But the functional units remain essentially the same today because they are made of the same building blocks: human knowledge and human communication. The difference now is the ubiquity of today's information technologies, which makes the lines between information and communication blur almost beyond distinction. It is becoming difficult, even artificial, to speak about one without the other. In response, we now think in terms of *information and communication technology* (ICT) as a framework, or, even more broadly, *social technology,* which more concisely captures the notion of sharing as a defining characteristic. I will define these in some detail in chapter 3.

How does ICT look in the lives of teenagers? Is there a difference between Dervin's 1970s model and today's highly connected world? In pre-Internet days, when students wanted to compare notes, work together on homework, or share secrets, they whispered together in the library, met at each others' houses after school, or called each other on the phone. They also passed notes in class, wrote letters to pen pals, and kept diaries. Teens used formal information systems, primarily in the library, for school-based research projects. In today's world, teenagers have much more technology at their disposal. They use both formal and informal information systems for school-based research, at the library and elsewhere. They communicate using landline and cell phones, handheld devices, and communications software. They send instant messages and e-mail, they maintain social network profiles on sites such as Facebook and MySpace, post to online forums, and share digital music. They have embraced the Web 2.0 credo that invites content *creation* as well as access to content.

With the availability of so much information and communication technology, these ought to be halcyon days in the library for teenagers. And yet, for a variety of reasons, libraries almost always have some prohibitions against the use of technology for communication purposes. These are important times to remember Chelton's admonition that social interaction among teenagers is developmentally appropriate, even necessary, and has a place in the library. Information and communication technologies are ideally suited to facilitate that development, just as much as teen spaces and study rooms in libraries do.

Making It Happen

In the conclusion of their book *Teens and Libraries: Getting It Right,* Walter and Meyers (2003) make a number of promises to teens on behalf of public libraries. One of these promises is that librarians will be adult professionals in all dealings with teens. This pledge means that librarians will respect teens by doing good work, by giving directions and advice but not being rigid or prescriptive, by providing structure and boundaries that promote development, and by having high expectations of them. This promise also means that librarians will simply be themselves, and not try to measure up to some (possibly ridiculous-looking) coolness factor. Librarians do not have to be cool themselves to provide cool library services.

Another promise Walter and Meyers make is that librarians will work *with* teens, not *for* them. This pledge has to do with shaping services that teenagers can own, that are informed by their habits and needs, and that they have had a voice in creating. Adolescence is characterized by a need to feel one can influence the world. Libraries can give teens an important opportunity to make a difference, to contribute to their communities, and to engage in meaningful participation. And everyone wins. By bringing their verve and insight to the library, teenagers have the power to make it cool in ways that librarians simply cannot.

But first things first. Let's go back to the beginning and look at how libraries and their information systems affect teen users.

2

information-
retrieval systems:
for better or for worse

A student of ours once ordered a book about the shipping tycoon Aristotle Onassis through interlibrary loan. I did not think this book was really what he wanted, because his history class was studying ancient Greece. When he came to pick it up, I asked him what his topic was. "Oh," he said, "it's Socrates," which he pronounced "So-crats." Restraining myself from smiling, I checked the cataloging-in-publication data on the back of the title page to see how a search on "Socrates" retrieved a book about Aristotle Onassis. It turns out that "Socrates" was Onassis's middle name (which may explain something about the kind of person he became). The combination of my student's lack of background knowledge and his propensity to use keyword searching was his undoing.

Libraries used to be less-complicated places than they are now. At least, the options for finding information in them were more finite. We used three basic tools to unlock their treasures: the card catalog, a few periodical indexes, and the reference collection. A few others—such as the vertical file, a regional union catalog, other specialized indexes, and maybe a community resource file—were also at hand but played less-prominent roles. These were the bread-and-butter tools librarians used and taught teenagers to use. Reliable warhorses, they worked reasonably well for conventional school assignments—the animal reports, the term papers on the death penalty, the maps for geography lessons.

Libraries are now densely populated with a variety of formal and informal information-retrieval systems, which teenagers find both a help and a hindrance. In this chapter, I will take a look at how teenagers use a variety of information-retrieval systems, how they select and evaluate the material they find, and how the interactive/communicative properties of information systems might affect teens' information-seeking experiences.

FORMAL INFORMATION-RETRIEVAL SYSTEMS

Organization Challenges

Formal information systems contribute to teenagers' not-always-positive attitudes toward libraries. Yet formal systems, both old and new, are also at the core of what has always defined libraries and made them work. Reconciling the disconnect between teenagers and formal information-retrieval systems is essential if libraries as institutions are to survive through the next century.

Library information-retrieval systems such as catalogs, periodical indexes, and other information databases may be the ultimate expression of formal information-retrieval systems. Levy (2001) put it this way: "Because of the scope of their enterprise, libraries have been forced to develop highly systematic methods of organization—methods that could work relatively satisfactorily for huge numbers of works, and that could transcend the skills and knowledge of particular individuals" (123). To maintain these methods of organization, elaborate profession-wide decision-making structures have evolved to govern cataloging practices. A goodly portion of this governance is devoted to subject access, an especially problematic area of cataloging because it relies on the vagaries of human linguistic interpretation. The Cataloging and Classification Section (CCS) of the Association for Library Collections and Technical Services, itself a division of the American Library Association (ALA), is the home of many committees and task forces charged with establishing and maintaining metadata structure and subject cataloging standards. The CCS works with other ALA committees, with representatives from the Library of Congress (LC), and with the H. W. Wilson Company, which publishes the *Sears List of Subject Headings.*

Consider these examples of the care and consideration taken by various entities involved in the establishment of American cataloging practices. In 1999, the CCS Subject Analysis Committee's Task Force on Library of Congress Subject Heading Revisions Relating to the Poor People's Policy was charged to review and make recommendations on thirty-three proposals for new and revised Library of Congress subject headings that described poor people. This task force produced a forty-eight-page report detailing the extensive discussion the committee members held regarding bias in subject headings (Association for Library Collections and Technical Services n.d.). On a more practical but no less complex level, in 2003 the Subcommittee on Subject Reference Structures in Automated Systems submitted a twenty-page report of "recommendations for providing access to, display of, navigation within and among, and modifications of existing practice regarding subject reference structures in automated systems" (Association for Library Collections and Technical Services 2003). It is important to note that these examples relate only to subject access in library catalogs. Similar intellectual effort is expended by a wide range of organizations, companies, and researchers in designing retrieval systems for other types of information repositories. Indexing and abstracting are disciplines in and of themselves. Clearly, no small amount of energy and focused intelligence has been devoted to refining and improving the formal information-retrieval systems we use.

Yet, with all the earnest effort these various initiatives and mechanisms represent, standard library information-retrieval systems are difficult for many people to use, particularly young people. Why is this? To be a successful searcher, and not just a lucky one, the user needs some understanding of the structure of a system before using it. The characteristics of formal information systems that seem to be especially tricky for users fall into three general categories:

Abstraction: A representation of the real thing
Vocabulary: Whose? And how much?
Classification: A book can only be shelved in one spot

Abstraction: A Representation of the Real Thing

Any catalog, database, or index is, by definition, an abstraction of the content it seeks to describe. A bibliographic system can be searched only by the metadata—the data about the data—that have been designed to represent the contents of the real thing. The contents of an entire book are represented by three, perhaps four subject headings. A magazine article is much shorter than a book, yet receives the same degree of representation. The user must therefore determine the appropriate level of abstraction (or specificity) for a search. If my goal is to find a recipe for marble chocolate cake in a cookbook, my search term will have to be broader than "marble chocolate cake," probably something like "cake." Much as I would prefer to think otherwise, it is unlikely that someone has written an entire book on marble chocolate cake—which is what a successful search on that topic in a catalog would signify. Understanding how the formal information-retrieval system is structured, I will know that individual recipes in cookbooks are not assigned their own subject headings. On the other hand, I may have some luck searching on "marble chocolate cake" in a periodical database. This is an example of the mental shifting that must occur—the user has to consider the degree to which specific pieces of information are represented in information-retrieval systems and how a subject might fit within a topical hierarchy.

To further confuse matters, formal systems now come in multiple flavors. In addition to the abstract bibliographic representation type, we have access to full-text systems and, more commonly, to hybrid systems in which both bibliographic and full-text information can be searched. Full-text searching means searching the real thing, not an abstraction or representation of it. But there are problems associated with such robust information retrieval. Here is what happened when I searched on the term "running" in a major periodical database of the hybrid type. The system defaults, as most do, to a keyword search, which encompasses the bibliographic record (title, author, subject headings, etc.) and the abstract. Karen Hunt calls this dependence on keyword searching the "tyranny of keyword searching"—deceptively easy for users to employ but ultimately unsatisfying in delivery (2006). Sure enough, using this default search, I retrieved 81,964 items, which varied from articles about people running for political office to articles about athletes running marathon races. My term generally popped up in the abstract field of these results, and less often in the subject field. When I restricted my search to the subject heading field, I retrieved 3,726 articles, all on the subject of running as a physical activity. When I chose the option of searching only the full text of the articles, I retrieved 524,086 hits. Searching the full text may be searching the real thing, but the price of high recall is pretty poor precision.

It can be difficult for users to fathom why their searches either work or do not work. Although formal information-retrieval systems cannot yet provide truly personalized feedback, many now employ automated "clustering" techniques to help users refocus their searches. These methods find text similarities within search results and display the subject terms (or even a link to the clustered results) that appear most frequently. My initial keyword search on "running" elicited a list of such subject terms, with an invitation to use them for narrowing the original set of results. Unfortunately, my list was not very helpful, as it included the names of political candidates and such seemingly random terms as "Computer scheduling" and "Leg—muscles." There were no suggested terms related to the physical act of running. I would have benefited from system feedback that told me instead to "click here to see the results of your search, this time using 'running' as a 'subject term search.'" Something like this happens if a user finds a relevant article in the results list, clicks on it, and acts on the resulting "Find more like this" link that is often supplied—or knows enough to notice and click on the appropriate subject term in the bibliographic record.

Without search results differentiating between subject headings and keywords, decent results are often buried in the midst of other, not-as-relevant hits. Naive users often resort to improving their searches through trial and error, a process that reinforces the feeling that "library searching" is a hit-or-miss affair. The ability to search both bibliographic information and full text is a wonderful thing, but users still need to understand the underlying structure of a system to obtain meaningful search results. I have seen search-savvy students do an end run around the online catalog by constructing their subject searches in the more forgiving Google

Books search (http://books.google.com) and then, armed with a list of book titles, searching by title in the online catalog.

Vocabulary: Whose? And How Much?

What do I look under? "Latinos" or "Hispanics"? "Movies" or "motion pictures"? "Chinese art" or "art, Chinese"? Controlled vocabulary is the tool that is used by formal information-retrieval systems to standardize terminology, ensuring consistency and stability throughout the system. Cataloging rules and conventions establish subject term structure, such as how subheadings are ordered. But even as these techniques solve problems, they also present difficulties for users. For the virtues of consistency and stability, we must accept a certain degree of inflexibility. Natural language gets translated into terms that can become awkward and, in some cases, archaic or offensive. The user must therefore be the more flexible partner in this relationship. If there is no cross-reference from "ear, nose, and throat" to "otolaryngology," the user must be prepared with an alternative terminology to test. The vocabulary problem is even more challenging for young users, who may not have the domain knowledge that can generate such alternatives. Abbas (2005) compared middle schoolers' research questions with their self-selected search terms as well as with the controlled vocabulary used in a digital library designed for middle school children. She found enough gaps in terms used across these three areas to conclude that the digital library's index terms were neither adequate nor age appropriate, and she suggests investigating the potential of using students' search terms to develop more age-appropriate controlled vocabularies.

The structure of subject headings can be hard for nonlibrarians to fathom. A student looking for books about African Americans and their participation in the Civil War will need to use this Library of Congress subject heading: "United States -- History -- Civil War, 1861–1865 -- Participation, African American -- Juvenile literature." The two key concepts are buried at the third and fourth levels of the string of headings. Commas instead of double dashes are used in two of the subdivisions. Our student could conduct a keyword search on "Civil War" (and even add "African Americans") but in a library of any size will retrieve far too many irrelevant hits. Pauline Cochrane (1986), in her text on improving Library of Congress subject headings for use in automated catalogs, suggests that subdivision coding be permuted (i.e., subject subdivisions be coded individually) for greater flexibility in retrieval. In describing preliminary discussions held at the Library of Congress about how this task might be accomplished, she reports: "Since the logic behind the [subject heading] string's construction is lost on most catalog users and some catalogers, a worksheet was devised to guide the cataloger who would analyze a work and assign subject headings in parts or 'elements.' These parts would then be available for computer manipulation to construct headings for catalog cards and for computer-based catalogs, with varying display options" (62).

Although this particular proposal did not move beyond the discussion phase, it is now being addressed through the development of faceted syntax in information-retrieval systems. Anderson and Hofmann describe facets as "fundamental categories, aspects, or 'faces' of phenomena similar to the journalist's 'who, what, where, when, why'" (2006, 8). Every term has the potential to become a main heading, with all the other terms in the string associated with it. OCLC is applying facets to the catalog environment through a subject-access system called FAST (Faceted Application of Subject Terminology), derived from Library of Congress Subject Headings (Jin 2008). The chief difference is the flexibility FAST affords the headings in combining them so they function more like keywords. So if our student searches on "Civil War" *and* on "African Americans" with the FAST implementation in place, a relevant results list is much more likely.

Cataloger Sanford Berman is perhaps the library field's most persistent (and sometimes controversial) voice for subject cataloging reform. In terms of cataloging for teenagers (1987), he identifies two major weaknesses in contemporary cataloging practice: the choice of vocabulary used for Library of Congress subject headings and the LC's stinginess in assigning headings. In his view, LC vocabulary is stilted and, at the time he was writing, rife with terms teens did not use. His examples include the LC's choices of "Adolescent boys" instead of "Teenage boys," "Teen-age marriage" (with the awkward hyphen) instead of "Teenage marriage," and "Youth" instead of "Teenagers." Many of his recommendations for changes have come to pass. The clinical term "Adolescence" is now reserved to describe books about child development. "Teenager" has finally become an official subject heading, though older records in many libraries' catalogs continue to bear the earlier terms. This duality, in which different materials on the same subject can be found under old as well as new terms, is another source of confusion for library users who are trying to make sense of the system.

Berman (1987) also views the sheer paucity of headings assigned to each record as being a huge problem for teenage library users. Fiction has only sporadically been assigned subject headings, which is a shame given the number of issue-oriented novels written for the teen audience. How would a teenager find a novel that features an anorexic protagonist if looking up "anorexia" yielded no fiction? For nonfiction, Berman criticizes the Library of Congress for assigning so few headings to each record. As an example, he uses the cataloging record for Elaine Landau's book *Different Drummer: Homosexuality in America* (1986), which was given the sole subject heading of "Homosexuality" by the Library of Congress. By contrast, the Hennepin County (Minnesota) Public Library, Berman's home library at the time, supplied eight subject headings: "Homophobia -- United States," "Gay teenagers," "Gay teenagers -- Interviews," "Gay teenagers -- Family relationships," "Lesbian teenagers," "Lesbian teenagers -- Interviews," "Lesbian teenagers -- Family relationships," and "AIDS."

Berman (1984) also needles the Library of Congress for its humorlessness, which he sees as part of the general rigidity of the institution's modus operandi. The book *Should You Shut Your Eyes When You Kiss? or, How to Survive "The Best Years of Your Life"* (Wallace 1983) is a sarcastic, tongue-in-cheek "survival guide" for teenagers. The following advice for navigating school cafeteria food is typical of the book's overall tone: "Go for food that was made somewhere else and brought in, sealed. Like milk, ice cream bars, potato chips. The next safest stuff is cold: sandwiches, coleslaw. Stay away from hot food except vegetables (but who wants to eat vegetables anyway?)" (23). The LC subject headings for this book are "Youth -- Life skills guides," "Students -- Life skills guides," and "Youth -- Family relationships." Although the author most likely intended a serious message to seep through, the book is written in a wholly satiric manner. The Hennepin County Library's subject headings for this book included "Teenagers -- Life skills guides -- Parodies" and "Teenagers -- Family relationships -- Humor."

Progress has been made since Berman wrote about subject cataloging for teenagers in 1987. "Gay teenagers" is now a Library of Congress subject heading. But change is slow. In the preface to the 1993 edition of his 1971 book, *Prejudices and Antipathies: A Tract on the LC Subject Heads*

Concerning People, Berman is pleased to report that some of his original recommendations have become reality. However, he notes that it took thirteen years for the Library of Congress to finally abolish "Jewish question" and eighteen to get rid of "Yellow Peril." He laments the rate at which the Library of Congress addresses reform and societal change. Indeed, efforts continue. In the late spring of 2008, the blog *Radical Reference* held a "Library of Congress Subject Heading Suggestion Blog-a-Thon" (http://radicalreference.info/lcsh/2008/blog-a-thon). Readers suggested subject headings and cross-references, which were then compiled and sent to the Library of Congress. Suggestions, with accompanying documentation and justification, included such terms as "Female sex organs" (rather than "Generative organs, female"), "Folksonomy," and "Bollywood films."

Even when headings change, individual libraries may or may not be equipped to retrofit their catalogs to reflect the changes. Thus, some books will still be found under "Homosexuality" while others will be found under "Gay teenagers." To the user, how can this not seem like a conspiracy to make things more difficult than they need to be? And some headings never change. I know how much my students are confused, and sometimes even offended, by the subdivision "Juvenile literature." They do not think of themselves as "juveniles."

I do not mean to single out the Library of Congress's subject cataloging practices as being particularly inadequate or uniquely odd. Most information-retrieval systems that use a controlled vocabulary are guilty of similar idiosyncrasies. In my search for information on teenagers' information-seeking behaviors and their uses of catalogs in the H. W. Wilson database *Library Literature,* headings were few in number (one to three per article) and similarly broad. In some cases, the headings were so broad as to be almost meaningless: "Microcomputers -- Children's Use," "Internet -- School Libraries," "End-user Searching -- Case Studies." Who still uses the term *microcomputers*? The 1,000-odd hits I retrieved from this search were far from all being on the topic I was actually interested in.

It is probably more equitable to scrutinize the complexity of formal information retrieval by comparing the way a topic is treated across different systems. Budd (1996) conducted an interesting experiment with the literary criticism term "reader-response criticism," which has alternate terminology in the field and is used somewhat inconsistently. His study compared the results of a search on the heading in the Library of Congress database to the citations in a bibliography from a highly regarded book on the topic. There was little overlap, with only three of the titles from the bibliography turning up on the list of 245 titles retrieved from the Library of Congress search. Of those 245 titles, many were not in English,

GUESSING GAME

Sometimes there seems to be a certain level of absurdity, even surrealism, in many of the Library of Congress subject headings we see. Try this guessing game. Which of the following are (or have been) genuine Library of Congress subject headings? The answers are printed at the end of the exercise.

Afro-American women in motion pictures

Booby traps

Cookery (Apples) -- Juvenile literature

Drive-by shootings

Education of princesses

Empty nesters

Freight-cars on truck trailers

Garbage can models of decision making

Internet addiction

Lesbian nuns

Milk as food

Poor teenagers -- United States -- History -- Twentieth century

Prostitutes' customers

Rednecks

Road rage

School shootings

Spin doctors

Virtual pets

Zorro television programs

ANSWER: IF YOU ANSWERED YES TO ALL, YOU WIN! ALL OF THESE HEADINGS ARE OR HAVE BEEN LEGITIMATE LIBRARY OF CONGRESS SUBJECT HEADINGS.

and many others were practical treatments of the theory not addressed by the bibliography.

Budd found more overlap when comparing the bibliography to the *Modern Language Association Bibliography*'s search results, though more than half of the books retrieved in the *MLA Bibliography* search were still not included in the Library of Congress results. When that half of the books were checked in the LC catalog, along with the missing titles from the book bibliography, Budd found that LC subject headings other than "Reader-response criticism" were used. Most of those headings were anchored by the word "Literature" and were typically quite broad (e.g., "Literature -- History and criticism -- Theory, etc."). These vague headings would not be of much use to someone looking for books on reader-response criticism.

What conclusions can be drawn from this experiment? Because the coverage of the *MLA Bibliography* is literature, its headings are granular and faceted. Library of Congress headings, on the other hand, cover a world of knowledge and are selected by catalogers who are not subject specialists of the same order as those who do the indexing for specialized databases. Budd observes that the questionable benefits of large results sets generated by such broad terms as "Literature -- History and criticism" are not worth the loss in the precision and relevance of those results. He concludes that "perhaps it is unrealistic to expect a structured resource, like a library's catalog, to be equipped to impose order on all complex inquiries" (Budd 1996, 115). He recommends, as a partial solution, increasing the number of subject access points. The results of Budd's experiment make it easy to understand the importance of the informal "invisible college" used by scholars and academics. As Case (2002) notes, "All kinds of scientists and scholars satisfy much of their information needs through contact with their colleagues in the workplace and at conferences" (238), and not through the catalogs and databases provided by libraries.

Classification: A Book Can Only Be Shelved in One Spot

Finally, we have the problem of classification. If it can be argued that there are not enough subject access points in a catalog, how can users be limited by a single classification designation? A shelver emerged from our library's stacks one day in a state of extreme frustration. "Books on countries are in at least three different places!" she exclaimed. She was right, of course. Books on the history of a country are in one section and books on "description and travel" in that country are in another section. Books on the economy of the country, on women in the country, on the music or art or literature of the country—all are given different classification numbers, which disperses them throughout the collection. Even books on seemingly narrow topics can be found in multiple physical locations. Budd found that the books on reader-response criticism were scattered among several Library of Congress call number areas.

Yet we know that users, both novice and expert, browse the shelves as a means of finding the information they want. And librarians have long taught the principles of classification systems and have posted Dewey decimal charts, in part to facilitate productive and serendipitous browsing. Once a user determines which call numbers are likely to yield success, those sections of the stacks become destinations. It could be said that Dewey classification, like Library of Congress subject classification, is a legacy system, reflecting similarly dated sensibilities. Unless a library reclassifies books as Dewey rules change, users might find books on the same topic in multiple locations. One option is to abandon Dewey classification altogether. The Phoenix, Arizona, Maricopa County Library District took this approach when it opened its Perry branch in 2007, organizing the shelves like a bookstore to facilitate browsing (Oder 2007). LibraryThing (www.librarything.com), a web-based open social cataloging system, initiated a public library–focused project called "Open Shelves Classification," a free, open-source, collaboratively written replacement for the proprietary Dewey decimal system (Spalding 2008). Though not suitable for all library settings, efforts like these might have the potential to enhance the browsing experience and make classification more reflective of the way a contemporary teenager thinks.

Searching Challenges

So what does happen when young people interact with formal information-retrieval systems? As mentioned earlier, the user must be the more flexible partner in this relationship. Formal systems are what they are. They can be changed, but to maintain the integrity of the system, they are not designed to change rapidly. The real question is how the user adapts his or her behavior to the demands of formal systems. We know more than we used to about children's and teenagers' search experiences, although

Walter (2003) points out that we still do not know much about their information needs. More research has probably been done on children's use of information systems than on teenagers' use of them. However, much of the research on children's use of online catalogs has relevance to the teenage (and maybe the adult) population.

The decade of the 1990s was a period of some rather intense research into children's use of library catalogs. It was important work, because research on this topic had previously focused primarily on adult users, and catalogs had always been designed with the adult user in mind. Moore and St. George (1991) found that children had trouble generating alternative search terms and would give up their searches rather than try again with new terms. Solomon (1993, 1994) divided children's catalog search failures into three types: (1) idiosyncrasies of the software, (2) the characteristics of Library of Congress subject headings, and (3) the skills of the users. I find it telling that two out of these three types of failures are related to the structural characteristics of formal information-retrieval systems and only one type of failure has to do with user attributes.

Searching Library Catalogs and Other Formal Systems

Solomon and others discovered access methods that were more suited to children's needs and abilities (Solomon 1993, 1994; Moore and St. George 1991; Raaijmakers and Schiffrin 1992). For example, children, even more than adults, are better at recognition tasks than at recall tasks. They can often recognize what they need when presented with a list of choices but are unable to produce information from memory without a prompting context. This recognition factor is why most people typically perform better on multiple choice or matching tests than on fill-in-the-blank tests.

In the information-retrieval environment, recognition skills mean that young users can identify terms they want from a list of terms as well as select alternative terms they might not otherwise have thought of. But coming up with terms without such a list is a much more difficult task. Similarly, teens and adults would benefit from browsable displays of pre-coordinated subject-heading strings, which show the true range and availability of topics in a way that keyword searching cannot replicate (Mann 2003). Children also do well with graphical displays of subject hierarchies because the hierarchies prompt recognition and can be populated with topics that are familiar to children (Walter and Borgman 1991; Borgman et al. 1995).

Hirsh (1999) found that students put much stock in the information provided in catalog notes fields in order to determine relevance. This is an important finding given how many catalog records do not contain data in that field. As Berman suggests, the more information a catalog record can provide, the better. Drabenstott, Simcox, and Fenton (1999) studied children's and adults' understanding of subdivided Library of Congress subject headings and made some interesting observations as well. Their empirical research supported Cochrane's recommendation to break up long subdivided headings because the logic of the order is confusing to users and does not increase their understanding. They also suggested that heavy users of catalogs—children, adults, and reference librarians—be involved in the establishment of new subject headings and subdivisions. Finally, they recommended that the punctuation between subject heading elements be reexamined. Users simply do not understand the logic of the ordered, double-hyphen convention.

Much of the research described above, particularly that conducted by Paul Solomon and the Science Library Catalog group at UCLA (Walter and Borgman 1991; Borgman et al. 1995), was very influential in the development of the commercial product called Kid's Catalog (Busey and Doerr 1993). Now called KCWeb (www.tlcdelivers.com), this software provides children with multiple modes of searching that meet the needs of different developmental levels. Users can search by keyword, explore a subject hierarchy of Dewey-inspired categories, or look through an alphabetical list of popular topic links. However, as important as the catalog research of the 1990s and the development of the Kid's Catalog were, this progress must be viewed in perspective. The focus-group data from the Science Library Catalog research revealed something that most of us know but are reluctant to acknowledge. The library catalog—in either card or electronic form—was always a resource of last resort for these kids. Their first choice was to browse the shelves, their second choice was to ask for help, and their third and always last choice was to use a catalog. It is probably safe to assume that in today's environment, kids would simply prefer to use the Internet.

Catalogs are not the only type of formal information-retrieval system that presents difficulties for young users. Databases, indexes, and electronic reference tools all present similar challenges. In her summary of the research literature on this topic, Branch (2002) noted that "novice searchers lack the ability to form effective search plans and queries, cope with searching obstacles, [and] assess, refine and select results and synthesize data" (14). Most of the participants in Branch's study did not use advanced features, preferred using a single search strategy, and became frustrated when they did not get the results they expected. Hirsh (1999) produced similar findings in her study of fifth-graders who became discouraged when their results did not match what they were expecting to see. Some of the students in this study were unclear about the contents of the periodical database they used, thinking it indexed books rather than magazine articles. At the high school and college levels, we often see this misconception in reverse, with students assuming that the catalog doubles as a periodical index. In actuality, the catalog may provide access to the titles (i.e., the library's holdings) of periodicals but not to their contents. Both situations demonstrate that the ability to formulate viable search strategies is only part of the equation. Students also need to have good mental models of the structure of the resources they are searching.

Affective Factors and Searching

How students feel about their task and about their own progress as they move through the search process influences their ability to be effective searchers. Branch and Hirsh both drew on the work of Kuhlthau, whose "Information Search Process Model" (Kuhlthau 1997, 2004) takes into account the critical role of the affective aspects of searching. The origin of the search task is also bound to have an impact on students' feelings about the task, as Melissa Gross learned in her imposed query research. Clearly, much of the research that young people do has been imposed by others, typically teachers in the context of schooling. This phenomenon may explain Walter's 2003 observation that we know very little about young people's own information needs. They never have a chance to express them!

Students' sense of ownership of a task will vary depending on the feelings and beliefs they have about their teachers and the level of understanding they have about the task. Gross also pointed out that "the query is in constant peril of mutation as it is passed along, transacted, and returned" (2006, 33). Parents frequently become involved in the research process, which results in a "double imposed query" situation (and possibly familial strife). These factors, which are unrelated to the nature and structure of formal information-retrieval systems, nevertheless have a profound impact on how young people use those systems.

What to Do?

Even the founders of our modern cataloging and classification systems acknowledged that no system could possibly be perfect. In terms of subject access, Charles Cutter (1876) declared: "No catalogue can exhibit all possible connections of thought. Enough if it exhibit the most common, and give some clew [sic] for tracing the rarer ones. Those that claim perfection for any system show that they have no idea of the difficulties to be overcome" (541). Melvil Dewey (1876) held a similar view of classification schemes: "The impossibility of making a satisfactory classification of all knowledge as preserved in books, has been appreciated from the first. . . . Theoretically, the division of every subject into just nine head[s] is absurd" (625).

I would add to the words of these sages that not even a psychic cataloger can predict how a book will eventually be used or regarded, even in terms of something so seemingly straightforward as its subject. Early child-care manuals, etiquette guides, and legal handbooks are later used to study social history, yet their subject access typically remains fixed as originally assigned. Exceptions occur when collections are cataloged at later dates. The "Historic American Sheet Music: 1850–1920" collection on the Library of Congress's American Memory website (http://memory.loc.gov/ammem/award97/ncdhtml) was cataloged as part of the digitization process by the holding library at Duke University. With the hindsight of late twentieth-century sensibilities, catalogers were able to develop a specialized thesaurus, which contains terms like "Legacies of Racism and Discrimination -- Afro-Americans." This heading was used to describe 362 pieces of sheet music, including songs with titles like "Go to Sleep, My Little Pickaninny" and "An Educated Coon Is Best of All." Had these items been cataloged at the time of their publication, the subject headings would certainly not have included the term *racism.*

If formal information-retrieval systems are so complex and counterintuitive, what can be done to improve them? That subject is fodder for another entire book; suffice it to say, there are many folks working on the problem. Federated search systems now allow users to enter a query that searches multiple resources—a solution that partially obviates users' confusion about the structure of the sources they are searching. For example, the University of Illinois at Urbana-Champaign Library catalog's "Easy Search" simultaneously retrieves results from the online catalog, a consortium catalog, a handful of e-book databases, a selection of multitopic periodical databases, and several web search engines (including Google Scholar). "Next generation" catalogs are gradually replacing legacy catalog systems. These new catalogs are characterized by faceting and clustering features, along with user-oriented, Web 2.0 enhancements that allow users to directly interact with bibliographic data in a number of ways. These capabilities are often managed through third-party vendors, whose systems allow relevance ranking of results, faceted navigation, and graphical word clouds that display clickable relevant terms from the results set. With such enhancements, even experienced researchers can discover relevant materials they had not previously found in their library catalogs (Olson 2007). Novice users and young people are provided with terms that prompt their recognition abilities. Researchers are even working on ways to effectively mix user-generated keyword tags with faceted classification schemes based on controlled vocabularies, providing searchers with the best of both worlds (Quintarelli, Resmini, and Rosati 2007).

Other catalog enhancements invite users to export records to personal information management tools, add comments about books, or even contribute their own tags to bibliographic records. The mission of the Toronto-based BiblioCommons Project (www.bibliocommons.com), which bills itself as "a social discovery system for libraries," focuses on the user's ability to add comments, tags, summaries, similar titles, personal lists, age suitability indicators, content notices, or quotations (Oder 2008). Readers can initiate their searches by referencing a user list like "Books I stayed up until 2:00 a.m. reading," checking the latest comments made by their favorite user-reviewer, or simply looking at a list of books recently returned to the library.

Next generation catalogs generally provide value-added content by linking bibliographic records to other resources. For example, the Hennepin County (Minnesota) Library catalog allows users to "preview" books in

Google Book search and provides tools users can install on home computers that display brief information about the library status of books or movies they find in Amazon, Barnes and Noble, and Netflix. Open-source systems from companies like Equinox Software (www.esilibrary.com) and LibLime (www.liblime.com) enable libraries to customize their software to take full advantage of NextGen options, rather than living by the boundaries set by traditional integrated library system vendors. Federated searching and next generation catalogs have the potential to help improve users' searching experiences, but further research is needed before we fully understand the efficacy of these innovations, particularly for young people.

INFORMAL INFORMATION-RETRIEVAL SYSTEMS

When discussing informal *systems* of information retrieval, the World Wide Web is the one environment worth a concentrated examination. Like the formal systems discussed already, the Web is intended for Searching-with-a-capital-S. And like other formal systems, the mechanisms for searching both help and hinder users.

Organization Challenges

It is hard to talk about the Web in terms of its organization when it is, as a whole, not an organized system. The Web is home to a great unwashed marketplace of ideas, a 24-7 information asylum that is open to all. The self-published information it hosts is not—in its totality—selected by anyone, nor is it cataloged according to the *Anglo-American Cataloguing Rules,* warehoused in a single location, or archived. Any of it may be modified at any time. There are no principles that guide the structure of the Web's information-retrieval tools, no Library of Congress catalogers, no American Library Association committees. To further confuse matters, the Web encompasses both formal and informal information-retrieval systems and resources. After all, the Web is where I consult the Library of Congress subject authority file and where I struggle with the subject headings in *Library Literature.* A large portion of what has become known as the invisible Web consists of the formal information-retrieval systems that reside on the Web—the proprietary databases and archives that are accessible only through their own search tools. But the visible Web is not well represented by these search tools. So how do people find what they want?

For all practical purposes, web searching began with Yahoo!—a subject directory service that employed human editors to index websites by topic within hierarchical categories. The web-searching field has since exploded. Search engines and subject directories abound, ungoverned by any centralized principle or authority. Furthermore, web search tools are generally commercial enterprises in competition with one another. They do not share their technical information or content, unless one search-engine company buys out another. The depth and breadth of the coverage of various search tools are difficult to assess because their systems are not open to public scrutiny.

Search-engine criteria for relevance determination vary widely, and change over time. Machines instead of people do the selecting (crawling) and indexing (ranking algorithms). Because human judgment is generally not directly involved, relevance criteria include not only word matching but also other factors that can be computer-calculated, such as the "link-to" frequency from other sites. "Sponsored" links, paid for by advertisers, generally appear at the tops of results lists, and paid placements can appear (unidentified) throughout lists. Imagine online catalog results that display "sponsored" titles first, followed by the most popular as well as the most relevant titles. The popularity index may actually not be a bad idea, but ad-peppered catalogs are unpleasant to imagine.

Web search tools come in some basic types:

Search engines: Search tools that retrieve websites by sending out automated "crawlers" to roam the Web and index pages. Results are ordered according to formulas that weigh search term placement and occurrence, links to a site from other major sites, popularity, and other factors.

Metasearch engines: Search engines that search several other search engines at one time.

Subject directories: Search tools in which human editors categorize websites into hierarchical, nested subject categories. Some subject directories are highly selective and specialized.

Internet portals: Gateways to the Web that offer several services, one of which is web searching. Commercial portals tend to focus on shopping, travel, and business-oriented activities.

These days, most search tools do not fall into "pure" types, and the field is in constant flux, with companies coming and going from the scene. A search engine may offer a subject directory service that is actually powered by an outside company. The reverse can also be true. For a time, Yahoo! originally a pure subject directory—used Google technology for its web-searching service. Search engines now support searching by type of information, such as images, government information, or file type. An interesting development in the subject directory world is the Open Directory Project (www.dmoz.org), a community-produced search directory with annotated links that are contributed by innumerable users and organized by thousands of volunteer editors. The Open Directory Project is open source, meaning its code can be shared and its structure and contents improved by the community. Individual users can import portions of it to a personal or school website, creating their own customizable index to the Web. Perhaps the greatest significance of this project is that now anyone can help index and organize the Web, in addition to contributing content.

I am only half joking by observing that the Open Directory Project represents the democratization of cataloging and information retrieval. But it really is only the beginning. For example, Google now offers a custom search-engine feature (www.google.com/coop/cse) that allows individuals (or librarians, teachers, or schools) to specify websites to be searched, while hosting the search box and results lists. Other user-centered enhancements, described in the following discussion of searching issues, give users much more control over the web search environment.

The web-searching field changes so fast that it is difficult for the average user to keep up. Services such as SearchEngineWatch.com and SearchEngineShowdown.com are devoted to evaluating search-engine performance, staying current on corporate buyouts in the sector, and reporting on cutting-edge technology and the other trends that can seem so dizzying to the rest of us.

Searching Challenges

Though web search tools seem easy to use, searching the Web effectively still requires some skill. The user must adapt his or her search strategies to fit the type of search tool that is used. Search engines are searched by keyword or phrase. Most search engines offer advanced features that enable users to focus their searches in a variety of ways, from specifying domain or file type to using Boolean operators. Subject directories are designed to be browsed, the user drilling down through hierarchical headings and viewing lists of related subtopics. However, most users tend to go straight for the search box, meaning they are actually using the search engines that general subject directories like Yahoo! provide. The results pages include links to the subject categories, so the user gets the best of both worlds (possibly without realizing it).

In teaching my students the differences between search tool types, I advise them to use a search engine when they are looking for something extremely specific (e.g., the name of the drummer of a rock band) and to use a subject directory when they are just "looking around" (e.g., exploring types of rap and hip-hop music). The pure subject directories, especially those that are highly selective or specialized, can be trickier to search because they index only the equivalent of bibliographic information—not the full content of each website. For example, ipl2: Information You Can Trust (http://ipl2.org), the result of a merger of the Internet Public Library (IPL) and the Librarians' Internet Index (LII), can be explored through a subject hierarchy, or users can type in search terms. But the terms are only matched against a bibliographic citation for each website plus a several-sentence description of the site. Users who expect search-engine-like results are inevitably disappointed.

Web searching is the "easy" way to find information, according to most teenagers. Any practicing librarian who has worked with teenagers for a significant length of time can report that the Internet has replaced the library's traditional finding tools as the primary tool for doing research for significant school projects. But how successful are teens' Internet searches? Searching the Web has been likened to "visiting a shopping mall the size of Seattle: Innumerable types of information, in a large variety of containers and in many different locations, are all available in one place" (Fidel et al. 1999, 24). The students in a study conducted by Fidel and her colleagues (1999) had little knowledge of how the Web worked, who put information on "it," and who "ran" it. Most seemed to think the Web was some sort of central repository.

Still, the students in this study approached web searching in a predictable pattern. Their searching was very goal-oriented. If they did not find the information they needed fairly quickly, they would switch to a different topic for the assignment. In other words, the students were focused on the requirements of the assignment, not on their interest in the particular topic. Right in line with Gross's (2006) imposed query theory, students scanned websites for the information that would "fill in the blanks" of the assignment (28). Their searching was "swift and flexible" (29). If one site did not have what they wanted, they would move on to another site. When all else failed, they would just start over, using new terms. All these behaviors are strikingly similar to the way we see teens search formal information-retrieval systems like catalogs and periodical databases.

Dresang (2005) reviewed the research on youth information-seeking behavior in the digital environment through the lens of her theory of "Radical Change," which is based on the digital-age principles of interactivity, connectivity, and access. The research generally points to the sorts of search deficits found by Fidel and her colleagues, that young people miss much of the richness of their information-saturated environments because of poorly developed information-seeking skills and a tendency (shared by adults) to take the easiest path possible. But she challenges us not to overlook "the new behaviors nurtured and facilitated by the digital environment and [not] to miss the golden nuggets embedded in these studies" (2005, 182). In particular, she highlights what the research has uncovered about the *social* nature of young people's information-seeking behavior and their interest in creating and collaborating in a digital environment—traits that exemplify the principles of interactivity and connectivity of the "Radical Change" model. The impact of these social attributes will be discussed in greater depth in chapter 4.

Many web search services now build in structures that support serendipitous discovery and sharing, such as the clustering algorithms that help users determine relevancy and refine their searches. Results pages now typically display both the traditional linear relevancy-based list of results as well as topical groupings of headings. Users are invited to narrow or expand searches by clicking on related terms within these lists of headings. Such prompts are available without requiring the user to find an advanced search page or type in newly constructed searches. At the content level, users can easily "push" the results of their search successes, utilizing the now-ubiquitous widgets supplied by Delicious, Diigo, Twitter, Facebook, and their counterparts. Some Web 2.0–style services take connectivity a step further by enabling users to take an active role in customizing their online experience. "Portal-generator" tools like iGoogle, Pageflakes, and NetVibes allow users to design a personal web environment, customizing their search experiences and harnessing the serendipitous power of RSS feeds. By using feeds to subscribe to services that meet their general parameters of interest, information comes to users that they may not even realize they want. More will be said about such tools in chapter 8.

How much do teens actually use these types of web tools and affordances? It's hard to say. It does not help that blindingly rapid changes in tool availability and development make it a difficult phenomenon to study.

SELECTION AND EVALUATION CRITERIA

Formal Systems

How do young people typically select and evaluate information retrieved from formal systems? Selection and evaluation criteria are influenced by the nature of the information need, the cognitive ability, and the developmental level of the student. Is the reading level of the material appropriate for me or is it too advanced or technical? Do I need a lot of information or a little? Do I need a popular treatment or a scholarly one? Students are taught the differences between magazines and journals. They are told not to use the health information they find in *Glamour* magazine if an assignment calls for rigorous biological research literature. At the most sophisticated level, students are taught to spot political perspective and determine point of view.

What is the reality of student searching? Librarians express much angst over students' tendency to simply snatch up the first several citations of a results list, barely checking for relevance, let alone suitability or authority. We watch students take home a pile of books, then return all but one or two the next day. We wince as they print out articles we know they do not need, discarding the "extra" paper in fairly short order. When students display these behaviors, they may simply be following principles of least effort as they rush through an uninteresting assignment. Or perhaps these tactics are their way of responding to the information overload caused by the volume of information they encounter. As people find more and more information, and have decreasing amounts of time to process it, they resort to simpler and less-reliable rules for making selections (Case 2002). A "collect-then-discard" strategy may be the most effective and practical way for young people to master the problem of information overload.

The findings of Hirsh's study of fifth-graders' relevance criteria are intriguing (1999). Besides relying heavily on the notes field in the bibliographic record, they used visual and organizational cues to assess the utility of a source. These elements include the book cover, its title, the table of contents, and the back-of-the-book index. They determined relevance primarily by examining the text for topicality, relying heavily on the assignment's requirements (the imposed query). But students also placed a high value on personal-interest attributes, the novelty of the information (i.e., that it was new to them), and the material's potential for peer interest (because they were required to make a presentation to their classmates). As students moved through an assignment, they were less concerned about topicality in general and became more focused on filling in specific gaps in their research. During the selection process, they did not consider authoritativeness, accuracy, or truthfulness of information when assessing materials for relevance. For the most part, they appeared to trust the information they found, regardless of source, and did not even think to question its validity.

Hirsh makes a distinction in students' selection and evaluation behaviors based on the nature of their task. She argues that even imposed query tasks can be personally interesting to students. Motivated information seekers will spend more time poring over lists of results and evaluating the information they retrieve. She posits that because the students in her study found their topic (famous athletes) to be interesting, their search behavior differed from that of students in other studies. Hirsh found that most of the students in her study expressed ownership of their topics and demonstrated care in their examination of bibliographic data and the visual and organizational attributes of sources. Her findings undermine our notion of the stereotypical student researcher who rushes through a task to get it out of the way as quickly as possible.

How has the evaluation of information retrieved from the formal library "canon" of books, periodicals, and reference tools changed with the advent of the Internet? I believe that some of our previous care in teaching evaluation skills has fallen away. Instead, we have had to turn our attention to the vast wash of the Internet, focusing on teaching students to first look for information that is merely credible. "Merely credible" is not much to ask for, but it must be addressed. We know with absolute certainty that students will encounter websites developed by such "authorities" as conspiracy theorists and people with axes to grind. Nevertheless, the "old" selection and evaluation issues have not disappeared. There is still a difference between *Newsweek* and the *Bulletin of the Atomic Scientists,* between the local community newspaper and the *New York Times.* But with the bar set so low to accommodate the Internet, perhaps teaching about those distinctions is endangered.

The Web

Credibility assessment is one of the greatest challenges young people face when searching for information on the Web. Although the core criteria are essentially the same as when evaluating any type of information—particularly in the context of schooling—the complexities presented by the technologies definitely present new challenges (Flanagin and Metzger 2007). Typical indicators of credibility (e.g., publication in a highly regarded or well-known source) may not be present, or may even replaced by more "distributed" credibility indicators like hyperlinks, public comments, or ranking systems. So it is not surprising that one of the biggest complaints teachers and librarians have about students and the Internet is kids' apparent lack of discrimination among the Internet's many resources. Educators' fears are supported by the research, which Hirsh (1999) summarizes by noting that "students, from elementary school to high school, do little evaluating of the accuracy of the information they find on the Internet; they tend to assume that the information they find is true and valid" (1267). In the Fidel study (1999), the students (and, interestingly enough, their teacher) evaluated sites according to whether or not the information they needed for the assignment was present. In other words, they used the assignment as an evaluation filter rather than using criteria like the authority of the website creator or the reliability of the information.

Agosto (2002) looked at Simon's model of decision making in her study of adolescent girls and their evaluation of websites. She focused on Simon's concept of "satisficing" (1979), or how people tend to use practical boundaries to simplify their decision making. Because it is not realistic to weigh all outcomes and fully explore every possibility, people generally choose to settle for something that is acceptable, even though it might not be optimal. The practical boundaries that Agosto's teenage girls identified were time constraints, information overload, and physical constraints. Her analysis echoes Case's summary of the effects of information overload (2002). Agosto is more optimistic than those of us who assume that teenagers just make choices based on the principle of least effort. Her "good enough" principle assumes a process anchored in reasoned criteria, whereas the "principle of least effort" assumes no process at all.

Agosto also studied the effect of these girls' personal preferences on their decision making, seeing these as reflective of the affective piece of Kuhlthau's process model (2004). Agosto found that personal preference played a large role in the girls' evaluation of individual sites, which they judged based on graphical and multimedia elements as well as their level of personal interest in the subject. She notes that "many of the participants dismissed the Women of NASA site solely based on its background color" (26). I wonder if these girls would have been so quick to reject a site if it was one they identified for their own needs rather than one they were looking at for an outside researcher.

We do not really need research to tell us that teenagers are not always careful or reasoned evaluators of information they find on the Web. And this discussion has not even touched on how teens make choices in chat rooms, how they evaluate the credibility of web forum postings, and what they do with queries from unknown e-mail or instant-messaging correspondents. But to play the devil's advocate, I would suggest that as individual teenagers become full participants on the Internet scene—the more they create their own web content and participate in online communities—the more sophisticated their perspectives become. By jumping in as real players, it is inevitable that they improve their understanding of the Internet's structure and content. We already know that many teens are skeptical of the information they see on websites because, having developed web content themselves, they know how easy it is to publish online (Lenhart, Rainie, and Lewis 2001). In the act of contributing their own material, their comprehension of the nature of other online content deepens. However, the depth of this comprehension is open to debate. As an example, librarians and teachers frequently express concern over the credibility of the content on Wikipedia, the online encyclopedia anyone can edit. But for many young people (and for adults as well), the very nature of Wikipedia's collaborative construction and community regulation are the factors that lend it credibility. They are living in a world in which expertise is distributed in ways never before imagined. At the same time, I do take issue with the students I've had who swear by the authority of an entry because they authored or edited it themselves!

INTERACTIVE AND COMMUNICATIVE FACTORS

Does it make sense to think about formal information systems in terms of their communicative and interactive properties? Or are we talking about a read-only, one-way environment? Yes, one can write letters to the editor of a newspaper (online or in print), an activity that is both interactive and communicative. But are we stretching to come up with this one example? Perhaps we are using definitions of *communication* and *interactivity* that are too narrow. If formal information systems and resources themselves are not technically "interactive," the searching and selecting processes certainly are. And with the expanding functionality of next generation catalogs, Web 2.0 attributes are even penetrating legacy information systems.

Sometimes the interactivity occurs *around* the information activity. Hirsh (1999) found that the fifth-grade students in her study shared resources as they searched and did not hesitate to ask their school librarian for help. One student reported that a friend identified a source for him while this friend was doing his own searching. When asked about his search strategy, the student concluded that "I kind of found it on accident" (1270). Yet why should his find be considered accidental? This type of collaboration is also a strategy, one that can be encouraged and enabled. These students, their teacher, and their librarian were exploiting the attributes of the library-as-place, a physical space in which information sharing is natural.

Fidel and her colleagues (1999) found that when students used the Web, "searching was both a social and an academic event. They [the students] conversed with one another while searching, asking questions and giving advice" (28). These teenagers were also proactive about asking for help from the librarian and the teacher. I think it can be argued that communication is just as important a tool in information searching as is the understanding of information systems. The Web 2.0 response to this behavior is seen in the rise of "folksonomies" (user-applied metadata, commonly known as tagging), review/recommendation websites, and the like. Such tools help with credibility determination as well as with search and discovery. For example, many searchers manage their personal web information worlds by tagging favorite websites in social bookmarking services. Because tags and user lists are public and shared (and can even be subscribed to through RSS feeds), searchers can benefit from one another's selections. Highly regarded social bookmarking account holders, such as libraries, drive traffic toward specific websites, lending credibility to those sites. In the same way, highly ranked reviewers on Amazon or sellers on eBay are considered credible sources of information and services. In cases like these (and in the absence of traditional credibility markers), the "wisdom of the crowd" speaks to credibility, enabled by social information tools.

As was discussed in chapter 1, teenagers are social beings, and their information behaviors are characterized by sharing and communication. Web 2.0 tools, built on sharing and communication principles, can bridge the gap between formal and informal information systems. The challenge for us is to remove roadblocks to such tools in libraries and enable the naturally occurring communication and information-seeking processes to work.

3

information technology meets communication technology

W hat happens when digital information technologies and communication technologies come together? They become more than the sum of their parts. In merged form they have come to be called information and communication technologies, or ICTs—environments in which people use communication technology to access information, manipulate it, transform it, and exchange it. In his foreword to *Literacy in the Information Age,* Allan Luke places the communication role at center stage: "Digital information technologies are communications technologies, new modalities and media of human communications, nothing more and nothing less" (2003, x). By any definition, ICTs are social information spaces. They are designed as much for the reciprocal sharing of information as they are for seeking and disseminating information. "Seeking" implies going to sources outside one's immediate social system. Sharing involves exchanging information both inside and outside your own social group and signifies that you have as much to offer as you are likely to receive from others. ICTs can be bona fide communities with unique social norms and customs, just like other human communities. Finally, ICTs take on many forms, having evolved organically in response to a wide range of user needs.

Some ICT tools, such as instant messaging and e-mail, were originally designed for communication purposes. But users have turned them into information tools as well, making them full-blown ICTs. People insert web links into their messages, send pictures to one another, and share other types of information. As with so many tools of technology, users have changed the designers' original intentions simply by adapting the tools to their everyday habits and needs. Product developers have responded by adding features to enable these behaviors. In this fashion, technologies and their associated uses evolve over time.

With at least 93 percent of American youth online, today's teens are growing up in a world that assumes integration of ICT tools (Macgill 2007). Teenagers use ICTs for maintaining friendships and for establishing new ones. Evidence of this phenomenon is all around us. Several years ago, a group of students at my school began a collaborative blog that consisted primarily of the typical banter, gossip, and party planning one would expect. When these students graduated, the blog became a way for them to keep up with one another from a distance and to organize reunions during college breaks. Today, my current and former students use Facebook and other social network services for the same purpose. Teens and members of Generation Y (ages eighteen to thirty-two) are the most likely to use the Internet for entertainment purposes and for communicating with friends and family (Jones and Fox 2009). Teens lead in the use of instant messaging, with 68 percent of online teens sending instant messages compared to the two groups most likely to be their parents— Gen Xers (ages thirty-three to forty-four) at 38 percent and younger baby boomers (ages forty-five to fifty-four) at 28 percent (Jones and Fox 2009).

Social network sites, online games, video-sharing sites, and handheld devices are now fixtures of youth culture. Teens still use online media to extend friendships and interests, develop autonomy, and participate in peer-based, self-directed learning (Ito et al. 2009). They are also frontrunners in the use of social networks and online games. Sixty-five percent of online teens use social networks, compared to 36 percent of Gen Xers; 78 percent of online teens play online games, compared to 38 percent of Gen Xers (Jones and Fox 2009). It's no wonder that popular social network sites embed plenty of online-gaming opportunities.

Recreation and social interaction are not the sole motivators for being online. In 2007, 64 percent of teens engaged in content creation of some type, up from 57 percent in 2004 (Lenhart et al. 2007). They upload original work as well as remixed content in a variety of forms, from photos and videos to writing and art. The feedback they receive online naturally encourages them to continue posting their creative work. Teenagers' academic lives also incorporate the use of ICTs. They use the tools informally to share information about assignments, to study together, and to work on group projects. More formally, students may now be assigned to develop wikis instead of turning in papers, check their teachers' web pages for course updates, access library resources, and turn in homework online. Schools and colleges routinely use course management software that provides a self-contained environment for sharing information, depositing work, and hosting both synchronous and asynchronous discussion. Distance-education platforms have become robust, fully featured creatures, especially in comparison to their video-delivered predecessors.

ORGANIZATION OF ICTS

What are some of these information and communication technologies? What is their value as information resources? For purposes of the present discussion, I have categorized the various services somewhat arbitrarily based on type of activity and patterns of communication. My intention is to focus on those services that have the greatest influence on teenage life online. Therefore, I do not discuss every possible ICT that currently exists, and I spend more time describing some ICTs than others. Most possess characteristics of informal information systems. Finally, I have left the mention of a couple of services, such as online gaming and virtual worlds, for further exploration in chapter 4.

It hardly needs to be said that technology is a swiftly moving target. The individual tools and applications I describe here will change. Future services will no doubt aggregate their functions in different ways and otherwise morph into forms I cannot begin to imagine. Given these caveats, I offer the following three-pronged framework in which to discuss current ICT trends that are especially important in the lives of teenagers. My inspiration for this structure comes from Linda W. Braun's very lucid discussion of technology and literacy in her book *Teens, Technology, and Literacy; or, Why Bad Grammar Isn't Always Bad* (2007).

> **Messaging:** Instant messaging and chat services, text messaging, e-mail

> **Sharing:** Social network services, online media sharing services (e.g., peer-to-peer networks), collaborative work spaces (e.g., wikis), web forums, tagging, and RSS

> **Out There for the World:** Personal websites and other "display" spaces, blogs

Messaging encompasses conversation of all types and with all manner of devices, and it can occur between single individuals or among groups of individuals. *Sharing* connotes community building. Sharing technologies help people maintain relationships, build common interests, and exchange information. *Out there for the world* consists of technologies that allow us to display ourselves and our work.

These categories are rather arbitrary, because most of the services listed share characteristics and features across the spectrum. From a teen's perspective, these tools are not even thought of as "technology." Rather, a teen's focus is on the *activity* that the technology is enabling, whether talking to a friend, listening to music, or sharing one's artwork.

Messaging

Instant Messaging and Chat Services

Instant messaging (IM) is a synchronous form of communication in which users type back and forth to one another while both are online. Though conversations typically occur between just two people, users often have more than one conversation going on at a time. Instant messaging is accomplished through dedicated hosting services (AIM, MSN, Google, etc.), through clients that can vet multiple hosting services on one interface, within existing social networks such as Facebook, and as a feature of some e-mail clients. Most dedicated IM services include a chat function, in which multiple people can participate in the same conversation. Though users typically type messages using a keyboard, advances in technology now support messaging via texting, voice transmission (Voice over Internet Protocol), and even live video connection. Unless a user deliberately logs an IM conversation, its contents disappear when the participants close their windows or log out. Still, users can send links, images, and other content to one another. IM is an ephemeral medium by nature, and the contents of unsaved conversations cannot be searched or retrieved later.

Although instant messaging does not incorporate information searching per se, it does allow the placement of information "bread crumbs." Teens sort their buddy lists into a hierarchy that tells them, in order of importance, who is currently available. Away messages are often used as announcement centers: "I'll be at the mall all afternoon" or "cell: 256-4212." Friends know they can check each other's IM settings to get useful, timely information without ever picking up the phone. Instant-messenger profiles, as well as away messages, can be bloglike, containing a description of the author's state of mind, bits of poetry, quotes from saved IM conversations, or links to his or her personal web presence. IM users typically only "see" or speak to others who use the same IM service or software (e.g., AIM, MSN, Google Chat, Yahoo!), but they can also install clients capable of displaying IM accounts from multiple services (e.g., Meebo, Adium, Pidgin).

These few paragraphs hardly capture the importance of instant messaging in many teenagers' lives. If a snapshot could be taken of all the teenagers who are online at a single moment, the vast majority would have some type of IM application enabled. For a long time, IM was the "killer app" for teenagers, the epicenter of their online world.

Online chat, also synchronous, can be a web-based or software-based communication service. Chat spaces are often organized around specific agendas or purposes, such as the chat room components of online distance-education courses. People go to chat rooms to accomplish a task, discuss a topic of mutual interest, or just hang out. The role of chat is generally centered on communication rather than on information, and so the focus is on the relationship rather than the task. In some cases, the participants all know one another. In more public chat spaces, users do not know each other and have no way of determining if their fellow chatters are who they say they are. In general, the days of high interest in joining public chat rooms with unknown others is waning.

Conversations held in chat rooms are typically neither captured nor archived, so their content cannot be searched later. There are notable exceptions, such as the chat room conversations held by students in distance-education classes, which can be searched later by students who missed class or by teachers who wish to check on student participation levels. But in general, chat room conversations are fleeting, like ordinary face-to-face group conversation but without even the impression of people's faces and voices.

Text Messaging

Text messaging, or SMS (short message service), is a mobile-phone-based service for sending short messages (up to 160 characters). Though not technically a "real time" (synchronous) technology, messages are generally delivered within minutes. Users send messages from one mobile device to another, paying for messages based on the calling plan they have with their service providers. American teenagers quickly adopted text messaging in the late 1990s, as mobile-phone use became more ubiquitous and pricing structures began to accommodate SMS. Texting is ideal for quick communication that does not require an immediate response. It allows teens to connect during off hours or while on the go and to do so without attracting much attention. Because cell-phone keypads are so small and message length is limited, users typically abbreviate commonly used terms and phrases. Many teens become adept thumb typists and don't even need to look at the keypad.

Texting is the second most popular use for cell phones, right after using them to check the time (Pressler 2007). In many ways, texting has become the "new IM" in teens' lives because it affords so much flexibility. Many parents have been caught short when the phone bill arrives, not realizing how heavily their children use this feature. Cell-phone companies have scurried to add unlimited texting plans to their suite of products. They have also introduced plans that allow some level of parental control. Parents might be able to restrict which cell-phone numbers can be called and limit the times of day the phone can be used for texting, calling, or web surfing (Tedeschi 2008). Teens are a vital part of the cell-phone market, but it is generally their parents who pay the bills, a fact providers cannot afford to ignore.

E-mail

E-mail, an asynchronous form of communication, was one of the early drivers of the Internet. Its roots date back to the late 1960s with the development of ARPANET (Bruce 2002). Messages are sent from one device to another device, from one designated point to another designated point or points. In other words, e-mail messages are not broadcast to the world at large, to be picked up by recipients. A single message can be sent to multiple recipients, but the sender determines who the recipients are. E-mail has grown beyond its text-only beginnings. Graphical and web-based software allows users to embed links and graphics and to easily send file attachments. Because e-mail resides on individual computers and servers, it is not searchable in the same way that postings to message boards and newsgroups are. Individuals can generally search their own saved e-mail records, but not those of others. E-mail is the most private form of online communication, yet it plays a pivotal role in information exchange. As will be discussed later, teenagers are avid e-mail users, but they generally regard it as most useful for formal communication, or communication that can "wait."

Sharing

Social Network Services

Social network services (SNSs) are web services in which individuals can create a public or semipublic personal profile, define a list of other users with whom they share a connection, and view and traverse their list of connections and those made by others within the system (boyd and Ellison 2007). In effect, SNSs build and support online communities, facilitating connections among members. I was rather amazed to realize that the first edition of this book makes no mention of the phrase "social network." In the few short years since its publication, hardly an online teenager now lives without a presence on MySpace or Facebook, making me wonder what the next few years will bring. When I try to explain social network services to older relatives, I describe them as yearbooks on steroids. Beyond the photo and brief list of affiliations, SNSs are interactive and value-added. Depending on the service, invited "friends" can leave comments, "poke" each other, send virtual gifts, compare movie preferences, play online games, chat, and send private messages to one another. They can join networks of like-minded users, create photo and music galleries, and find old friends. They can post a current status (similar to use of the IM profile and away features) and—most important—view a rolling list of status changes among their friends.

Besides those services whose sole purpose is social networking, many web-based services have social networking features or attributes. These attributes are built on personal data generated by users. For example, the entry for *The Kite Runner,* by Khaled Hosseini, on Amazon has the following socially generated information: "Customers who bought this item also bought" book suggestions, a list of subject tags customers associate with the product, a graphical display of customer rankings of the book, customer reviews, rankings of customer reviewers, a discussion forum, and user-generated lists of related or recommended books. So where Facebook and MySpace are about friends' networks, sites like YouTube, Flickr, Last.fm (music), and even Amazon are primarily about media sharing or discovery. Socially generated information like this is increasingly common, so much so that it has become an expected part of the web experience—and another indicator of how formal library information systems appear to be increasingly anachronistic.

Teenagers have been heavy adopters of social network services. Currently, the two most popular networks are MySpace and Facebook, though their long-term prominence in the SNS arena is hardly assured. MySpace was an early attraction for teens, particularly with its focus on connecting music, bands, and fans. Rather than rejecting young users, MySpace changed its user agreement to allow minors (boyd and Ellison 2007). Teens could copy and paste HTML, personalizing their spaces. MySpace later became the focus of media attention around safety issues and sexual predation. Facebook had its roots in the higher-education community but later opened its doors to other users. Unlike MySpace, full Facebook profiles cannot be made open to nonmembers. Facebook also led the way in opening its doors to outside application developers. The huge variety of available "apps" allows users to customize their sites and engage in tasks such as tracking a pregnancy, growing a virtual plant, competing in virtual Scrabble, or comparing expertise about television sitcoms. Teens are not alone in their appreciation of social networks. Time spent on SNSs by all users has now surpassed time spent on e-mail, representing a major paradigm shift in how consumers interact with the

Internet (Wayne 2009). General search tools like Google even provide ways to include results from personal social networks. This information is already publicly available within defined social circles but can now be conveniently aggregated using connections from a user's public profiles.

Unlike online forums, which—as discussed below—are discussion communities centered on shared interests, SNSs are organized around *people* and their connections. The focus is on relationships rather than on information.

Online Media Sharing Services

Web 2.0 has revolutionized the way we think about artistry and entertainment. Although passive media watching and listening are still activities enjoyed by many, consumers now interact with their media by commenting on it, ranking it, and sharing it. A mini industry has developed to support this culture of sharing. Hosting sites need only to embed the widgets, or tools, provided by these intermediaries to enable their users to share content with a single click (see figure 3.1). Indeed, the sharing phenomenon has challenged traditional marketing practices and notions of commercial success. A video on YouTube can achieve "viral" status overnight, without its producers spending a dime on advertising. Instead, producers supply the tags and other metadata, users share links across their personal networks, and a new star is born. The rub is that users are rather fickle. Their attention needs to be captured in order to trigger the desired cycle of events. Sometimes the feedback loop can have unintended consequences,

Figure 3.1

Sample screen showing the variety of icons used for sharing content through different social media sites.

as in those unfortunate instances when a video goes viral because its subject has become an object of public ridicule. This type of occurrence will be discussed in greater detail in chapter 5.

Teens have always shared music; technology-based solutions have certainly facilitated that passion. Peer-to-peer (P2P) file sharing is a mode of information exchange in which computer users with the same networking software can access files on one another's hard drives, without the use of a central server. Unfortunately, peer-to-peer sharing has earned most of its media attention for the illegal exchange of copyrighted media and software, and it can also expose personal computers to virus and other "malware" attacks. Devices like MP3 players make sharing fairly straightforward and less risky than peer-to-peer file sharing. Fans also use e-mail or instant-messenger clients to swap music. They access fee-based online repositories of music from services like iTunes or Rhapsody. Or they can find a plethora of (fee-based or free) download websites and blogs, some legal, others chock-full of pirated music files. These various options have contributed to a slight decline in the use of peer-to-peer networks (Madden and Rainie 2005).

Consumers are personally conflicted about illegal file sharing. Fifty-seven percent of all broadband users (who are more likely to engage in file sharing than other consumers) believe there is little or nothing the government can do about the problem (Madden and Rainie 2005). In defense of their bottom line, media producers are experimenting with a wide variety of digital-rights management solutions to prevent users from copying and distributing files. Sony BMG sold CDs with hidden antipiracy software that left computers susceptible to future attacks and damaged or crashed computers when customers tried to remove it (Krebs 2005). Such draconian practices have created a backlash from consumers, who then find it easier to justify illegal sharing.

Internet radio from services like Pandora, Last.fm, and Slacker.com represent a new and very Web 2.0 model of the music experience. Social features encourage listeners to share music interests. Trusted members (similar to trusted book reviewers on bookseller sites) generate the "if she likes this new tune, then maybe I will, too" phenomenon. Musical attributes selected by the service, user tags, and other such classification techniques either enable the stations to "learn" listener preferences to improve the experience or enable the listener to find music with similar characteristics and thereby customize personal radio stations or playlists. In information science terms, Internet radio is a discovery system. Some directed searching is involved (e.g., artist name, song name), but much of the retrieval occurs in the background as user preferences generate the aggregation of tags. Most services link to music sellers like iTunes or Amazon, completing the cycle to ownership. They have also gone mobile, enabling users to listen on cell phones with data plans.

Web Forums

When people are trying to solve everyday life information problems, web forums often fill the need. Also called web boards and discussion boards (and, in the old days, online bulletin boards and newsgroups), forums are essentially asynchronous group-discussion environments. They are information-sharing spaces where readers post questions, opinions, and other commentary on topics of mutual interest. Forums can be open to the world or restricted to a few individuals. Discussions are often "threaded," meaning replies appear nested under original postings so readers can more easily follow the flow of conversation. Participants can also respond directly to individual posters by using embedded e-mail functionality. This option is employed when conversation ceases to become valuable to the group as a whole but remains cogent for the primary participants. For example, someone may post a request to a collector's newsgroup for a specific item. Those who have the item to sell or trade will communicate directly with the poster through e-mail because these transactions will not be of interest to the community at large. When message boards and news-groups are moderated, the tone and character of the discourse may change. Off-topic postings, spam, and offensive content are less likely to appear, but conversation will be more restrained than it otherwise would be.

Web forums can be found on countless websites or be self-hosted. Google Groups (http://groups.google.com) contains the archives of Usenet, one of the oldest of such services on the Internet, as well as a huge variety of discussion groups anyone can start and manage. Yahoo! Groups (http://groups.yahoo.com) also hosts free public and private discussion groups. Web forum users need to be aware that their messages can live on long after their initial relevance. The Usenet messages of John Walker Lindh, the "American Taliban," were later used to trace his descent into extremism.

Web forums for teenagers abound, typically offered as part of a suite of social network tools. Studentcenter.org is an example of a service that hosts forums as well as blogs, chats, e-mail, photo albums, and videos. The message boards are organized by topic, covering everything from fashion to GLBT (gay, lesbian, bisexual, transgender) issues. Nonprofit advocacy sites as well as commercial sites feature message boards. Teens can discuss their cancer treatment, share video-game tips, or argue about vampires and werewolves on a forum devoted to *Twilight* series author Stephenie Meyer. Discussants are likely to learn about forums from friends and others with similar interests. Today's discussion forums are distributed throughout the Web, meaning there is no good way to locate them unless one already knows the URL or can find them through a general web search (e.g., by searching "forum" and "cartooning"). Message content can only be searched collectively through standard search engines. Because forums typically reside on individual websites, archiving practices are determined by individual website owners.

Besides filling information needs, web forums are virtual communities. Many are populated by regulars who participate in the discussions on a consistent basis. These individuals may develop considerable expertise and be highly regarded members of the community. Other regulars may dominate the conversation in less-helpful ways, effectively hijacking useful discussion. Web search tools can match words and links to find potentially relevant contributions but, unfortunately, cannot screen out rants and frivolous postings. Users are forced to develop their own filtering strategies to find interesting or worthwhile discussion threads. Many become familiar enough with a forum to know who the "trusted" members are. Some forums have better reputations than others and attract a better class of contributors.

Collaborative Work Spaces

The Web is a natural environment for collaboration. It provides a neutral platform for shared activities and community building. Wikis are perhaps the Web's quintessential collaboration tool because they provide the means for members of a community to add and update content remotely and at will. The world's most well-known wiki is Wikipedia, the encyclopedia anyone can add to and edit. *The Economist* gave its 2008 "Business Process" award to Jimmy Wales, cofounder of Wikipedia, "for the promotion of online public collaboration as a means of content development" (*Economist* 2008). The dispersed Wikipedia community is able to work around the clock to catalog events as quickly as they happen, with members adhering to its only nonnegotiable policy—retaining a neutral point of view (Lih 2009). According to the Wikipedia website, versions of the website now exist in more than 260 languages, with more than 85,000 active contributors working on the more than fourteen million articles.

It seems that every day a new collaborative web tool is born. Ning.com allows communities to create their own social networks in which members can host blogs, upload pictures and video, and discuss common concerns in a forum. Google offers several productivity collaboration tools, including Google Docs, which hosts shared documents, presentations, forms, and spreadsheets. Google Calendar is widely used by groups of people for scheduling and planning purposes. "Cloud computing" services like these mean that consumers no longer have to e-mail documents to one another, keep track of different versions of documents, or worry over names being dropped from distribution lists.

Collaborative work spaces can be closed or open, depending on the needs of the community. Schools and universities often use closed systems to maintain the privacy of their users, share proprietary information, and conduct business that has no relevance for the general public. Most open collaborative work spaces are searchable. Indeed, Wikipedia articles frequently appear at the top of results lists because the proliferation of website links to Wikipedia articles boost their rankings in search-engine algorithms. But even information on Nings and other social spaces can be unearthed by search engines.

Tagging and RSS

Tagging, as described in chapter 2, is a way for users to describe and classify Internet content. At heart a "cataloging" activity, tagging becomes a social activity when tags are shared and accessed by others. As individuals, users tag the photos they upload to Flickr, a photo-sharing website. They use social bookmarking services like Delicious.com to tag favorite websites and be able to find them from any Internet-connected computer. They tag blog entries to make it easy to find all their postings on specific topics. The magic occurs when others avail themselves of these tags. For example, I can go to Flickr and search for all the photos that have been tagged with the term *cute* (and there are plenty!). When I find a user who is particularly good at taking cute photos, I can see what other tags this person uses and follow those trails. Again, the "trusted user" principle is at work, as we reason that "if this trusted person likes these things she's tagged, then maybe I will like them, too."

RSS (Really Simple Syndication or Rich Site Summary) is a way of subscribing to web content as it is updated. An application of XML (Extensible Markup Language), RSS inserts coding that packages the content as a list of data elements (e.g., date, heading, summary, entry, location—not so different from author, title, subject, and call number!). RSS aggregators, more commonly called readers, are used to query RSS-enabled web content and display updated information the user has not yet seen. RSS readers can be downloaded as stand-alone software or accessed on the Web through services like Google Reader and Bloglines. By using an RSS reader, viewers know when favorite blogs, websites, and podcasting services have been updated and can access new content without having to check individual websites. Sites like YouTube and Flickr allow users to subscribe to the work of favorite videographers and photographers. It is not clear how much teenagers use RSS readers or are even aware of their existence. I've been mildly surprised by watching my students visit each of their favorite online comic sites in turn, rather than catching up on all the new comics at once by using an RSS reader. Teens (as well as others) are more likely to use feeds that are embedded in conventional websites. For example, a library's posted new book list might be generated using RSS technology, as are the scrolling news items on many websites.

Out There for the World

Personal Websites and Other "Display" Spaces

The ability to post personally created content has been a key attribute of the Web since it began and is perhaps the ultimate expression of the Web's role as a democratizing agent in modern society. Personal web pages became prevalent with the widespread availability of free website-hosting services and graphical website-design software. Individuals are now sharing their own media productions in unprecedented numbers. Obviously, the value of personal websites as information sources is widely divergent. Fame no longer depends on formal training (or, in some cases, even talent). Personal websites vary from the site of a fourth-grader who posts a page about her dog to the site of a serious meteorology enthusiast whose local storm data is as reliable as comparable data from the National Weather Service.

As noted earlier, teenagers participate heavily in the culture of content creation, with 64 percent of online teens engaging in at least one type (Lenhart et al. 2007). The percentages are impressive: 39 percent of online teens share their own artistic creations online (such as artwork, photos, stories, or videos), and 26 percent of online teens remix content they find online into their own creations. For teens, the social aspect of media services is key. Not only are they sharing their creative work but they are participating in conversations generated by that content (Lenhart et al. 2007).

Though it is hard to track precisely, many users these days are highly likely to post their creative work on hosted aggregator sites like YouTube or Flickr, which typically offer social networking features and relieve the individual user from coding and hosting chores. A good example is deviantART.com, an online art community that is popular with my students. Members can post and sell art, license it, comment on one another's work, participate in a series of active forums, follow the site on Twitter, and become a fan on Facebook. The artwork is categorized by medium or genre and ranked by popularity. Teens can find creative homes with services like deviantART, which cost them little in dollars but can have a big payoff in terms of building an audience and community.

Finding information in websites like these is the job of search engines. Content creators improve the chances that search engines will retrieve their sites by employing technical search-engine optimization techniques and by (somehow) making sure their sites are linked to from other highly trafficked sites. Individual content creators, including teens, might find it easiest not to go it alone but to use hosting services that ensure "findability" through such means as RSS feeds, a higher profile with search engines, and integrated social networking features.

Blogs

A weblog, or blog, is a personal website that consists of brief entries generally written by one person. Blogs are "personal" only insofar as they reflect an identifiable voice or tone. Institutional and commercial blogs, commonly authored by multiple individuals, still reveal a characteristic voice. "Microblogging" services like Twitter (also referred to as "status updating" services) allow users to post short updates (generally no more than 140 characters) via the Web, text messaging, and a variety of third-party applications. Readers subscribe to these updates, which can provide a running account of the poster's day.

A defining trait of the blog is its format, with new entries appearing at the top of the page. Most blogs are characterized by short journal entries focusing on the writer's daily life and observations. Other blogs are characterized by longer entries with more topical content, usually about issues going on in the larger world. Many blogs have a "blogroll," a sidebar containing a list of links to like-minded blogs. The writer's personal commentary takes center stage, but nearly all bloggers link to the source material they discuss. As editorialists, bloggers provide a context for their sources. Rebecca Blood (2002) notes that "a good weblog on any subject provides a combination of relevance, intelligent juxtaposition, and serendipity" (12). Blogs attract readers with similar interests and points of view and build followings based on trust in the taste, judgment, and presentation of the creator. "When a weblogger and his readers share a point of view, a weblog constantly points its readers to items they didn't know they wanted to see" (13).

How do teenagers use blogs? Little research has been done on this to date, but quick scans through the many thousands of blogs that exist show that the ones created by teens are primarily of the diary type. Teen blogs frequently feature interactive elements like polls, where readers cast votes on issues ranging from the hottest new music act to the latest crisis in the Middle East. Xanga.com is a good example of a blog-hosting service that seems to attract a large teenage following. Many entries are written in the slang styles that characterize online communication among teenagers. Teen bloggers relate events from their school social lives, express personal hopes and fears, and complain about their parents. They can also be quite serious in their writing, using the forum as an outlet for creative writing, political musings, or other earnest pursuits.

If one is to judge solely by the blogs they link to, teens read and follow blogs that are like their own, migrating to the blog services their friends use. They report "having a Xanga" or "an LJ" (Livejournal), rather than using the generic "weblog" or "blog." There are also many mainstream blogs that appeal to teen viewers, such as those created by celebrities or authors. For example, the writer Neil Gaiman maintains an online journal (http://journal.neilgaiman.com) in which he answers questions from readers, teens among them.

Blogs are not necessarily designed for targeted, deliberate searching. They are meant to be followed, integrated into one's daily online activity and routine. They meet information needs in the way that personal magazine and newspaper subscriptions do. Increasingly, however, bloggers are tagging their entries with keywords. They also extend their reach through RSS feeds, which, for the individual blogger, is not as difficult as it sounds. Most blogging software now accommodates the coding, and the very most a blogger needs to do to activate the feed is check a box in his or her profile. Bloggers can also embed "permalinks" with each entry, which allows others to link to that specific entry no matter where it resides on the blog. Blog fans can use a blog tracking service like Technorati (http://technorati.com) to search blogs and identify the most influential voices on a variety of topics. Besides searching syndicated blogs by keyword, Technorati can search by URL to reveal who is linking to whom.

As search functionality becomes more common in the blog environment, it will be interesting to see if teenagers take advantage of it. We do not know much about teenagers' interest in searching blogs. Do they ever try to find something specific, or are they sticking with the core functions of writing, reading, linking, and commenting? We may not get a chance to find out. Increasingly, teens favor spending time on social network sites like MySpace and Facebook, which require less daily upkeep than maintaining stand-alone blogs and provide them with similar (or better) connections to friends and followers.

What are the consequences of all this interconnectedness? Is teenage culture truly changing, or are ICTs just new ways of accomplishing the same old things? In part 2 of this book, I take an in-depth look at the consequences, both intended and unintended, of ICTs in teenage life and some of their ramifications for society at large.

PART TWO

consequences

4

the fallout:
intended and unintended
consequences

Today's information and communication
technology (ICT) tools have lofty origins.
The Internet itself began as a military research endeavor called ARPANET.
Its purpose was to provide the U.S. military's research and development
community with a secure and survivable means of communication. As
a bonus, scientists would be able to use the technology to share data
sets and research findings. The Internet still serves these purposes, but it
has also absorbed countless other roles that were never envisioned by its
original designers. Scientific researchers tend to conceive of their labors
in terms of serious and important purposes. But the people who actually
use the tools find ways to employ them that were never imagined in the
laboratory. An interesting example of this is closed-captioning for television, which was developed for deaf viewers. Its biggest implementation
is in noisy bars, allowing patrons of those establishments to keep up with
the game despite the din.

Consumers, including teenagers, have managed similar end runs with
other ICT tools, transforming many advanced technologies into tools of

social connection. Smart product developers observe the old adage—first watch where the people walk before laying the sidewalks. I once observed one of my students use his cell phone to take a photograph of a printed special bell schedule rather than laboriously hand-copying all the time changes. It seems doubtful that cell-phone designers had this type of utilitarian use in mind when they added the camera function to their communication device, but I thought it was a clever (and ecofriendly) course of action. Teenagers can be consummate trend drivers, particularly when it comes to information and communication technologies. Marketing executives have learned that where teenagers go, the business world will follow. So a cycle begins. Designs are modified, new products are created, and campaigns are launched, all in response to the vagaries of the modern teenage mind.

It is interesting to observe the factors that drive the media choices of teenagers. Teens are dependent on market factors (what is actually available), economics (i.e., parent purchasing power and willingness), and family dynamics (protecting family time, sharing the media). Simple logistics also play a part. Many teens, as well as adults, favor cell-phone text messaging because they do not always have access to a computer, although their cell phones are readily available. Teenagers are also motivated by what is happening within their peer group. If most people in the group use one type of technology, the others need to use the same type. There comes a tipping point when a specific technology wins the allegiance of the cohort. New members must conform if they want to belong.

Media choice is also heavily influenced by the user's goals. For example, magazines are an initial destination for current information on trends, fashions, and celebrities. In turn, magazines help direct a more focused online searching experience (Harris Interactive 2003). As early as 2002, Grinter and Palen found that teenagers favor e-mail for formal activities, such as communicating with teachers. It is ironic that most adults, including system designers, continue to think of e-mail as a vehicle of informal communication. Now, however, it is the medium of choice when the user needs to be able to edit, spell-check, and produce a more polished product. And all e-mail is not equal. One of my students told me that having an e-mail address from school "looks so much better than something off of yahoo or hotmail, makes you look a little more serious . . . or so I think."

In contrast, teenagers choose texting and instant messaging for spontaneous one-on-one conversations or for group chats with friends they know in real life. If they want to speak casually with people they do not know, they go to online forums or other more open chat environments. These online spaces are typically organized around defined topics that provide a link for participants who otherwise have no common ground from which to initiate conversations. Organized forums and public chat rooms are treated as destinations, as goals in and of themselves. Instant messaging, texting, and e-mail are processes, means to an end.

In their extensive ethnographic study of youth and digital media, Ito et al. (2009) report two major findings. The first is that youth use online media to *extend* existing friendships and interests. In other words, teens are almost always hanging out online with people they know in their off-line lives, and they are using the media to explore interests or find information that goes beyond what they learn at school or in their communities. Second, young people use digital media to engage in peer-based, self-directed learning online. They tinker, add new media skills to their repertoire, share what they create, and get feedback from peers whose opinions and authority they value. One important take-home message from this study is that, for teens, technology in and of itself is not the goal. Rather, they seek the personal connections and activities that technology enables. This self-report from one of my students echoes the study's findings:

> I spend lots of time on Gmail, chatting with friends, reading/posting fanfiction on fanfiction.net, listening to music on playlist.com or Pandora, Twittering, playing on nitrome.com, being a Harry Potter fan on Mugglespace, doing stuff on GoogleDocs, and watching YouTube videos. However, if I made a pie chart of how much time I spent on each site, Gmail would DEFINITELY win, since I leave it open while doing homework and talk to people.

It is also important to remember that not all teenagers are digital media experts. One can find great variation in interests, skills, and backgrounds, making it foolish to speak of an entire generation in one-dimensional terms. Cultural historian and media scholar Siva Vaidhyanathan observes that the students he has taught exhibit a wide range of comfort with and understanding of digital media, and that they are more com-plicated than they are often portrayed to be (2008). He urges us to drop our simplistic attachment to categorizing people by generation in favor of more accurate and nuanced assessments of young peoples' needs. Technologies, he says, do not emerge in a vacuum but are subject to mar-ket forces, political ideologies, and policy incentives. To think otherwise can lead to polarized views of technology as well as of teenagers.

WHAT R U SAYING?

Each time a new communication technology comes along, two extremes inevitably emerge. First are those who immediately jump on the band-wagon, purchasing unreliable beta-level products and wondering where everyone else is. Then there are those who cling to their old tools, wring-ing their hands over the impending loss of civilized communication, even of all civilization. We hear perennial concerns about the deterioration of social skills, the loss of intimacy and depth in communication, and the erosion of genuine human connection. Where educators and pundits once worried about the loss of face-to-face contact as telephone use increased, they now mourn the lost art of letter writing as e-mail use has grown. Others argue that e-mail is merely the successor to pen and paper and that letter writing is now more robust than ever. Online correspondence is also a strange mixture of the private and the public. It is immediate, often impulsive, yet it can be planned and meticulously crafted. It can scroll off a screen into the ether or it can be saved and shared later, and not always by its creator.

New technologies *do* change patterns of language and written com-munication. Some changes are welcome, some are not, and some are just odd. After a period of use, we often forget the origins of such changes, and they become business as usual. Naysayers rightly point to the prepon-derance of poor spelling and slipshod grammar in electronic communica-tion. The immediacy of the medium and its perceived informality (at least in the minds of adults) certainly can contribute to a lack of attention to detail. But, as teenagers have realized, spell-checking and other editing tools are changing both perceptions and habits. And now, cell-phone text messaging (SMS, or short message service) makes the most primitive e-mail communication tools look eloquent. Between the per-character pricing structure and the minimalist writing palette, the writer is forced to be cryptic. But with improvements in technology—features as simple as hot keys (e.g., single letters that make complete words)—even this medium is bound to become more expressive.

In some cases, habits should change as a result of technology, but do not. The invention of the typewriter brought a do-it-yourself form of professional printing into the business-office environment and the home. Work-arounds were developed to compensate for the typesetting tricks that typewriters could not manage, and some of these oddly persist in an era of desktop publishing and word processing. For example, writers still commonly insert double spaces between sentences, which had to be done on typewriters to create adequate visual separation. But unlike mono-spaced typescript, letters produced by word processors are proportional, and the extra space is not needed (Williams 1990). It was only with the 2009 revision of the Modern Language Association's style manual (*MLA Handbook* 2009) that MLA's requirement to underline titles instead of using italics was lifted—a prescription that was nothing more than a hold-over from the days of single-font manual typewriters.

The list goes on. Many commonly used abbreviations began life as a means of saving scarce space on the printed page. Their use became codified, and they persevere in a digital world that does not require their space-saving attributes. Depending on the discipline and the format, bib-liographic citations are still littered with abbreviations for journal titles, state names, and other terms (e.g., "Univ." for "University" and "Pr." for "Press"). Scientific styles still mandate using authors' initials instead of full first names, much to the dismay of interlibrary loan librarians.

Something Lost, Something Gained

Does change always signify decline? Or does change sometimes just mean change? Although new technology takes away some things, it also gives back others. In the virtual environment, we lose visual cues, changes in tone of voice, and other subtle nuances that are clear in face-to-face interaction. But the virtual setting brings along its own cues and conven-tions. Participants are often more direct with one another, more candid, and so more "honest" than they would be otherwise. Contacts may be more frequent and spontaneous, if only because they are easier to initi-ate. There is simply less inertia to overcome, less start-up time. Everyone is infected by this ease, not just teenagers. Using Facebook, e-mail, and instant messaging, I have kept up with my far-flung middle-aged cousins, former students, and—horrors—people I went to high school with. One no longer needs a "reason" to make the contact, or, as my young adult nieces would say, it's just not such a big hairy deal anymore. Online com-munication has great potential for increasing intimacy and closeness in human relationships.

I tire of the two-camp dichotomy—the split between those who con-demn ICTs outright and those who regard them as the great modern panacea. Such positions are neither helpful nor illuminating. Technology makes communication and other aspects of modern life *different*. Yes, some things are better and, yes, some things are worse, but mostly things are different. Only future historians will be able to assess the impact of the accommodations, the attitude changes, and the behavioral shifts we have made. In the meantime, I subscribe to the perspective articulated by Nardi and O'Day (1999), who tell us to situate information (and com-munication) technology within ecologies of human activity. If a healthy, diverse system of users and functions is present, then we can be assured of a productive and beneficial outcome.

We do not need a crystal ball or the insight of a future historian to know some things about what ICTs mean in the life of a teenager. Today's ICTs provide teenagers with remarkable tools for personal and social development. Teenagers look to ICTs to help them accomplish two key, age-old functions of adolescence: personal identity formulation and connection to others. These two functions can seem mutually exclusive or, at the least, contradictory. Even as teens strive to be different, to be unique and independent, they want to belong, to be one in a group of many. When I sent an e-mail message to the students at my school asking them questions about their use of ICTs, I was showered with fascinating testaments that all pointed to these basic motivators and their inherent conflicts.

It is important to note that the students' comments (many of which are reproduced here) and my accompanying interpretations refer to specific tools and technologies, which are destined to be superseded by or exchanged with other technologies. When I wrote the first edition of this book, personal blogs were all the rage. Now, social networks like Facebook and MySpace have all but eclipsed personal blogging by teenagers. Therefore, the examples used here are primarily for illustration. No matter what the present or future form of the technologies, they tell the same story—about the need teenagers have to find a sense of identity and community and how they do so through the use of ICTs.

IDENTITY

Adolescence is a crucial transition period from childhood to adulthood. It is during this time that we separate ourselves from our parents and find out who we are without them. Palfrey and Gasser write about identity in terms of *personal* identity and *social* identity (2008). Personal identity is associated with the characteristics that make each person unique, whereas social identity is a factor of one's relationships and associations. The exploration of independent identity is perhaps the most pressing developmental factor of a teen's life. There is much about the online world that allows for this exploration and experimentation. Teens who are fortunate enough to be "connected" have been quick to exploit these avenues. When they meet one another, they exchange social network identities, e-mail addresses, and instant-message screen names. All are symbols of identity and status, and all are windows into the inner lives of each person.

Social network user-profile templates include the opportunity to share loads of data about oneself: name, birth date, gender, e-mail address, website address, instant-message screen name, home address, relationship status, education, employment history, and personal preferences ranging from music to religious affiliation. Even simple profiles are rarely used merely to describe one's demographics ("I'm a girl, I'm fifteen years old, and I live in Peoria"). Instead, they are creative outlets, literary devices for recording what one feels and thinks. Even IM profiles and away messages are used for much more than what their supposed functions indicate. They are laden with pieces of self; they are used to share political viewpoints, original poetry, and links to websites of personal importance. They are also used to solicit sympathy or express solidarity with others, and to entertain and amuse. Icons and avatars reflect moods of the moment, alter egos, and current idols. Social net-work services like MySpace support customization of each user's space with colors, animation, themes, and "skins" (graphical designs that indi-vidualize the look of a site).When describing her instant-message pro-file, one student told me:

> hmmmm, as for profiles. for me and a lot of people it's just a form of self expression i'd say. just to get whatever off your mind. or as you mentioned to show people weird links or something. song lyrics lots of time. or just weird stuff you find online that you paste the text out of. most of the time it's something i write though, just like whats on my mind. . . . sometimes just random stuff like "AGGGGGGHH HOME-WORK!" or countdowns till school ends.

In Control

ICTs afford an independence to teenagers that is otherwise difficult for them to achieve. Their school day is highly structured, leaving little time for socializing. Life outside of school can also be heavily scheduled with work, sports, lessons, family obligations, and other activities. ICTs can give teenagers control over the discretionary time they do have.

> It's not like watching television, Millennials [twenty-first-century teens] explain, where you have to wait for the weather to come on. And it's not like the radio where play lists are dictated to them. With the 'Net, it's their schedule, their music, and their friends, essentially when they want it. (Harris Interactive 2003, 19)

Instant messaging, social network services, chat services, and texting can all be used outside times that teenagers are normally permitted to be together, such as late at night, and are, for the most part, unobtrusive. Unlike a ringing telephone, instant messages and chats do not disturb the family dinner. Cell-phone text messaging makes no sound in class, much to the chagrin of many educators who have concerns about this modern form of note passing. SMS is also useful for the teenager who is stuck somewhere, usually with parents. One student told me about sending her boyfriend text messages from the car during family trips. The technology gives her the wherewithal to maintain what control she can over the private part of her life.

Keeping Parents at Bay

A major focus of adolescence is separating from one's parents and establishing an identity apart from them. Online communication provides a convenient door to an outside world over which parents have only limited control. Because teens are often the technology experts in their homes, deceiving parents can be remarkably easy. Tech-savvy teens know how to erase cache files on web browsers, track their parents' online presence and mask their own, turn off telltale sounds, sidestep filtering software, set up false "G-rated" social network profiles, and hide their activities by closing windows and sprinkling their online conversations with coded language. Messaging technologies like IM and texting function below the radar in most homes. They can be used covertly, especially if sound is turned off and the teen does not share computers or portable devices with others in the home. Particularly adept teens can text without looking at the keypads on their cell phones. *New York Times* writer Laura M. Holson tells a story about a fourteen-year-old and her friends moving their backseat carpool conversation to texting so her father could not hear them (2008). Even when messaging is used openly, teens typically try not to draw too much attention to their online communications within the family circle. It is their private space within a public world. One of my students shared her personal technique for keeping her parents from bothering her about online activities:

> When parents wander into my computer room, i quickly switch to the academic site and begin to moan about homework. I often have the history site open simply because my parents consider history very boring. If I had a science article open they might be more prone to come over and discuss it with me. I can also pull up papers that i have already written, the point is just to discourage my parents from giving me the "You should be managing your time more efficiently" lecture.

For all these reasons and more, parents often find that the Internet is a flash point of conflict with their children. Parents naturally worry about the questionable content that can be accessed online, who their children are "meeting," and what other unsavory activities their sons and daughters might be engaged in. In some respects, parents' worst fears are true. Ordinarily mild-mannered teenagers swear like sailors online. They let the world know that their parents truly are stupid and clueless. They share intimate details of their lives, including what they have done that they have been expressly forbidden to do. They seem to think of the very public Internet as a private place simply because their parents are not there. From the teenage perspective, the Internet is a gateway to independence. From the parental perspective, the Internet is a morass of unknowns over which they have no control.

Having It All

This is an exciting time to be growing up, a time full of options for enriching one's personal life. And teens want to take advantage of all of them. So, rather than make choices, many have become habitual multitaskers. Media reports have focused on this phenomenon, some raising the alarm about decreasing attention spans and others labeling it a fact of life for today's young people. Jennifer Burek Pierce draws on brain research in her observations of the multitasking phenomenon, noting that there are limits to what teens can learn while managing more than one activity (2008). A study by the Kaiser Family Foundation found that the way young people multitask with computers is very different from the way they do so with more traditional forms of media, such as television (Foehr 2006). When teens watch TV or read, for example, their secondary activities tend to be nonmedia activities like eating or doing chores. When using a computer, teens' most consistent secondary activities are more likely to also involve the computer. In other words, the computer appears to be a serious media multitasking promoter. A teen may be searching the Web for a school project in one window, instant messaging with friends in other windows, and checking e-mail in yet another window. Conversely, certain media activities, such as video gaming, are much less likely to lend themselves to multitasking behaviors. Gaming is more intensely visual, auditory, and interactive, and therefore more consuming than most other media (Foehr 2006).

I think of teens as being adept "serial multitaskers," moving from one cluster of activities to the next. Except for gaming, no single activity receives their undivided attention. The student who told me about keeping her parents at arm's length described her out-of-school routine thusly:

> My internet usage generally goes like this. I like opening multiple windows at once because then i never get bored and feel that I am being more efficient. Generally I will open one window that is devoted to checking my email, after I am done with that I will browse the student newspaper or other online school stuff. Another window will be facebook. Another window will be the studious looking window which i attempt not to look at too often. I normally have another window devoted to music, this is normally i-tunes, pandora radio, or sometimes youtube (i search the songs I want to listen to, and then just do other things instead of watching the music video).

Is this a generation adapted to overstimulation? Can teens really do so many things at once? Maybe not well, but certainly with less anxiety than adults. They have learned to develop highly effective compensatory strategies. For example, IM discourse is distinguished by its real-time yet more-sequential-than-synchronous nature. Conversations "hiccup" as responses often come two or three comments below their direct antecedents. When I asked students about this, they were untroubled. One student wrote:

> hiccup conversations, as you call them, are extremely common but not a big deal. its difficult for me to think of any really absurd or funny ones because i just dont think of them that way. the receiver always gets it in the context of three lines ago or whatever instead of processing it as current, so it seems to make sense, at least to me.

Still, life can get very interesting when teenagers participate in multiple IM conversations. Keeping windows straight is a challenge, not to mention following the topic and tenor of each conversation. Making a mistake can have grave social consequences. If teens who are engaged in a group chat hold side conversations with some of the participants, a misplaced snide comment is difficult to explain.

Getting There without Going Anywhere

Teenagers typically lack control over where they can go and how and when they can go there. If they are not too young to drive, they must share the family car. They generally have to negotiate their time away from home. ICTs allow teens another kind of mobility, one in which family rules and physical distances are irrelevant. Teens use technology to share life experiences as they occur. Being together in person is not a requirement for this kind of personal simulcasting, as long as social network services and text messaging provide the tools for constant updating. As an added bonus, keeping in touch with friends who are far away is just as easy as keeping in touch with someone who lives a block away. We are looking at a generation that does not understand the significance of long-distance calling to previous generations. My mother still has to keep herself from watching the clock during long-distance calls. Today's teenager sees no difference between calling someone across the street and calling someone across the country. Virtual mobility also gives teens opportunities to communicate with people they do not know in real life, no matter what the location of the various parties.

ICTs are, of course, also used to facilitate face-to-face meetings. A friend of mine remarked that 90 percent of his kids' cell-phone conversations with friends are about establishing where each person is. "I'm at the mall." "Hey, me too!" "Where?" "Lower level, food court." "OK, stay there, I'm coming down." And so on. Cell phones make it even easier for teens not to plan activities in advance, much to the consternation of their parents, who often feel blindsided by sudden turns of events. Though parents often get family cell-phone plans for security purposes, teenagers quickly begin to use them to strengthen personal communities outside of their families.

COMMUNITY

As much as teens want to be special, different, and unique, they also want to fit in. They need to belong, to feel they are part of something larger than themselves, and to know that they matter to the group. On one side of the equation, we have the adolescent's compulsion to formulate a sense of personal identity. On the other side is the equally strong drive to stay connected to others. ICTs provide plenty of opportunities for meeting both needs.

No longer can computer users be described as antisocial hermits. These days, teens who are closeted in their rooms with their computers are not typically "alone" with the computer. They are often online with others. They become part of a community by watching others, mimicking what they see, and finding ways to collaborate and share their expertise. The path is not always a smooth one. Others do not always let you in, and sometimes you do not want to participate. The news still seems to feature those occasional stories about Internet addiction and about teens who are socially isolated because they spend too much time online. Early research pinpointed high use of the Internet leading to increased cases of teenage depression and declines in social support (Subrahmanyam et al. 2002). But ICTs have since become so prevalent and so inseparable from other forms of communication that all bets are off. It is time to revisit the role of the Internet in teenagers' social development.

Let Me In

Online life is rich with micro-communities, with opportunities to join, to affiliate, to simply belong. Social network services are tapestries woven out of friend-linkages, predicated on the notion that "friends of mine are likely to be people you will like." There is an implicit assumption of trust, that the people in these relatively vetted and self-determined communities and subcommunities are unlikely to be axe murderers or otherwise unsavory characters. Once a critical mass of linked friends accumulates in particular networks, those networks perpetuate simply because they are where everyone of consequence hangs out. One of my students remarked:

> Facebook has become the most common way I communicate w/ friends out of school. Not for any inherent merit in the technology, but just because that's what my friends use.

If this student wants to connect with his friends, he must meet them at the virtual corner drugstore they are known to patronize—even if he happens to like another corner drugstore more. Some online communities have the added cachet of exclusivity because they are built on invitation-only membership structures. Teenagers (and others) create such closed communities for their groups of friends, and only members of the community can interact within them.

Besides controlling membership and access, there are other, more subtle ways to define affiliation. Teenagers populate their social network profiles, signature files, and other online identities with in-jokes, quotes from one another, and running commentary on events that only a select few can appreciate. As noted, they tend to migrate to the social network services their friends use, and they create links or "friends" lists that connect back to their friends. In her observations about teen blogging, Nussbaum somewhat sarcastically notes that "linked journals also form a community, an intriguing, unchecked experiment in silent group therapy—a hive mind in which everyone commiserates about how it feels to be an outsider, in perfect choral unison" (2004, 33). A less-cynical take on this would be to observe that although teens want to retain their sense of identity as unique individuals, they also need to feel secure. Security comes from knowing that you are not so different from others, that you belong to the group, that you fit in.

SNSs typically offer features that specifically promote community building. For example, Facebook users can affiliate with "networks" that are based on location or institution, and they can join "groups" that are based on interests. A user's "groups" page shows updates to groups that the user is a member of, as well as providing a list of groups the member's friends have recently joined. The business models of some SNSs also support third-party applications, or "apps," that further strengthen bonds among users. Friends send one another "gifts" and links to activities with names like "Can You Finish the Lyrics?" "How Well Do You Know [name of friend]?" "Movie Compatibility Quiz," and "What Kind of Junk Food Are You?"—all designed to highlight shared personal connections. Popular apps tend to migrate from friend to friend within networks, some reaching viral proportions as they spread across the social network landscape.

The spread of virtual affiliation does not, however, mean that social networks are the equivalent of social equalizers. Teens affiliate with online communities based on the same social markers they adhere to in their off-line lives. Certain services are associated with particular crowds, such as preppies, jocks, nerds, goths, or punks. Part of identifying self and community lies in identifying who we are *not* like. As social circles evolve and trends change, teens may switch services in order to align with the community of the moment, the group that resonates with their current identity affiliation. At the same time, persistent issues of race and class may determine long-term alliances in the online realm just as they do in the off-line realm. In the cases of MySpace and Facebook, scholars are beginning to record some of these distinctions, giving lie to the *New Yorker* comic caption, "On the Internet, no one knows you're a dog" (boyd 2008a; Hargittai 2007). A social space is still a social space, online or off-line, and can be just as stratified in one place as the other.

On the other hand, the social nature of the Web allows teens to join online communities with people they do not know in "real" life but whose interests and passions they share. As much as the Internet has a reputation for hosting sexual predators, it is probably more likely that teens will find safe and healthy places to conduct their own social experimentation and information gathering. Ito and her colleagues (2009) found that young people can be just as motivated by interests as by friendship and that new relationships are often formed based on mutual interests, hobbies, and career aspirations: "In contrast to friendship-driven practices, with interest-driven genres of participation, specialized activities, interests, or niche and marginalized identities come first" (Ito et al. 2009, 21). These points of shared discovery occur in many online locales, from web boards and photo- and video-sharing sites to arts-based communities, such as fanfiction.net and deviantART.com.

Certainly, among my students, web-based communities and connections are sources of information as well as methods for sharing their own creative work. When I asked students if they had any friends online that they did not also know in real life, reports were along these lines:

Actually yes, which is strange because I always told myself having on-line friends isn't safe. I "met" these people through my online school's newspaper and IM with them more than with people I know face to face. But the relationship is totally not the same, you just can't read people through their IM text like you can in person.

*

I have one friend I haven't met. We worked a little bit on making a videogame together, along with some other far away people I never got to know and one other friend here. He's in Colorado. We don't talk a whole lot. It's really when our projects and interests converge that we work together.

They also responded to my questions about their use of online communities:

I'm not into public chat spaces, but I go to a number of online bulletin boards, mostly related to a specific topic for information. In particular, the Woodwind.org message boards (and archives) are ridiculously useful to me as a clarinetist.

*

i'll go to web boards if i'm having technology troubles and am looking for troubleshooting info, like when my sidekick went black and died. . . . those web boards saved it.

*

I do put my art on deviantart, but that's mostly just so I can send people links instead of the actual kind of large files.

Let Me Out

Teens have a strong urge to share because it gives them a sense of belonging. At the same time, teens need privacy in order to protect a developing (and tender) sense of identity. There are two types of privacy in the context we are discussing. One is privacy within the online environment. There are times when one wants to share online and times when one does not. For teenagers, this duality is fraught with ambivalence, a push-me, pull-you tension. The other type of privacy that teenagers desire is protection from the adult world, from a world of outside authority. As noted earlier, ICTs afford teens protection from the prying eyes of adults.

Though teens want to be part of the group, sometimes they just need a break from being within reach, from performing. And sometimes they just need protection from interruptions when they are engaged in other activities. One student wrote to me:

i usually am away when i have an away message up, but sometimes im just working on the computer and dont want to talk to someone who happens to be online then. it can be really annoying if youre trying to work and someone keeps talking to you.

One of my students opined that away messages, no matter what the tone or content, are used simply to convey the idea that "I'm away; please don't clog up my desktop with dozens of windows."

If teens do not want to be disturbed, why do they sign on and then make themselves unavailable? My theory about this phenomenon is that no one wants to be left out. At a minimum, one wants to be the proverbial fly on the wall and know who else is online. Here is another take on the subject:

I usually use away messages so I can get some homework done. Every now and then, when I have a question to ask, I take off my message to see if anyone is online who can answer. I suppose I'm away, but not from my computer, just from the "talking zone."

I like the distinction this teenager makes between the literal truth and the real meaning of her action. Yet she does not actually sign off, which is telling. She chooses to remain connected, just not active.

The plethora of SNS applications has certainly given some teens "app fatigue," particularly because many apps require separate registration (further obligating them to share personal information) and can result in a significant time commitment. The user has to weigh the potential of an app's status value against its cost in terms of the time investment and its coolness factor. No one wants to circulate an app that is considered yesterday's hot phenomenon. Several of my students shared their decreasing desire to participate in the app culture:

I don't do quizzes, they're really bad and you have to add each one as a separate app. That bothers my OCD nerve. Most of the groups invites I get are also useless.

*

I used to use a lot of apps and take a lot of quizzes and stuff, but I've tried to stop myself doing that because the newsfeed and my profile were so extremely cluttered.

*

My usage of Facebook has kind of been reduced to checking other people's photos, though I also use the birthday feature.

I especially appreciated this damning assessment:

I don't use apps/games because they are a twin star system that blinds passers-by and sucks up time with their tremendous forces.

Get Them Out! Let Them In

Teens also develop strategies to manage their online intake and output. As with the IM examples above, they learn to regulate the who, what, and when of their online interactions.

I really don't like status updating, it always annoys me when other people constantly change their status, people really dont care that much about them. Therefore, in order not to annoy like minded people i generally just keep my status clear unless I have a particularly witty or important thought. the last status i posted was, "HEY SOPHO-MORES, WHAT DATES DO WE NEED TO KNOW FOR THE HISTORY TEST TOMORROW?"

ICTs can also be used to exclude people from a community. Sometimes this use of the technology is nothing more than teens finding a way to control who they talk to and under what circumstances. It has become common to hide one's online presence and availability by using away messages to screen incoming inquirers, by logging on with alternative screen names that are known only to a select few, or by just using a different social networking tool to communicate with favored friends. Here is an away message that one of my students sometimes uses:

Things I might be doing:
  Making food
  Eating that food
  Cleaning my room
  HOMEWORK
  Watching TV (while doing HOMEWORK)
  Sitting here at the computer staring at you because you think
    I'm away but I'm NOT. Hahahaha.

This exclusionary use of ICTs can have less-friendly implications. For example, on IM it is possible to block individuals, which means that the person who is blocked simply cannot see that the blocker is online. Used judiciously, this tool is a benign way of keeping someone at arm's length (and an improvement over the days when we had to beg our parents to tell a caller we were not home). The blocking feature on IM can also be used more malevolently when social circles morph. Someone can be blocked temporarily, by one person or by an entire clique, but if blocked for too long that person will eventually figure out that he or she is the victim of a technological version of shunning. More subtly, SNS friends lists can be ranked, allowing users to visibly showcase their favorite friends and, by implication, "demote" former favorites. Or, a "friend" can be "unfriended." Online bullying, which will be discussed further in chapter 5, is also a growing concern.

On the other hand, it might be possible that ICTs elicit the softer side of the teen psyche as much as the meaner side. There is often a great deal of hand-holding and mutual encouragement. SNS apps provide plenty of opportunity for these types of exchanges, allowing users to send one another virtual gifts, flowers, pieces of "flair," and friendly "pokes." When blogging was more prevalent among teens, I read one girl's rant about an immature boy who had become "incredibly annoying." The subject of this boy's behavior passed from blog to blog, with a number of participants coming to his defense. One boy noted that the target's self-esteem was "nonexistent" and pleaded for understanding on his behalf.

Socializing

As play is a child's work, socializing is a teenager's work. Socializing is how teens learn to negotiate within the larger society, how they learn to learn the rules. All parents can recall the time of transition when they ceased to be the center of their children's lives, their places taken by their children's friends. This shift in focus is painful for parents, but it is an essential part of growing up. Without it, young adults would not become mature adults, prepared to form their own family units (and to raise ungrateful children like themselves!). Through time, teenagers have found many ways to learn and practice these important socializing skills. New technologies probably allow them to practice to a fault, as reported by several of my students:

> i have lots to say especially about aim because i waste my whole life online. i haven't done my homework for three days.

*

> I use Facebook far too much, and once I've signed onto a computer, I check Facebook every few minutes or so. It's the best method of communication with a lot of people.

*

> I think I'm friends with everyone in my class, and I have 50 or so out of the 60ish on my friends list. So that helps a lot.

One particularly articulate student makes the following distinction between the use of ICTs for communication and for socializing:

> I really find the internet to facilitate communication, not socializing. That communication helps organize and maintain existing social structures, but it's no competitor to them. Facebook especially is designed not just to communicate w/ friends but to help keep track of them. It collects status messages and reports them in a feed. It retrieves contact info and reminds you of birthdays. It looks for new friends based on old friends (and if you use certain apps, similar interests). It tries to do a lot of the grunt work of being a social creature. It's a rolodex on crack really.

The Internet is not the first technological environment to encourage social behavior or even to enable the formation of virtual friendships. Early telegraph operators swapped chitchat during slow times and developed their own shorthand vocabulary, which was not all that different in nature from the coded talk of today's online messaging environment (Joinson 2003). Romances were even known to develop over the telegraph. The codes and norms developed by telegraph operators, ham radio enthusiasts, and today's ICT users are much more nuanced than they might appear. Much information is exchanged in these terse, deceptively rich communiqués. As discussed at the beginning of this chapter, the social uses of communication technologies were never on the original drawing board. Developers viewed their inventions as business tools, survival tools, and tools for "serious" activity. But end users have never been particularly concerned whether their use of a product fit the vision of its maker.

Teens have access to a wide variety of ICTs for socializing with their peers. Instant-messaging software is a very popular tool, because it is generally free and is now available through SNSs like Facebook and MySpace. Its use is down since 2006, but 60 percent of online teens still send instant messages to their friends, with 42 percent of teens who use SNSs sending messages via SNS on a daily basis (Lenhart 2009). There is a bit of a chicken-and-egg question here too. Teenagers may drive ICT communication, but they are also driven by it because of a desire to conform as well as to increase their socializing opportunities. In other words, if you are not online, you are "out." You miss not only the social experience but the chance to plan group social events. Those who are not online become invisible, and their social capital suffers. To keep things in perspective, 51 percent of teens with cell phones still report speaking directly to one another each day, and 29 percent report getting together in person for social activities (Lenhart 2009). Even so, much of the coordination for those in-person activities is managed through ICTs.

Online communication among teens shares some fundamental characteristics with face-to-face teenage communication. It is filled with the same drama, complexity, and import. Only the medium is different. Lewis and Fabos (2000) describe the experiences of Sam and Karrie, two teenage girls who use IM extensively. Both girls feel that IM is important in defining their social status. They manipulate their standing in a number of ways, such as adopting different language styles or adjusting the subject matter depending on who they are instant messaging with. Sam waits to respond to messages from popular people so she won't appear too eager, like a "loser." The assumption is that instant messagers are engaged in multiple simultaneous conversations, and she wants to appear just as engaged as everyone else. This behavior is not so different from tactics of earlier times—waiting to answer the phone until it has rung several times, not answering the door immediately, making a boyfriend wait a few minutes when he arrives for a date. Sam's choice to respond either promptly or slowly is just as calculated.

Jargon

Jargon has always been a way to establish credibility as a member of a community, to elevate one's status in it, or to unwittingly reveal one's utter cluelessness. Holson (2008) notes that the abbreviated terminology of text messaging has become this generation's version of pig Latin, another mechanism for keeping parents at bay. We are familiar with the typical shorthand of online speech—"lol" for *laugh out loud,* "imho" for *in my humble opinion,* ":-P" for sticking one's tongue out, "w/e" for *whatever,* "pos" for *parent over shoulder* (and something less savory, as well). In the online environment, the organic development of jargon is also influenced by mechanics and has a tendency to become ritualized. Here is a story from one of my students about the birth of one particular speech pattern:

> some time ago, when you wanted to say something loudly you'd say it and then add exclamation points by holding shift and "1" like so: !!!!!!!!!!!!!!!!!!
>
> but every so often, you'd let go of shift before you let go of "1" and get this: !!!!!!!!!!!!1111.
>
> then people started adding the "1's" intentionally. and now it has gone so far that people type: !!!!!!1111oneoneone.

In similar fashion, certain misspellings become codified: "teh" is used for *the,* and "pwn" for *own* (as in to defeat badly, usually in a game). Certain stylistic conventions characterize online speech as well. One student sent me these examples:

We also use asterisks to denote action. The text is in the third person:

wads up piece of paper and throws it into the trash
blinks
eats her sandwich slowly

Those who are adept online writers can communicate effectively and efficiently, even elegantly, using these stylistic conventions. Those who are new at it, who are not sufficiently observant, or who overuse them will make gaffes and lose status points in some online communities.

What's Real, What's Not

Many forms of online conversation are ephemeral. Unless someone deliberately saves most instant-messaging sessions or copies them, they disappear forever when windows are closed. Online, it is easier for shy teens to flirt and for the inarticulate to do things that are difficult to do in person, such as break up with a boyfriend or girlfriend. The fleeting nature of these interactions also makes it easier for teens to be rude, to tease, and to bait one another. It is not always easy to tell what is truly meant, what is sarcasm, and what is a game of online banter. For example, I have seen girls' Facebook profiles indicate that they are "married" to other girls, a relationship status that may or may not have anything to do with their sexual orientation or the actual identity of a significant other. Along the same lines, AIM instant messaging allows one user to "warn" another if that person is being objectionable or offensive in some way. After an individual's warning level has exceeded a certain threshold, he or she is no longer able to send messages until a system-determined period of time has passed. Users sometime participate in warning "wars" simply for the fun of it. Or, they may temporarily block access to someone who is proving to be an irritation.

Teenagers must learn the drill—when to take actions seriously, when not to, when things cross the line. Based on responses from my students, most seem to have these distinctions well in hand:

I've had all kinds of arguments and fights over e-mail and instant messaging services. I block people, I warn people, I've been blocked, I've been warned—both for fun and more seriously. It's the nature of instant messaging.

*

> I used to chat, but now I stay offline because the chat program has so many bugs that the person on the other line thinks I'm giving them the silent treatment when really facebook just dropped the message.

Is this type of social interaction so different from real-world teenage social jockeying? Perhaps the tools are different, but the patter is the same.

Privacy and Intimacy

ICTs make some communications seem more ephemeral than they actually are. As a warning to our students, we tell them the following story when they are first issued school e-mail accounts. Several years ago, one of our teachers noticed a piece of paper tacked to the bulletin board in the computer lab. It was a printed copy of an e-mail message in which a boy sheepishly asked a girl to go with him to a school dance. The teacher happened to notice that the boy was sitting in the computer lab and handed him the paper. The boy looked at it blankly for a moment, then pointed to the date at the top of the message. He had written the e-mail message two years earlier (which, in Internet terms as well as teenage terms, is a very long time!). Somehow, this message had survived the two years and then been printed and posted in a public place. It could have just as easily been forwarded electronically.

Just as e-mail communication is not truly private, the breakups, fights, and other dramas that are reported on SNSs suddenly become community property. Discussions and dissensions hop SNS walls, and before long everyone has a vested interest in the outcome. There is also a tendency to overanalyze status updates, with people looking for themselves in the subtext. One girl told me this story about a blog entry she wrote:

> blogs are really good for telling people stuff without having to do it directly and without people really knowing. but sometimes people overanalyze. like once i was listening to a song by the white stripes. . . . the song is jack white singing to and about holly and holly singing to and about jack white. so i said something like "and who is this holly that jack white keeps talking about?"
>
> and then my friend jake, who was sort of involved with a girl named holly at the time, said: "am I jack white? and if so, why do I have a

codename? I'm fairly sure that I am but have no idea whatsoever of the significance of this; i'm pretty interested to find out though." so then i posted the lyrics to the whole song so he'd get the picture. which i didnt like doing. it was way too obvious and i like to be more cryptic. but it's really easy to seem too full of one's self when responding to blog posts that one imagines are aimed towards oneself.

I was surprised and moved, however, to hear another side of the blogging picture, one that echoes the behavior of the students who defended the "really annoying" boy.

blogs are usually places for personal reflections, to talk about what's happened in one's day, new events, new things, new places. in one of my classes the other day we were discussing blogs, and the teacher said that they thought blogs were a lot like slam books—places to say nasty things about people that you wouldn't say to their faces. actually, that's not true. the blogs ive read rarely say a lot of negative things. people are too aware of how many other people might read it. its surprising how much people visit each other's blogs, but they do, and they'll get mad if they see their name in a bad light. i've found that blogs tend to be written in a style completely different from what the person's actually like. people reveal a lot of insecurities on their blogs, about how they're shy, lonely, depressed. . . . i think the main reason that blogs are written and read is that its interesting to see a whole new side of someone you thought you knew, and that its exciting to share that side with people.

Notions of privacy seem to have taken on a whole new meaning in today's world, particularly for teenagers who seem so willing to share the intimate details of their lives on the Internet. Conversely, they are often strongly motivated to keep parents away from their online personas. They use privacy settings not so much with an eye toward fending off the proverbial creepy stranger as for the purpose of preventing parents and other authority figures from seeing their personal information. For many teens, parents are the "public," and what might conventionally be thought of as the "public" has a more abstract meaning.

The concept of "friend" is also different in the SNS environment. Besides including real-world friends, it can encompass friends of friends or friends through association. In other words, SNS friends might be individuals a teen never spends time with in real life or has never even met in person but who are connected to the teen through legitimate associations. A relatively small proportion of teens accept friend requests from absolute strangers (Lenhart and Madden 2007). One of my students describes it this way:

> I don't add people to my "friends" unless I know them. That might sound odd, I have over 500 friends, but I do know or know of them, so it's not creepy.

danah boyd uses the phrase "networked publics" to describe "the spaces and audiences that are bound together through technological networks" (boyd 2008b, 125). The properties of social network services, a particular type of networked public, are that activities are persistent (speech and actions are "recorded"), searchable, replicable (forwarded, copied, duplicated), and available to invisible audiences. The challenge for teens is to create some level of privacy in these public spaces, spaces that have a permanence and an accessibility that other forms of ICTs do not.

Many teens do not seem to be aware that SNSs allow some customization of privacy settings. For example, wall posts, photo galleries, and status updates can be restricted to a subset of friends rather than left at the default, which is to remain open to all friends. Little of the information on an SNS profile is actually required. Such options allow teens to have it both ways; they can be cool within their preferred social circle and still maintain standards of appropriateness expected by other figures in their lives. Some of the students who friend me seem to forget they have done so, and I find myself rather bemused by what they post online.

What about those creepy strangers? If one is to believe the popular media, child predators are lurking behind every computer screen. Indeed, the "moral panic" that has arisen over this issue spawned any number of legislative initiatives, most notably the Deleting Online Predators Act of 2006 and 2007 (Marwick 2008). These well-intentioned efforts generally mandate that "social networking" sites be blocked in schools and libraries. Recent research is providing a more accurate portrayal of the actual risks involved in using such sites as well as giving us a better picture of how criminals use ICTs to lure their victims. A study conducted under the auspices of the National School Boards Association (2007) found that both students and parents experienced fewer problems, such as cyberbullying and unwelcome personal encounters, than school fears and policies seemed to imply. In fact, the vast majority of students surveyed were safely involved in social networking activities, content creation, and online discussions about education and learning.

Wolak and her colleagues (2008) presented an overview of research relating to Internet-initiated sex crimes, including a focus on the characteristics of victims and offenders. They concluded that young people who use SNSs are unlikely to be increasing their risk of being targeted by online predators. Rather, typical predators are adult men who are quite open about their interest in sex, use more direct methods of communication (e-mail, instant messages, chat rooms) with potential victims than SNSs, and seldom pose as young people or abduct their victims. Instead, predators develop connections with susceptible teens who see the relationships as romantic adventures and, for a variety of reasons, already have a tendency to take risks in both their online and off-line lives. The researchers recommend identifying and counseling these at-risk teens. They also advise focusing prevention measures on online interactions, because Internet-initiated sex crimes typically come about through direct communication between offenders and victims. They found no evidence that posting personal information on SNSs put teens at risk for sexual victimization.

Do these findings mean that teens should feel free to post any manner of personal information on their SNSs? Common sense would say no. If sexual predators are not paying close attention to social network profiles, unhappy peers, future employers, and college admissions officers may be. In a study of health-risk behaviors on MySpace by adolescents, researchers found that 54 percent of teens' profiles contained "risk behavior information," with 24 percent of the profiles referencing sexual behaviors (Moreno et al. 2009a). In a follow-up study, researchers tested an intervention strategy—sending a single e-mail message to a test group of subjects who had posted sexual or substance abuse references on their profile pages (Moreno et al. 2009b). This message identified the sender as "Dr.

Meg" (with a link to full identification), a doctor who studies how youth talk about health issues, particularly sexual health. It provided information regarding the risky nature of posting personal information online and included a link to information about sexually transmitted infections. Three months after the intervention, the profiles were examined again. Those who received the intervention were 4.2 times more likely to remove all sexual references than were those in the control group. The e-mail message from Dr. Meg, who was unknown to the subjects and who wrote, "If I could see your profile, nearly anybody could," was a reality check about the public nature of SNSs. These teens' perceptions of networked publics were quickly realigned.

Given the growing body of research that is providing us with a more nuanced understanding of the risks and benefits of using SNSs, I find it ironic that most of the public focus continues to remain on adult-child sexual predation. Yes, it is critical to protect young people from sexual predators, including emphasizing the steps teens themselves can take to protect themselves. But we should not forget the importance of teaching young people to be good cybercitizens. The mix of the daily "stuff" of teenage life and the power of ICTs can create the perfect conditions for breeding misunderstandings and misconduct.

Perhaps the real question to ask about ICTs is what they have meant for the *quality* of interpersonal communication. Are teens substituting shallower online friendships for in-person, higher-quality relationships? What good is it to have an online relationship that achieves a level of ease or intimacy that cannot be replicated in real life? Teenage boys, for example, may be more willing to be sweet or open online, and then clam up at school. But without the online venue, such boys would not be any more likely to open up at school; the new media give them the chance to test the waters a bit. We now understand that teens' use of social media is highly friendship-driven, with teens generally associating with people they already know off-line (Ito et al. 2009). They use the new media to "hang out" and extend existing friendships. A friendship that flourishes in multiple environments is bound to be more robust. And what about those SNS profiles, status updates, and blogs? Just because teens share their innermost secrets online, are they getting the kind of feedback and support they would get from face-to-face interactions? On the other hand, would online teens who are suffering from depression share in person what they write online? It's hard to say. As noted earlier, some things are lost and some are gained with the use of new technologies. It will be some time before we understand their implications.

Collaborating

One tried-and-true method for achieving a sense of community is collaborating with others toward the attainment of a common goal. There is little doubt that the online environment facilitates collaboration, particularly around schoolwork. When I queried my students about their use of ICTs, they indicated consciously maintaining a continuous state of readiness for collaboration opportunities by keeping e-mail clients, SNSs, and instant message windows open, even when not actively using them. They scolded me for not including schoolwork in my list of examples of online activities, several noting that this was one of their major uses of social media. Students may have IM conversations open while they work through math problems together. They initiate conversations to work on group projects, clarify assignments, check answers, discuss readings, and prepare for tests.

> often we make study guides before tests by opening a chat window and writing IDs (i.e. definitions, little snippets of information, etc. that we think will be on the test). Someone copies everything and formats it so we all have something to study.

> *

> Facebook is often used for school purposes, and i think alot of adults dont really understand this. The last time I forgot and assignment at school, i simply went on facebook, figured who was online that i knew had the assignment. Chatted with them. And within a few minutes they had scanned the assignment and sent it to my email and I printed it. the whole exchange took maybe 4 minutes from the time I got on the computer to the time the assignment was printing. It is very convenient.

> *

> GoogleDocs is very important for me for assignments, because I can access the documents anywhere. I can also write collaborative stories

with my friends on GoogleDocs. It is probably my favorite Google thing
other than Gmail.

Teenagers quickly learned to use SNSs for organizing off-line events,
online study sessions, and the like. No more inefficient and annoying telephone tag. Online "meetings" can be held when teens are unable to get
together in person because of distance, or transportation or because meeting times are outside the normally permitted gathering times.

Music, Media, and Sharing

Popular music plays a powerful role in teen life. It mirrors, amplifies,
and responds to their emotions and experiences. The continuous cycles
of development and production ensure its role as a kind of generational
social glue. At one time, teens had to depend on radio broadcasts and live
performances to hear their favorite music. Recording technologies gave
those with ready cash the ability to own and play music at will. Then the
Internet came along and put a huge wrench into prevailing music business
models and concepts of music ownership. The unit of sale seems to be in
a constant state of flux. It may be an "album," it may be a song, it may be
a physical object like a CD, or it may be an electronic file to download. In
some cases, and for a variety of reasons, creators or vendors intentionally
give away their music. Reporting for the Pew Internet and American Life
project, Madden (2009) observes that in the Internet age, selling recorded
music has become as much of an art as making the music itself.

With every modern recording technology, music piracy has existed in
some form. I remember kids who would set up a tape recorder next to their
portable radios. The quality wasn't very good, but it was a lot cheaper
than buying the vinyl version. Today, it's a snap to transfer high-quality
music files from a CD or a file-sharing service to a computer or handheld
device. Quality and speed issues aside, the piracy issues are identical.
Teens have a great deal of sympathy for the file-sharing movement, which
operates outside the standard power structure. As minors, teens' rights
are limited. They cannot vote, their ability to earn is restricted, and they
simply do not have the control over their lives that adults enjoy. A system
that flourishes independently of the status quo is very appealing to those
who are otherwise bound by it. Peer-to-peer (P2P) networks are decentral-
ized grassroots endeavors based on egalitarian participation (assuming, of

course, that the participants have access to adequate computing equipment and high-speed networks). Teens are treated as full partners in the P2P realm, without the stigma of their usual second-class citizenship.

Peer-to-peer file sharing systems have also opened up more than music for media-hungry teens. With technologies like BitTorrent bringing the transfer of large files into the mainstream, teens can now access television shows and full-length movies. Seeming contradictions in copyright law make it difficult for users to make sense of prohibitions against downloading unlicensed content. It is permissible to record off-air programming for later viewing, so why not grab the programs online at one's convenience? Still, quality is hard to guarantee, particularly in the case of full-length movies, as one student told me:

> there are a few illegal sites my friends have told me about for movies, but they tend to be of hilariously bad quality—filmed from inside a theater, so silhouettes keep getting up and walking around in front of the camera.

CD sales were the first casualties of online music availability. Now, newer business models may be slowing down both the purchase of online music and P2P file sharing activities, legal or otherwise. Internet radio and television are becoming destinations of choice for many teens. Like their off-line counterparts, online radio and television run in the background, making them suitable for multitasking, and can be accessed at will just by tuning in. Unlike their off-line counterparts, users can customize their media experiences, carry them on mobile devices, and share in a social network that connects them to expanded media options. One market research study found that 52 percent of teens listened to online radio in 2008, compared to 34 percent in 2007, and that downloading or listening to music on social networks increased from 26 percent in 2007 to 46 percent in 2008 (NPD Group 2009). Still, teens like to own music, whether or not it comes from legal sources, because a high value is placed on the ability to create and share personalized playlists.

Gaming

Video gaming in all its forms is immensely popular among American teenagers, with fully 97 percent of young people ages twelve to seventeen playing computer, web, portable, or console games (Lenhart et al. 2008). "Gaming" no longer means one kid sitting in front of one electronic device playing a solitary game. In confessing his own online gaming seduction experience, *InfoWorld* columnist Chad Dickerson (2004) claims that systems such as Xbox provide extremely rich collaboration environments that deserve close watching by business managers. Gaming is often a social experience, whether online or not, and games can be played online with friends as well as strangers, across wide physical distances. In 2008, 65 percent of game-playing teens reported playing with other people who were in the room with them; 47 percent of teens played online games with people they knew in their off-line lives; and 27 percent of teens played online games with people they first met online (Lenhart et al. 2008). Players establish lists of "trusted friends," similar to buddy lists in instant messaging or social network friends lists. Friends can then immediately see who is online and available for real-time play.

Massively multiplayer online games (MMOG) and a subgenre, massively multiplayer online role-playing games (MMORPG), are particularly suited to collaborative sensibilities. An up-to-date listing of them, astonishing in its depth and range, is available from the Multiplayer Online Games Directory, at www.mpogd.com. Multiplayer gaming is the ultimate environment for establishing virtual friendships and a sense of community with people you have never met. One student told me about the many friends he has made and how he belongs to several "clans." "i can join a game in ravenshield and ppl are like 'yo [user name]!! hows it going?'" Gamers tend to identify with one genre or another, rarely crossing over. This particular student favors strategy games and first-person shooter games. Role-playing game (RPG) devotees are equally loyal in their affiliations.

The psychological dimensions of online game playing are complex and are fodder for many books and articles. Role-playing games provide a means of exploring identity and experimenting with or "trying on" different personas. Unless taken to extremes, RPGs are a safe way to immerse oneself in a fantasy world, to achieve (virtual) power, and to exert control in a world of one's own making. Online strategy games, however, are designed more for team building and collaboration than they are for personal identity exploration. As one student told me, "If I want individual glory in my games, I'll play a nice peaceful game of Civilization [an off-line game] instead."

In many game environments, as a novice gains competence, play typically becomes more difficult and increasingly dependent on group collaboration. Each milestone is therefore much more of a team effort, resulting in a sense of belonging that some teens find rare in their real-world lives. But players can find it difficult to leave games because they develop virtual obligations or are concerned about being "outleveled" while they are away. One of my sons told me that online gamers tend to specialize in just one game because there are simply not enough hours in the day to become competitive at more than one. In some cases, the game and the relationships developed through the game can become more important and satisfying than real life.

Scholars are finding that gaming activities can do a great deal to enhance learning. James Paul Gee (2008) notes that learning is a process of reflection and interpretation, skills that can be enhanced by the social settings and practices in which games are situated:

> Reflection and interpretation are encouraged, not just through in-game design features, but also through socially shared practices like FAQs and strategy guides, cheats, forums, and other players (in and out of multiplayer settings). Gamers often organize themselves into communities of practice that create social identities with distinctive ways of talking, interacting, interpreting experiences, and applying values, knowledge, and skill to achieve goals and solve problems. (23–24)

Clearly, the collaborative nature of many gaming systems may offer much more than recreational value for teens.

BEYOND FALLOUT

There is a great deal about ICT-enabled life that is less than desirable. On one end of the spectrum is the merely annoying, and on the other end is the outright abhorrent, which will be examined more closely in the next two chapters. There are plenty of items to list under the "merely annoying" end of the continuum. Much online conversation is vapid. Teenagers waste a lot of time on SNSs. They flame with the best of the old-timers and post compromising pictures of friends. But if the Internet disappeared tomorrow, these behaviors would find other homes; indeed, they have sprung from previous homes. On the other hand, ICTs also have enormous potential for enhancing teens' lives and helping them mature into interesting, productive adults. But it is up to them to decide if that is how they will use the tools.

5

from mischief to mayhem: behavior

I remember a disciplinary case at our school in which two students illicitly gained system-administrator-level access to the computer network. The students were shocked to find themselves called in for remedial action because they felt they had not "done" anything—they did not change settings, delete files, or otherwise tamper with the system. In their minds, it was all about seeing if they could crack the system and poke around a bit. The process was their goal, as was the subsequent gloating. But because they did not technically break anything, why should they be in trouble? Indeed, they felt they had done the school a favor by finding the security holes in the network. This story raises two questions in my mind:

- Is the Internet an intrinsically different environment from other shared human environments? In other words, does the Internet introduce a uniquely new moral sensibility?
- What is it about adolescence that makes teens particularly prone to unethical online behavior?

Internet observers note important distinctions between Internet-related moral issues and Internet-dependent moral issues (Van Der Hoven 2000). Internet-related issues are those in which the moral issues are the same as they would be in parallel, off-line contexts. Downloading other people's files or e-mail is an invasion of privacy, morally identical to going through others' desk drawers or postal mail. Internet-dependent issues are actions that cannot occur without the Internet, yet the underlying ethical issues are familiar and perennial. Without the Internet, there would be no viruses, no spamming, no flame wars, and no hacking. But not all Internet users engage in these behaviors. The Internet offers unique opportunities for unethical behavior, but it does not require its users to be unethical. The options for making moral choices exist as much on the Internet as they do in other arenas of human endeavor.

Technology innovators often deny or ignore the ethical implications of their work. Mary Shelley's Frankenstein story is a seminal example of how literature richly captures these morality tales. Dr. Frankenstein did not consider the consequences of his actions aside from the contributions he believed he was making to the advancement of scientific knowledge. Consumers of scientific knowledge, in their turn, leave technical development to the experts, effectively abandoning their own role in making moral choices. A student of mine once remarked that if music is "on the Internet," it is fair game for downloading—dismissing the circumstances that might have put it there. The fact of the technology seems to mean that subsequent actions are allowable, even intended.

Many of the moral issues we are now dealing with are not new but have taken on new dimensions. Specific features of information and communication technologies (ICTs), like anonymity and speed, inject unfamiliar characteristics into conventional situations. Hamelink (2000) anticipates that genuinely new moral questions will eventually arise, particularly in the area of artificial intelligence and other intelligent systems. For example, what lies in store for human interaction with virtual beings? Who will be responsible for decisions made by intelligent digital assistants? For the time being, however, uniquely new moral issues are not at the heart of our problems. Instead, we are revisiting old moral dilemmas, made more complicated by new technologies.

Why does it seem that teenagers are especially susceptible to the lures of cybermisbehavior? During adolescence, individuals formulate moral perspectives on many aspects of life. But intellectual growth often outpaces moral development. Psychologists and educators have long puzzled over minds that are so capable of knowledge absorption yet relatively undeveloped in the subtler skills of moral judgment and decision making. Sociologist Émile Durkheim (1925/1961) believed that morality grew from attachment to a group and respect for its rules and symbols of authority. His views influenced behaviorist psychology and gave rise to the character education movement, associated most strongly with William Bennett.

In contrast, psychologist Jean Piaget (1932) believed that children define morality by actively struggling with issues of fairness. He felt that education should focus on ways of thinking about moral issues such as justice and human rights, methods of relating to others, and strategies for choosing what is moral. Piaget's theories belong to the cognitive-developmental traditions of thinkers like John Dewey, and his work prompted the influential psychologist Lawrence Kohlberg's research into the stages of cognitive-moral development (1958, 1984).

MORAL DEVELOPMENT AND ICTS

A great deal of what we now understand about adolescent behavior in the online world comes from these theoretical perspectives. The rules we establish to maintain order are influenced by behaviorist psychology. Rules give adolescents clear boundaries and expectations, which they need to understand their place in the world. Codes of conduct, more nuanced than rules, reflect the cognitive-psychology tradition, as they parse out the differences between truly immoral behavior (e.g., stealing credit-card numbers) and mere violations of social convention (e.g., using all capital letters in an e-mail message). Rapidly changing technologies, and changing uses of those technologies in different contexts, can confuse these distinctions.

Early on in this business, attorney and Internet ethics expert Nancy Willard identified four key factors that influence online misbehavior (1998, 217):

1. a lack of affective feedback and remoteness from harm;
2. a reduced fear of risk of detection and punishment;

3. a new environment means new rules;
4. perceptions of social injustice and corruption.

Willard proposed that, as a consequence of *a lack of affective feedback and remoteness from harm,* the user does not see the hurtful impact of his or her actions, leaving him or her with an impression that there is none. This perspective is a result of not actively engaging in consideration of issues of fairness and justice. In an environment of *reduced fear of risk of detection and punishment,* negative consequences of unethical behavior are less likely and therefore do not act as a deterrent. The user fears the consequences of getting caught, but does not acknowledge the moral rationale behind the rules and regulations. Operating under the conception that *a new environment means new rules,* users rationalize that "real-world" concepts and values do not have any standing in cyberspace. Therefore, rule violations are seen as violations of (unimportant) social conventions, not of universal moral principles. *Perceptions of social injustice and corruption* prompt users to justify unethical behavior by claiming they are righting the wrongs of the world and shifting the balance of power away from the corrupt "haves" to the "have-nots." Context mitigates the moral implications of actions. Willard's analysis holds up well, even as the digital landscape continues to shift and alter modes of human interaction.

Popularized responses to the impact of new forms of digital media tend to portray it either as the solution to all of society's ills or proof of its imminent downfall. Of course, it is neither of these. Cyberspace is more nuanced than a petri dish of situational ethics in which users find it increasingly difficult to discern underlying moral values. Cultural anthropologist Mimi Ito observes that young people, in their interactions with new media, are actually developing social norms that are quite different from adult values and behaviors (Viadero 2008). Researchers at the GoodPlay Project (www.goodworkproject.org/research/digital.htm) have captured this dynamic in an explication of Web 2.0–related ethical issues that provides a more granular understanding of the forces at play. Their report identifies five core issues, or "fault lines," that are salient in the new media environment: identity, privacy, ownership and authorship, credibility, and participation (James 2009). For each, the report presents a fictionalized vignette, then compares the traditional (off-line)

conceptions of the ethical issue with the newer, online conceptions of the issue, finishing with an exploration of the promises as well as the perils of online conceptions. For example, in the vignette that describes a case of identity play, the promise of the online environment is shown as a potentially low-risk opportunity to experiment with personal identity, engage in self-reflection, and receive valuable feedback from others in a way that is not possible in the off-line world. The perils of the online environment are demonstrated in parallel fashion. Experiments with personal identity can lead to deception, self-reflective behaviors can be usurped by the expectations of the virtual audience, and feedback can be misguided or even harmful. I think that this kind of in-depth examination is the best way to acquire a meaningful and helpful understanding of a complex landscape.

TROUBLE IN CYBERSPACE

What are some of the behaviors and situations that typify trouble seemingly unique to cyberspace? Most of these technological hot spots have been covered extensively by the media. They are numerous and, like all things connected with the Internet, subject to change. This chapter examines some of the most prominent and troublesome of them, with a focus on how they are perceived through the lens of adolescence. The adolescent perspective is illustrated in this chapter by a series of examples that contain excerpts of students' responses to hypothetical cyberethics dilemmas. I extracted these nuggets from students' online responses to the ethical dilemmas posed in a unit of our school's required computer literacy course. I believe they are a good representation of how many teenagers respond to the morally ambiguous cyberspace landscape. (For a current listing of the scenarios that have been used in this curriculum, see www.uni.illinois.edu/library/computerlit/scenarios.html.)

Cheating

The popular perception is that if teenagers are not looking at pornography on the Internet, then they are using it to plagiarize schoolwork or download copyrighted music. Plagiarism has certainly been made easier

PARTY ON

Lester sends e-mail to the entire student body inviting them to a BYOB party at his house while his parents are out of town. He receives a message from a system administrator calling him in for a meeting with school officials. Lester objects because he feels that his e-mail is his own private business.

I agree with Lester in that it is his own business and the school shouldnt be checking emails for party invitations. If he hosts a party and his parents arent there, let him get in trouble with his parents, not the school. the school is not supposed to control your life outside of school.

*

Not a smart thing to do. I normally think that you should let people do whatever they want unless it harms someone else, but seriously, if your going to throw a party that's as questionable as this you could at least try to be discreet. Facebook, gmail, word of mouth, the list of ways to do something like this that doesn't obviously alert teachers is practically endless.

*

I agree that he was a bit stupid, not realizing the possible consequences, but i still think that the school should not get involved. I mean, he hasn't harmed the school, right?

*

IT WAS A DRINKING PARTY!!! The kids are around our age! Plus, he sent it to the whole school, it was not private.

*

Well, if he sent the e-mail to the whole school, it's not his own business; it's everyone who received its business. Even though the System Admin didn't receive the message, it would be assumed that lots of people would receive it. Also, by using the school network, the user has already agreed to allow the administrator to view his/her files if a need arises.

*

This is illegal if hes too young, and still not right if his parents dont know. They arent even home, and they have no idea what their son is doing while they are away. Hes drinking, and hes inviting others to come to his house w/o his parents knowing, to drink and party with him! sending school emails is NOWHERE close to this violation.

by the Internet. Students can copy and paste from many sources; they can also download prewritten or customized term papers (often at outrageous prices). Teachers fight back in a number of ways. They collect in-class writing assignments so they will have original writing samples for comparison. They use search engines to find unique strings of words from suspect papers, and they use the services of companies like Turnitin .com, which conduct more exhaustive searches for evidence of plagiarism. Teachers also retool assignments to make them more immune to plagiarism. A student who has to write an imaginary dialogue between two philosophers will have more difficulty plagiarizing her paper than if she is assigned to write a traditional comparison of the two philosophers' perspectives.

David Callahan's book *The Cheating Culture* (2004) sets this behavior in the context of a larger societal trend. From his extensive data gathering, he concludes that cheating has become an American way of life. He blames the competitive economy and the fact that most cheaters are neither caught nor punished. In other words, crime *does* pay and, furthermore, puts those who do not participate at a distinct disadvantage. Many people who consider themselves law-abiding and honest citizens find themselves slipping into cheating in small ways, whether by fudging a bit on their tax forms, exaggerating their children's accomplishments for a competitive admissions process, or failing to return incorrect change at the grocery store. The everyone-does-it mentality is so seductive that cheating and other forms of small-time dishonesty have lost their aura of disrepute.

"Doing Honest Work," the theme of the January/February 2009 issue of *Knowledge Quest,* addresses the difficulties of defining originality in student research and writing in the remix age. Leila Christenbury (2009) notes that, though there will always be students who try to game the system, defining *plagiarism* is hardly as simple as it seems. She examines plagiarism as an instructional issue as well as a strictly ethical one. She reminds us that concepts of originality shift over time and across cultures (citing Shakespeare's unattributed lifting of a popular version of *Hamlet*) and that preventing plagiarism requires active instruction on the part of teachers, who must then require practice on the part of their students. She exhorts teachers to take responsibility for creating assignments where blatant plagiarism is less likely to occur. Holtzman (2009) writes from

a high school student's point of view in describing how expectations of "original work" shifted during his years of schooling, creating confusion in the minds of students. As a senior, he concludes:

> Ultimately, I realized that "original work" lies in how a student pulls together the varied strands of the thesis and supports each strand with evidence—in other words, creative synthesis. Research and citations are history's version of "showing your work" in math, rather than just writing down an answer. (63)

He recommends that teachers and librarians emphasize the centrality of expertise, the role of citations as acknowledgment of previous work, and the importance of synthesis and perspective to help students come to a deeper understanding of the meaning of "original work."

Improper Use of Intellectual Property

The old-time Internet ethos purports that information "wants" to be free. The open-source movement, in which computer code is made transparent and available to the public for modification and improvement, is a reflection of this perspective—that anything worth creating is worth sharing. Hamelink opines that "CyberSpace is one enormous photocopying machine" (2000, 157) and reminds us that copying intellectual work has an honorable heritage:

> Bach copied and reworked music made by others and did this with great respect, creativity and innovation. Many of his choral melodies were taken from other composers. If copyrights were indeed very strictly enforced, jazz musicians would be in deep trouble. In line with the current regime jazz legend Bill Evans should have copyrighted his brilliant harmonic discoveries and any time somewhere in the world a pianist used his way of playing a B flat chord, money would have to be paid to Evans' publisher or record company. (161)

Teens are among the most prolific users of file-sharing software, which has become a primary means of acquiring music without having to pay for it. The concept of ownership of intellectual property can be a particularly

NEW MUSIC

Ken doesn't have much money to buy new music. Instead, he checks out CDs from the public library and rips them or copies music files from free sharing sites or friends' computers. When he does have money, he either buys CDs the library doesn't have or downloads songs from iTunes for under a dollar apiece.

Many people burn cds, and so I think its ok for Ken to do this, Ken isn't the only person out there who rips cds.

*

This could actually be pretty bad. Ripping songs isn't much of a crime, but it takes money from the artist. The artist could actually have large losses, because ripping songs is so popular.

*

Sure, it is illegal, but many artists do not care. It is still bad, but it pales in comparison to other things. I think instead of going after people who do a little bit of copyright violation, we should be going after people stealing enormous amounts of money and violent offenders.

*

although it may not be the right thing to do, its not hurting anyone. i mean, if the band is big enough to be getting their cds into a library, they most likely have plenty of money already and it wouldn't hurt them to have ken ripping their cds. plus, what if the band is dead? then it most definitely isnt hurting them.

*

The artists aren't going to starve to death because of people ripping songs, but also he should do the right thing (when convenient . . . just kidding). He could live with listening to songs on Youtube until he gets enough money. It's his own moral decision.

difficult one for them to grasp. Most see no reason to protect the small body of intellectual work they themselves might have created by this point in their lives. So why should others mind? Instead, creators should be gratified that others appreciate their work enough to want to have it.

Unfortunately, modern copyright law and its enforcement through measures like digital-rights management can seem so draconian and invasive that many people find it easy to excuse law-breaking behavior. The prevailing tension is reminiscent of the early days of VCR technology, when Hollywood moguls feared the demise of their studios once consumers abandoned theaters for the comforts of home and bootlegged videos. The industry found a way to accommodate marketing practices to the new technology, and now fee-based video rentals, downloads, online streaming, and pay-per-play options account for a sizable portion of their profits. As noted in chapter 3, the music industry is catching on as well, with online-purchasing models and other forms of (legal) music acquisition.

The latest "copyright frontier" is defining fair use as it applies to remixing portions of copyrighted work. A study conducted by the Center for Social Media (2008) found that many uses of copyrighted material in today's online videos are eligible for fair use consideration. The research uncovered a wide variety of practices that could be considered legal in many circumstances. These practices include satire, parody, negative and positive commentary, discussion triggers, illustration, diaries, archiving, and the pastiche or collage format that has come to be known as remixes and mashups. The circumstances that constitute fair use require that the new use be *transformative*. Transformative use means adding value to what was taken and using the new work for a different purpose than the original.

It is important to keep in mind the intent of copyright law, which is that creators deserve the right to be compensated for their work and have some control over how it is used. Though it is easy to claim that the recording companies are the "bad guys" and deserve to be cheated, such excuses can easily be covers for other, less-noble motives. Like many of the ethical issues discussed here, this one carries a complexity that deserves close and careful attention.

Hacking

The unadorned, original meaning of the term *hacking* is merely this: clever programming, a willingness to share it, and an appreciation of the same

COMMEMORATIVE VIDEO

The sophomore class officers decide to make a commemorative video of the year's activities. The video will consist of a combination of still photos taken during the year as well as video interviews of class members. The background music for the photo shots will include several popular songs that really enhance the mood of the video. Students will be able to watch the video online or purchase it for $.50 (the cost of the DVD disk).

> This commemorative video is perfectly fine. The students do not make any profit from selling the DVD.

*

> I don't get why everyone is uptight about the music. They never said they got it illegally. It's the problems of the sites who distribute illegal music anyways, not the people tempted to take it!

*

> What I mean is that I think I shouldn't be illegal to do that. Really, who cares how much money you make off your songs? Don't musicians just want to express themselves? Or am I just really naive . . . ?

*

> Even so, the music is still getting out there without the money going to the artist, even though they aren't profiting, they're taking profits away from the artists of those songs.

*

> I really don't like the idea that they shouldn't do it because it's illegal. I go by what's right, not what the law says.

talent in others. But the term has assumed other associations in the public mind. Many confuse it with the more malevolent *cracking* or *black-hat* hacking, which is invasive and destructive. Hacker ethics have their roots in Willard's third factor, that the online environment signifies new rules and codes of conduct. The new code of conduct values the sharing of expertise and information. There are, of course, many shades of difference in hacker ethics. Some feel that it is perfectly acceptable to break into systems for purposes of exploration and learning as long as no vandalism or breach of confidentiality occurs. Others regard this attitude as gussied-up cybervandalism.

"Hacktivists," more purposeful in their outlook, often view the end as justifying the means, particularly when they act out of a strong sense of moral obligation to an overarching cause. For example, it is not uncommon for activist-minded groups or individuals to expose transgressors such as child pornographers, publishing names and descriptions of wrongdoing. These Robin Hood–style vigilante tactics are similar to those used by other extreme-leaning activists, from ecoterrorists to political advocates of various stripes. Hacktivists may deface political websites, initiate denial-of-service attacks, or even impersonate and subvert an opponent's online identity. In the Web 2.0 world, they may merely open up channels of communication to parts of the world that are under electronic "siege." During the 2009 contested presidential election in Iran, activists outside Iran set up proxy servers that masked the identities of those inside Iran who were posting updates to Twitter and other social network services (Sydell 2009). The distributed nature of this activist network made it impossible for Iranian officials to stop the flow of information out of the country, and it transformed the simple microblogging service into a rather major player in the unfolding events.

The hacker ethic holds particular appeal for computer-savvy adolescents, who savor the sense of power and entitlement that seems to come with the territory. They see it as their obligation to test the limits of online systems by finding security weaknesses and otherwise dabbling in spaces where they are not authorized to be. School administrators now find themselves engaged in "nerd discipline" and are confronted with a troublesome mind-set that seems to defy standard corrective approaches. Perpetrators regard school computing rules as applying only to others (who are idiots and need to be controlled), not to themselves (who are brilliant and should be paid to take care of the system).

In Van Buren's (2001) exploration of high-school hacker ethics, the students she interviewed revealed numerous ways they could wreak havoc, including bringing the entire school network to a halt. Their focus

PASSWORD PRIVILEGES

Some students find a way to obtain system administrator passwords to the school computer network. They learn how to mask the identity of the computers they are logging in from, so no one can trace their actions or figure out who they are. The students use the passwords to poke around the system, including reading and copying some teachers' files and tests. When they finally get caught, they are in big trouble. The students know they have broken the rules, but they claim that they did not delete or change files, look at personal e-mail or student records, or even personally benefit from seeing the tests. Therefore, they feel their punishment should not be too severe.

> What's wrong? They got a few passwords and tried to solve the puzzle of how to get into the administrator accounts and had some fun. Why should they be punished?

*

> I think that their punishments should be just as severe as it would of been if they had used the information. I think this because when they did this, they knew what could happen and they could of used the information, you don't know if they are lying for not. I think that also the kids should have not been poking around that area in the first place. Anyway if they were smart enough to do all of that, and not get traced and stuff, they should of been smart enough to not get caught.

*

> I can see why students would do this. The pressure of getting good grades and the reactions we often get from our parents is motivation to cheat like this. Regardless of this stress, this doesn't justify hacking into the school's computer system and messing with people's PRIVATE accounts.

*

> Weeell, the kids didnt change anything, but they were stilling messing around in other peoples files. Their punishment shouldn't be too bad, but they should still be punished.

*

> This isn't a big deal. Actually, I think the teachers are at fault for not coming up with better security . . .

was on the potential power of their actions, the fact that they could cause damage but did not. When asked point-blank how poorly funded institutions could solve problems of network security, they had no suggestions. Their counterargument was that most student hackers, like themselves, were not malicious, offering "the fact that nothing serious had happened to the school networks as evidence of their peer groups' beneficent nature" (Van Buren 2001, 69). The possibility that they, or other like-minded individuals, engaged in immoral behavior was not a notion worth considering. Teens do not even have to be particularly skilled to adopt this attitude. The disciplinary case I described at the beginning of this chapter required no special technical background. The students used a device called a "key catcher," a small physical component that plugs into a computer keyboard cable and records key strokes. Their success rested on an ability to attach the unobtrusive device to the teacher's workstation and scan through all the captured keystrokes to locate the root password. I can imagine an "old school" hacker regarding this scenario with dismay and wondering why kids these days don't possess real skills.

Some teen hackers, though, have no qualms about mischief making, either for its own sake or for more malevolent purposes. Online identity theft is a good example of this mind-set. Simple impersonation can easily occur when someone forgets to log off a networked computer and another sends out e-mail in that person's name, alters files, or otherwise tampers with the account—often just to "teach the loser a lesson." Or an account can truly be hacked, using deliberate means for a variety of malicious purposes. In either case, not only have the victim's personal space and information been invaded but his or her identity has been assumed and misrepresented.

Freedom of Expression versus Freedom from Expression

The Internet has introduced unrivaled opportunities for personal expression, but these opportunities are not without cost or conflict. One person's right to free speech is a potential invasion of another person's privacy. Speech can be hurtful, even if accidentally so. Children first learn that they are never to lie. Later, they come to understand that utter honesty is not always the best policy, that there is a time and place for every expression. But the facelessness of online communication removes inhibitions, making it easier than ever to speak before thinking, disregarding or minimizing your target's reactions. Sensitivity to others' feelings has taken a backseat to the efficiency of the *send* command and a general trend toward what might be called "offensiveness deflation." In sum, ICTs have the potential to cause unintentional hurt, to violate or betray confidences, and to be used as vehicles of outright bullying.

Social network services (SNSs) and cell-phone technologies have multiplied the modes in which personal information can be shared. It is now a simple matter to take pictures or shoot videos and forward them, post them, and otherwise spread them around the digitized universe. The subjects of these artifacts have little to say about the context in which their images are displayed. The rise of "sexting," sending sexually explicit photos and messages through cell phones, has escalated the problem to new heights. As relationships deteriorate, photos may be distributed to wider audiences. Some teen sexters have even found themselves facing child pornography charges, both for taking and sending photos as well as for receiving and possessing them (St. George 2009). In the worst cases, videos and photos go viral, saturating the Internet and altering lives in profound ways (Bennett 2008).

In response, SNSs have developed a few features that give users some measure of control over their digital images as long as they are members of the particular service. For example, Facebook allows users to "untag" (i.e., render unsearchable) the images of themselves that are posted on other users' profiles. But they cannot remove the photos, modify the captions, or even delete their names. Many teens are quite sanguine about this phenomenon. As noted earlier, notions of privacy are in transition, and teens may not be terribly concerned about the probing eyes of an abstract public. But users often do not realize how open a "closed" network can be. In the case of Facebook, photos can be viewed by users who are outside a direct "friend" relationship if other second-order linkages are created via status updates, networks, and other means. In general, once the images are "out," they are permanently beyond a subject's control.

Grinter and Palen (2002) report the concerns teens have about IM conversations among friends being saved or copied and then shown to others. Teens therefore might view the phone as being a safer medium for exchanging sensitive or confidential information. And, of course, the ability to save, forward, or alter private messages can be debilitating to those involved. One of my students commented:

> I've lately noticed how dangerous it is to try to have a serious con-
> versation with somebody when you don't know how closely they value
> the information that goes on between you two. I mean, if you type
> it and send it to the person, that means they can save it and show it
> to someone else or copy and paste. It makes any committing words
> a serious hazard to your privacy. Just because they say they won't,
> doesn't mean they won't. I don't know, AIM and E-mail give you in-
> credible powers of invasion of privacy.

Bullying is a plague that has long been an unfortunate feature of childhood and adolescence. Now, with ICTs, bullying can go on twenty-four hours a day rather than being confined to the school day. The victim's home is no longer a place of escape and sanctuary. Homophobic taunts, for example, reach far beyond the hallway or gym class now that is possible to "out" others by posting their names online. Rachel Simmons, author of *Odd Girl Out: The Hidden Culture of Aggression in Girls* (2002), reports that bullies tend to be products of the middle class. They engage in "alternative" or unconventional (i.e., nonphysical) aggression because their culture does not always allow them to display anger in a more open way. These same "good kids" lose their inhibitions and sense of accountability in the online environment, writing things they would never say to one another in person (Simmons 2003). Perpetrators can later behave as though nothing has happened or even claim that someone else was using their screen name or e-mail account (claiming to be victims themselves).

In fact, the pervasive concerns regarding adults preying on children are giving way to a growing awareness that it is the peers of children and adolescents who should be the focus of that concern. A study conducted by the Cyber Safety and Ethics Initiative at Rochester Institute of Technology confirms that peers of approximately the same age or grade level perpetrate the majority of cyberoffenses, and that cyberbullying peaks in middle school, which is also when the online exchange of sex-related content begins (McQuade 2008). At the same time, it is important to remember bullying remains a feature of adolescence both off-line and online. Of online teens, 67 percent feel that bullying and harassment

POPULARITY POLL

Joe uses a web board to conduct a popularity poll. He asks, "Who are the people you like most in the sophomore class? Who are the people you like least?" A couple of names predominate on the "least liked" list. Suzy, who is one of those people, starts missing a lot of school. Her parents are puzzled because the doctor can find nothing physically wrong with her. School officials warn them that Suzy will have to repeat the year if her attendance doesn't improve.

I think Joe should have probably done something else for his poll. Some people would find the results offensive. What he could have done instead was just ask who people thought was popular, and not who was unpopular. That way the "unpopular" people wouldn't get their feelings hurt, and the people who were on the poll would be glad to see their name on the list.

*

I agree that they should take least popular off, but I think that the whole thing should be gotten rid of. It could still hurt people. It could get people talking and the "least likes" might get out.

*

I believe that Suzie has to talk to the other sophomores and find out why she is disliked. After that, the school should heavily punish the person who started the "popularity poll" in the first place, for creating such a thing. He should also get a lecture about creating situations that might be offending or hurtful.

*

I think that Suzy should receive some help and support and Joe should receive some kind of punishment for what he has done. If she explains why she has missed that much school, she shouldn't have to repeat the year.

happen to teens their age more off-line than online (Lenhart 2007). Of the one-third who report being the victims of cyberbullying, girls are more likely than boys to be targets, as are those who more actively share their thoughts and identities online.

As in the off-line world, many cases of harassment go unreported. Research commissioned by the Girl Scouts of the USA found that 30 percent of girls who were sexually harassed in a chat room simply left the chat room and did not tell anyone about their experience (Girl Scout Research Institute 2002). But 21 percent said they did nothing because "it happens all the time" and "is no big deal"—a sentiment often expressed by both harassers and victims in parallel non-Internet situations. Why don't victims just block the abusers' screen names, un-"friend" former "friends," ignore their text messages, and delete offensive e-mail? It is not so simple. If too many technical blocks and filters are in place, legitimate communication cannot get through. Most of all, the victim remains continuously aware of the abuser's presence. If a group of bullies is involved, the whispering and pointing has a virtual life as well as a physical one.

Teachers can also be the victims of bullying. Student bullies may post their teachers' home telephone numbers to sex-oriented public forums. They can create or add to websites that satirize or defame real people, such as ratemyteachers.com, where students publicly critique their teachers, or badbadteacher.com, where anyone can accuse an educator of sexual misconduct. As with bullied peers, the subjects of these sites are not celebrities whose lives become something of public property but ordinary citizens who should have more of an expectation of personal privacy. An extreme case of how unfettered free expression can impinge on the rights of others occurred when a student, from his home, created a website called Teacher Sux. The site contained offensive and threatening comments about his principal and his algebra teacher, depicting the latter with her head severed and her face morphing into Adolf Hitler's face. The boy showed the site to other students at school, where it was subsequently viewed by the principal and the teacher in question. His parents sued the school district for suspending their son, claiming his constitutional rights were violated. The Pennsylvania Supreme Court ruled against them in *J. S. v. Bethlehem Area School District* (569 Pa. 638 2002; 807 A.2d 847 2002), finding that obscene and libelous speech was not constitutionally protected. Even though the site was created without the use of school computing facilities, the fact of its accessibility at school and the deleterious impact of its content was enough to convince the courts that irreparable harm had been done to those depicted and to the school climate.

School administrators are especially frustrated by the unique challenges of this particular battleground. First, they do not necessarily

FACEBOOK PHOTOS

Chester, Agatha, and Ridley are hanging out at the park one day and meet up with Chester's friend Troy. Troy takes a bunch of pictures with his cell phone and uploads them to Facebook, adding suggestive captions to the photos. Agatha starts getting friend requests from guys she doesn't know. She also gets a phone call from one of the families she babysits for, canceling her upcoming job with them.

Agatha should ask Troy to take the pictures off or remove the captions. However, it is her fault for getting in the pictures. She should choose her friends more wisely and be responsible for her actions.

*

i think that troy should be the one getting in trouble, not agatha. he was the one taking pictures and putting the suggestive captions on them.

*

She could just remove the tags, and tell Troy that he shouldn't have been doing that, b/c it's causing her problems. Obviously she might want to make sure she never hangs around Troy anymore. It wasnt her fault b/c she didnt know her pictures were going to be posted, but she should have been more careful.

*

I think Agatha just should not accept the friend requests and remove her tags. Its really not that bad though. Its Troy's fault for the suggestive captions so he should deal with the consequences for that. I think whoever she is babysitting for is over reacting.

*

Most of the time when I am tagged in photos, I remove my tag because anybody can view photos. If you are friends with somebody, you can view their photos of a person who you don't know. If a photo is bad or maybe offensive, I might ask the uploader to remove it.

understand that an unsafe environment at school can be created outside of school (as the courts determined in the case of the Teacher Sux author). Second, precisely because most of these activities happen outside school, officials may not learn of the harassment, and if they do, they lack the evidence required to pursue disciplinary action. It is difficult to establish a paper trail in an ephemeral online environment like instant messaging. Teens often share screen names and passwords, further complicating investigations. Third, the pursuit of harassers may be inhibited by schools' fears of being accused of violating privacy rights. Finally, in an atmosphere of moral panic and finger-pointing, school personnel may have justifiable concerns about even getting involved. Freedom High School (Loudon County, Virginia) assistant principal Ting-Yi Oei (2009) was arrested on child pornography charges during his investigation of a student sexting incident because he naively placed the photo in question on his own cell phone. Local law enforcement seemed to be more interested in placating a disgruntled parent and finding a fall guy than in conducting a legitimate investigation of the incident. His outstanding record notwithstanding, his reputation and career were turned upside down.

Access to Inappropriate Content

The potential ability to access online pornography and other questionable content is one of the most volatile Internet-based issues that schools and libraries have had to deal with. The problem is actually a much bigger one than the simple availability of pornography on the Internet. It has to do with minors' rights to access a wide variety of information, the conflicting and confusing content that is thrown at them by well-meaning as well as unscrupulous content providers, how types of information are interpreted by the community, and kids' personal ability to deal with what they are exposed to. Because these concerns are so broad and of such importance, the next chapter is devoted to their examination.

ANOREXIA

Several students have discovered a website that promotes anorexia as a lifestyle choice rather than as an eating disorder. The site includes tips for weight loss, pictures that glamorize the anorexic look, a discussion board that members use to support one another, and other materials that promote "anorexic pride." School counselors have asked that this site and others like it be blocked on the school network. They point out that anorexia is a deadly disease and that some students are particularly susceptible to this type of misinformation.

I think that the school counselors should be able to block the websites on the school computers because they think they are protecting the students from harmful information. As long as they don't restrict people's computers outside of school, I think that they should be able to do so in school.

*

The students can be told that this is a bad choice, but this website in no way should be blocked. If it is blocked, then the students' subconscious will think that some thing good is being kept from them, and then we will have a problem. Also, the students should make their own decisions.

*

I feel that the school is taking the right action. The school is responsible for the children while they are attending the school and anorexia could be very harmful to students and even deadly. The website in a way is brainwashing them and should be banned from the school network immediately.

*

Although I do think it's the students' choice whether to be anorexic or not, that's not the point. Even though I think that they should educate the kids about the dangers of anorexia rather than shielding them from a website, the point is that the school administrators have the right to block the site on school computers. They're SCHOOL computers! The school can do what they want with them!

*

If the school counselors blocked this site from the network, they would have to block all sites dealing with this topic. We must respect freedom of speech and accept there are many sites with inappropriate content on the web. It is not fair or efficient to block this site, and students would most likely simply find another site similar to it. Either the school [should] develop a system which generally blocks sites dealing with this topic, or not block it at all.

6

the deep end:
content

C ontent, loads of it. The Internet has given us this gift. It is a wonderful gift, representing a transformation of the information landscape perhaps as profound as the invention of the printing press. Like many gifts, however, there is a catch. Not all the content is of high (or even reasonable) quality, and not all of it is what it appears to be. The onus is on the consumer to make wise choices, to pick out credible content from the onslaught of the crassly commercial, the banal, the suspect, and the unsavory. The consumer must also learn to understand how intent and context influence meaning. For example, a riot may be the subject of a news article, a pundit's blog, a local newspaper editorial, a video taken by a passerby, and Twitter messages that emanate from a variety of origins. Any one of these sources might be considered credible or useful in some way—or not—depending on a user's interests and purposes.

The focus of this chapter is on the implications of open access to online information of all types and changing notions of credibility. How does a young person make choices in an information universe that is unvetted and without apparent structure? In their excellent overview of digital media, youth, and credibility, Flanagin and Metzger (2008) note that young people do not seem to be terribly concerned about credibility as it has historically been construed. Many teens feel that digital media are shattering traditional models of authority. In some circumstances young people can have more authority than adults, and in other cases nonexperts may be more credible than experts. Still, even with evolving perceptions of credibility, consumers of all ages need to be able to decode what they see and experience online. At first glance, every website in a list of search-engine results looks the same, with only the implicit rank order distinguishing one site from another. The Web has no fiction section, no nonfiction section, no biography section. Visual and contextual cues that do exist can be misleading or confusing. A search on "abortion" may lead to an advocacy organization's website, a medical website, or a church website. Finally, purveyors of questionable content employ an arsenal of tactics to make their wares palatable, marketable, and ultimately acceptable to significant numbers of people, including (and maybe especially) teens.

It's important to keep in mind that this information landscape is not divided into pure categories of "good" and "bad." Not all credible content is equally credible, and not all questionable content is equally questionable. For purposes of discussion, I have sorted this continuum of material into somewhat arbitrary categories, followed by a similar sorting of the variety of techniques used by content providers to persuade and manipulate. Ultimately, young people need to be able to protect themselves by sharpening their media and information literacy skills and becoming savvy consumers of online information. Teaching these skills will be the subject of chapter 7.

DEFINING APPROPRIATE AND INAPPROPRIATE

No discussion of young people and online content can be conducted without addressing issues of "appropriateness." Everyone has something to say about kids and what they should or should not be looking at online. First, it is important to acknowledge that terms like *questionable* and *inappropriate* have different meanings in different contexts. What is considered acceptable content at home may not be considered acceptable at school or in the workplace. Furthermore, there is disagreement about what constitutes inappropriate Internet content within formal schooling environments.

I appreciate the framework articulated by Doug Johnson (2003), in which he classifies the uses of technology in terms of place, audience, and purpose. *Place* is an issue of ethical resource allocation. Because the demand for technology has outpaced its acquisition, priority for its use must be given to academic needs. The inappropriate use of personal technologies also distracts from classroom activities. Cell-phone use in schools, for example, may need to be regulated to protect classroom learning. The issue of *audience* arises with concerns about the appropriateness of content. Johnson advises schools to define and teachers to help students understand the characteristics and conditions under which content becomes unsuitable for school use. Content and language that are used outside of school are not always appropriate in schools, where a wide range of value systems must coexist. *Purpose* has to do with how students use technology and how schools control that use. Although schools must respect students' rights to personal expression and their explorations of identity, students must also understand when exercising those rights becomes harmful to themselves or others.

Johnson also reminds us that technology itself is neutral, that it can be used for constructive as well as destructive purposes. This admonition is important to keep in mind as technologies develop and become increasingly ubiquitous in a wide variety of settings. Views of technology tools should adapt as well. Scarcity of computing facilities in schools has become less and less of an equity concern and can no longer routinely be used as a sole reason for prohibiting use that is not directly related to the curriculum. Similarly, educational applications for handheld devices (including cell phones) now seem to be released on a daily basis, making it much harder to justify the outright ban of such devices in schools. It helps me to remember how, not so long ago, it was unthinkable to allow the use of e-mail on any library's computers. Now e-mail is commonplace in libraries—may even be seen as a core service in public libraries—and is integrated into the functionality of research tools such as online databases.

Sometimes it is tempting to fall back on policies that are either easy to enforce or are implemented merely to prevent situations that are difficult to control. For example, educators can be very prescriptive about what students are allowed to look at online while at school. Many school acceptable-use policies restrict all use of the Internet to academic purposes. The rationale for such policies can be a factor of limited computer resources, as Johnson notes, but I suspect it is at least as often a consequence of our own beliefs and prejudices about what students should be doing during school hours, in the school building, and, not inconsequentially, with taxpayer-funded resources. When a school board member is touring the school, it can be hard to justify a library scene in which students are browsing eBay, comparing electronics prices, or checking the latest NFL scores. From the student point of view, however, restrictive policies lump nonacademic websites in with the truly odious—the pornographic, the violent, the hateful. It does not appear to them that their teachers and administrators draw any distinctions among these wildly disparate Internet-based resources and activities. They have only to look at the print resources in the school library that are not curriculum related—the sports and car magazines, the teen girl magazines, even the fiction section, with its nonrequired reading choices—to have their impressions confirmed.

It is also important to remember that many topics that were once vilified have become mainstream, erstwhile taboos have insinuated themselves into the popular culture, and alternative lifestyles are well represented on the Internet. Though much of this content is suspect, as will be discussed later in this chapter, a great deal of it is useful, legitimate, and well intentioned. The Internet has given curious teens the wherewithal to dabble or to dive wholeheartedly into the esoteric, the avant-garde, and the unusual. Witchcraft is a good illustration of these changing mores. Though still a forbidden subject in some communities, witchcraft has otherwise become almost conventional, popularized by the Harry Potter books and by television shows like *Buffy the Vampire Slayer* and *Charmed.* Mattel even introduced a Secret Spells Barbie in the fall of 2003. Information about Wicca, the practice of witchcraft, has blossomed online. Teen Wiccans, most of them girls, congregate on the Internet, where they swap e-mails, ideas, and spells (Hagerty 2004). They flock to the Witch's Voice (www.witchvox.com), a "proactive educational network" that also links far-flung practitioners to like-minded groups and individuals. It even has a section for essays written by teen pagans.

One strategy for dealing with the disconnect between "inappropriate" content and the school environment is to deliberately incorporate nonacademic content into the educational process, where its use can be supervised and mined for pedagogical purposes. The examples above—online auctions, product cost and feature analysis, sports scores—all present opportunities for mathematics and economics instruction, at the very least. Even presumed nonacademic services like social networking and instant messaging can be put to academic use. In the next two chapters, I will discuss such options, along with techniques for teaching content evaluation. For now, suffice it to say that highly restrictive access policies can block a huge range of potentially valuable web resources and Internet services and create an institutionalized impediment to teaching students credibility assessment strategies (Harris 2008).

Ultimately, schools and libraries must define the principles and standards that best fit their individual settings and circumstances. In my own case, practices have emerged from some underlying personal philosophies. First, students shall do no harm, either to themselves or others. Next, the Internet is provided at school for learning. Last, personal growth and identity exploration are components of learning and literacy. In fact, notions of reading and literacy are evolving, partly in response to changes in technology. Reading and writing online, even for "nonacademic" purposes, are increasingly becoming understood as exercises in literacy, particularly when literacy is defined as reading and writing habits that connect to the reader's/writer's real world (Braun 2007). As an example, Lewis and Fabos (2005) found that IM literacy was, in part, an extension of schooled literacy practices, reflecting a level of literacy engagement educators may find encouraging.

A couple of examples illustrate how my perspectives play themselves out in practice. The first is my choice to allow students to use the computers in our library to pursue personal interests. David, who consults sports sites like ESPN (http://espn.go.com), is typical of these users. During baseball season, he navigates from ESPN's major league baseball scores pages to its message boards site. From there, he selects "MLB teams," then "Chicago Cubs." By following the Cubs message board, he not only keeps up with the news of his favorite team but, more important, he learns the banter of this (largely adult) community, discovers what is important to its members, and gains a more nuanced understanding of baseball issues than he might pick up from traditional news sources. Though David posts a question every once in a while, he generally confines himself to reading and learning. If David were a student at a school that restricts computer use to curriculum-related purposes, he would not be allowed to further this aspect of his "education." From my perspective, as long as others do not need his computer for school-related work, David can continue to follow the conversations on these message boards as much as he likes.

Although I defend the rights of the student who hones his baseball knowledge in my library, I prohibit most computer gaming. Why this distinction? The difference lies in the impact of the activity on the environment around it. Unless it is carefully managed (which can be done), gaming can turn the library, the computer lab, and the classroom into an arcade. My personal experience is that the space becomes loud and raucous, and eventually even smelly from the close congregation of agitated bodies. No one else who wants to use the space for its intended purpose has a chance. Picturing the scene without computers makes the differences more obvious. The Chicago Cubs fan would be using magazines and newspapers to conduct his research (although, apart from the letters-to-the-editor section, those sources would not provide him with the community dialogue he finds on the message boards). The game players would be chasing each other around the library, wielding sound-enabled toy laser weapons. The ground rules are evident: learn, and do no harm.

WISDOM OF THE CROWD

As we teach young people to evaluate online information, it is important to keep in mind that we are operating in a very different information environment than the one in which most of us grew up. Contemporary conceptions of authority and credibility have been profoundly affected by the wide-open nature of the Internet and the culture of sharing afforded by Web 2.0 tools. Internet users now seek answers from "the wisdom of the crowd" rather than from more traditional (and centralized) sources of authority. The judgment of the many is often regarded as equal to or even better than the judgment of any single individual or entity. This phenomenon plays out in a variety of ways. If a list of hits on Google turns up the same information multiple times, a user is inclined to accept that information at face value—without even having to click through to any of the links to the actual websites. This behavior is fueled by the assumption that if a lot of people say something is true, then it must be, and stems from the same thinking as the "satisficing" behaviors described in chapter

2. To the consternation of librarians, it is a strategy that may work more often than not. If I want to know the capital of North Dakota, the first screen of search-engine results clearly points to Bismarck.

More typically, "crowd wisdom" is defined as information that is provided by users or peers rather than by traditional information providers. Wikipedia is perhaps the best-known example of this phenomenon. As the online encyclopedia that anyone can edit, its self-correcting properties have earned it the respect of many. Links to the site from other reputable sources virtually guarantee it first-page (if not first-place) rankings on Google searches. The business world has gotten into the act through the practice of "crowdsourcing," or outsourcing work to an unspecified work force or public by putting out a general call for input. Educators and others have followed suit by posting surveys, polls, or just open questions on blogs and professional learning networks. The information gathered through such exercises may not be considered scientifically valid, but it meets the needs of its intended purpose. At its heart, the phenomenon of crowd wisdom reflects the informal information-seeking practices described in chapter 2. It certainly comprises a significant way in which young people use the Internet for information gathering.

At its best, the wisdom of the crowd advances knowledge and has become the subject of serious research. The MIT Center for Collective Intelligence (http://cci.mit.edu) was created for the purpose of studying how people and computers can be connected so that, as a collective, they have the potential to act with more intelligence than they would as individuals, separate groups, or computers. However, the involvement of the many drives both quantity and quality of content, which can be problematic. The same crowd origins that make Wikipedia so valuable also define its weakness. The "crowd" may be a corporate interest, a disgruntled politician, or a vandal. One of the most famous cases of Wikipedia inaccuracy was an anonymously written entry on writer and journalist John Seigenthaler (Seigenthaler 2005). Seigenthaler served as an administrative assistant to Robert Kennedy, and the article falsely connected him to the assassination of John F. Kennedy, an inaccuracy that went uncorrected for months. Likewise, information that is shared by citizen-journalists is hard to verify independently and does not undergo any kind of editorial review. Finally, crowd wisdom can be susceptible to various types of groupthink, including a pervasive sense of complacency ("someone else will take care of that"), peer pressure, and even hysteria. One of the more vocal critics of crowd-style democratization of the Internet is Andrew Keen, author of *The Cult of the Amateur,* who decries what he perceives as the loss of expertise and culture and predicts an enormous drain on the economy as people refuse to pay for either (2007). He describes the current state of affairs as the "law of digital Darwinism, the survival of the loudest and most opinionated" (2007, 8).

INFORMATION NEIGHBORHOODS

The Web is home to huge classes of information that have never been included in the traditional publishing models that libraries employ for building collections. Now, library collections are unlimited and virtual as well as selective and physical. Users blithely conduct web searches that retrieve information from a wide spectrum of origination, ranging from commercial sites to advocacy organizations to online communities. As an illustration, one of my students was delighted to find a map online of a river he was studying for a science project. As I helped him with the detective work of uncovering authorship for his bibliographic citation, he discovered that the map came from a brochure created by a riverboat tour guide company. The geographical markers on the map represented boat stops and other features of the tour, pitched to entice potential customers. As such, they did not really touch on the scientific perspective he needed for his project. The map—as an information artifact—was not lacking in intrinsic value. But its particular value lay in a set of informational data points that were selected and contextualized for an entirely different purpose and audience, making the map inappropriate for his needs. Still, it was hard for me to convince him that his "relevant" selection was not really relevant (even with its high placement on his results list and with all keywords present) and that he could find a more suitable source with a little effort and thought. In pre-Internet days, my library would not have had access to this brochure, and the student would not have been faced with determining its relevance to him. On the other hand, that same online access allowed him to renegotiate his search and locate the truly relevant material that in pre-Internet days also would not have been available to him.

A model I find useful when categorizing web content is one that was developed by the SUNY Stonybrook School of Journalism Center for News Literacy for its pioneering news literacy course (www.stonybrook.edu/journalism/newsliteracy). The course employs a "news neighborhood" metaphor, in which news is divided into six neighborhoods: news, propaganda, advertising, publicity, entertainment, and raw information. For example, "news" is defined as information that is gathered by journalists and can be verified by authoritative and independent sources, whereas "propaganda" is defined as information created by government or political entities using manipulation and deception in order to generate support or trigger action. Students are shown examples of news media stories and asked to sort them by neighborhood, an exercise that helps them better understand content and intent. It is not really realistic to try to devise a similar set of discrete categories for the broad spectrum of "information neighborhoods," but the concept is very similar to what is already done on a smaller scale. For example, librarians and other educators have long asked students to distinguish between peer-reviewed journals and popular magazines. In the web universe, any number of rubrics could be designed to help young people better discern one information neighborhood from another.

Although I will not try to create such a rubric here, I will attempt to highlight some of the unique neighborhoods that make the online information world so challenging for consumers of all ages to travel through.

Advocacy

The Internet is a haven and a boon for advocacy activities of all types. The physical library hosts no parallel functionality, certainly not at a comparable level. In contrast, the online advocacy neighborhood hosts huge repositories of content that exists solely to represent specific interests, to persuade others of the merits of those interests, and to share information about them. Advocacy sites are as varied as the entire range of human interest and concern. Neighborhood residents include such diverse inhabitants as the National Rifle Association, La Leche League, the Animal Liberation Front, and the American Society of Anesthesiologists.

For young information consumers, the challenge is to recognize how the mission of these organizations might influence the nature of the content they deliver. As an example, whenever I see students searching the open web for environmental information, they invariably find themselves on the websites of advocacy organizations like the World Wildlife Fund and Greenpeace. Whatever credible and authoritative information exists on these sites is contextualized to support the prime directive of the organizations. The National Confectioners Association's website (www.candyusa .org) tells me what I want to hear about the benefits of candy and chocolate, drawing on reputable scientific documentation. But it minimizes the information I do not want to hear about the dangers of overindulgence. The site's information may be absolutely factual, if not entirely complete. Even a site like the Bulletin of the Atomic Scientists (www.thebulletin.org), with a board of sponsors that includes 18 Nobel laureates, filters information through its own lens. The discerning consumer will be tipped off to the organization's perspective just by noting the name of its famous Doomsday Clock, which appears on the cover of every issue of the periodical and as a "favicon" (URL icon) in the web browser's address bar.

Commercialism

On the open web, commercial websites are given the same billing as the websites of education and government institutions, nonprofit advocacy organizations, hobbyists, and others. The science students who find themselves on the website of the World Wildlife Fund may then land on the website of a company that manufactures devices for water pollution control systems. They need to understand that the data such a company provides are selected to support the success of the commercial venture, not necessarily to contribute to broader scientific knowledge. Things get very sticky when residents of the commercial "neighborhood" masquerade as residents of other neighborhoods. This phenomenon is not a new one in contemporary media. When children's television programs revolve around product lines, the advertising neighborhood is recasting itself as the entertainment neighborhood. These same programs have now moved online, along with their commercial messages.

The advertising neighborhood often portrays itself as either a research or news neighborhood. A web search on "alcohol statistics" retrieves a site called Alcoholstats.com, created by the Anheuser-Busch company. The site contains a rich collection of state-by-state data about alcohol use as well as numerous articles on subjects such as alcohol consumption, advertising, education, and health. The state data are compiled from various government agency reports and include statistics about teen drunk driving and related topics. The articles originate from a variety of external sources, with a healthy representation from survey research firms like Nielsen and Harris Interactive. Although all this information is independently collected and published, an interesting trend emerges when viewed in the aggregate on the website. Here is a sampling of the brief descriptions of the articles on alcohol advertising:

> "Anheuser-Busch places beer advertising in magazines, on television, and on radio programs where at least 70 percent of the audience is expected to be adults of legal purchase age."

> "The majority of Americans (79 percent) support better education about alcohol and stricter punishment of offenders over raising taxes and limiting advertising of alcohol beverages."

> "The majority of youth . . . cite their parents as the leading influence in their decisions about whether they drink alcohol or not. Sixty-seven percent of college-bound youth (ages 13–17) identified their parents as the leading influence in their decisions about drinking alcohol."

> "Alcohol advertising on all media comprise 1.17 percent of all ads."

Collectively, the message of these statistics-laden articles is that the advertising produced by Anheuser-Busch is not responsible for underage drinking, that the public understands this, and therefore that the company's advertising should not be restricted in any way. The question is: are young people equipped to recognize this subtext and the way in which these messages are packaged? Or are they more likely to take (and use) this information at face value?

The underbelly of the commercial neighborhood is the unwanted content that arrives hidden in spam, pop-up advertising, spyware, and the like. It is one thing when young people actively look for trouble, but it is another to have trouble come marching in unbidden and unexpected. Consumers of all ages often share personal information online without considering the privacy practices (or "nonpractices") that can precipitate this onslaught. My students respond to these aggravations with relative equanimity: "Yeah, sometimes spammers send me porn links and stuff . . . it's so annoying." Reactions like this one tell me that the shock value of spam has declined, as it has for flame wars. Instead, this generation has become accustomed to the intrusion and seems to regard it as a necessary evil of the online environment.

As sanguine as my students may appear to be about these invasive phenomena, their impact is likely to have a lasting effect on the future of communication technologies. Spam is rendering e-mail nearly useless in some cases. The deluge is frustrating and resource-draining at the least, and outright destructive at worst. At whatever level, spam can take the control of the online experience out of users' hands.

The Dark Side

Beyond any debates about appropriateness, the Web is host to an undeniably scary world. There is little quibbling about the unsuitability of the Internet's seamiest neighborhoods—the hard-core pornography, the violent imagery, the place of refuge for scoundrels and villains of all types. For a variety of reasons that will be discussed later in this chapter, much of this content is hard to detect immediately. Or it arrives quite uninvited, invading our private online space. For these reasons and more, it is important to understand the nature of the Internet's dark side. Let's take a quick tour through some of these content types.

Pornography

Ah, pornography, the Great Evil of the Internet. Our worries about it spring from two different areas of concern. First, we worry about intrusive pornography that arrives, like spam, without being summoned by the user. Online porn is more than accessible—it can sometimes actually be hard to avoid. As casual as teens may purport to be about invasive information and communication technology (ICT) phenomena, they are not always comfortable with it. Of Internet users ages ten to seventeen who encounter pornography online, the majority report that it is unwanted and unsolicited (Wolak, Mitchell, and Finkelhor 2007). Peer-to-peer networks have become major conveyers of online pornography and are the source of much of the unwanted content. Teens can unwittingly acquire hard-core video clips, many of which have innocuous file names or names similar to something they might be looking for. Teens do not need credit cards to share these files, nor does most filtering software recognize or block them.

The second source of our worry about pornography has to do with our knowledge (and memories!) of the teenage mind. We all recognize that curiosity about sexuality is a normal part of growing up. When I was a teenager, boys were sneaking copies of their fathers' *Playboy* magazines and girls were reading contraband copies of *Peyton Place* to find out about sex. These days, societal standards about sexual content in the public forum have loosened considerably, partly as a consequence of the mixed messages broadcast by today's media. Teens need look no further than the nearest billboard, grocery-store magazine rack, music video, Calvin Klein ad—or even the current cover of *Rolling Stone* in their school library—to find rather explicit sexual imagery. Online, commercial websites targeted at tweens feature highly sexualized characterizations of young women (see figure 6.1). What was once taboo has become commonplace. Accessibility has dulled our shock meters, inevitably leading to new standards of acceptability.

Even though standards of sexual explicitness have relaxed, viewing hard-core pornography is still a stigmatized activity. The pornography industry has long taken advantage of technology to minimize the effects of that stigma. Videocassettes changed pornography access from a public affair to a private one, bringing it first to booths at the adult store and then to VCRs in the home. The Web provides this same privacy and convenience to teenagers, who are barred from the adult sections of video stores. The online environment reduces their fear of detection and encourages a sense of disinhibition. But the stakes are higher in the online environment because of the sheer availability of so much extremely explicit material. Online pornography can make *Playboy* and *Penthouse* look like *Good Housekeeping* magazine.

Figure 6.1
Sexualized image of teenage girl trying on clothes at Zwinky.com. The site shows different articles of clothing going on and coming off of the figure of the girl.

Crackpots, Wackos, and the Demons of Adolescence

Unfortunately, the Web is a mecca for old-fashioned and newfangled crackpots peddling questionable products, information, and solutions for all of life's ills. Curious teens will discover ideas and instructions for body piercing, tattooing, and branding. Troubled souls will locate plenty of information on weaponry, military equipment, and spy gear. Occult interests are easily satisfied by the plethora of websites on satanism, voodoo, and demonology. The information found online about over-the-edge topics is by no means monolithic in opinion, tone, or intent. While perusing a discussion forum on tattooing, I was amused to read the outraged comments of principled tattoo artists condemning the "scabwrenchers," "scratchers," and "hepatitis vendors" who give tattoos to minors. But the same forum contained threads about whether or not to shave a body part that has been "inked" (yes, shave it for best effect), the pros and cons of tattooing feet, and one member's link to his private gallery of pornographic, misogynistic tattoos. The question is whether or not teen observers and participants can sort these threads into the sane and the insane, the reasonable and the unreasonable, and the advice that is legitimately helpful and that which is self-destructive.

Teens who fall prey to the modern plagues of adolescence—eating disorders, self-injury, illegal drugs, and the like—now have unimaginable resources at their fingertips. They can join support groups for the anorexic "lifestyle," they can consult how-to sites on cutting and other forms of self-injury, and they can look up formulas for prescription-drug cocktails. On a community "pro-anorexia" blog I found the following entry:

> I want the fabric of my coat to drape over my shoulders, I want my collar bones to be apparent. . . . I want my dress to not be able to stay on my body. I want to appear delicate . . . weak . . . only I will know just how strong I am.

In other entries on this blog, participants post lists of the foods they have eaten that day and ask questions about one another's dieting and fasting techniques. Does the one-bagel-a-day diet work? Is water-fasting unsafe? Where do you get Dexatrim and how much does it cost? Will you be my Ana (anorexia) buddy? Without the Internet, such support and validation would be much more difficult to come by. Worst of all, parents, other knowledgeable adults, and friends face difficult odds in the face of such a formidable, omnipresent influence as an Internet-based community.

Hatemongering

The Internet is a great public square. The values that inspired its creation do not discriminate among belief systems. As a result, bigots have the same place at the table as those who work for social justice. Perhaps the most troubling by-product of the Internet era has been the new lease on life it has given to extremist hate groups. Although ethnic hatred and racism have always been with us, extremists once had to go to great lengths to find one another and organize their efforts. They have now found both community and platform through the Internet, with teens as a particular target audience. Kindred spirits are a click away, and calls to action are easy to instigate with the help of social network sites and tools. Compare yesterday's laborious distribution of racist leaflets on a few college campuses to today's Internet-enabled delivery. Extremists create professional-looking websites that are hard to distinguish from those of reputable organizations. Their presence on mainstream social networking sites gives them a reach and kind of legitimacy that was once unimaginable.

In its 2009 annual "Year in Hate" report (Holthouse 2009), the Southern Poverty Law Center identified 926 active hate groups in the United States, up 4 percent from 2007 and a whopping 50 percent from 2000, when there were 602 groups. The national immigration debate drove much of the hate discourse during this time period, but the economic recession and Barack Obama's successful campaign to become the nation's first African American president raised the stakes to new levels of intensity. The Leadership Conference on Civil Rights Education Fund, which represents nearly 200 national organizations, used part of its 2009 report on hate crimes in America to clarify how hate groups have exploited the Internet to spread their message and recruit new members. Besides hosting traditional websites, hate groups are active on social network sites like MySpace and Facebook and in online discussion groups hosted on such mainstream websites as Google, AOL, and Yahoo! Their members take advantage of open online venues like newspapers to post anti-Semitic or racist comments. The Florida-based *Palm Beach Post* had to disable its comments section because of the avalanche of anti-Semitic comments that appeared in the wake of the Bernard Madoff Ponzi scheme scandal (Leadership Conference on Civil Rights Education Fund 2009). Hate groups post videos to social sites like YouTube, often using misleading tags and titles to expose the content to those who would not otherwise seek it out. As have other information providers, they have adapted content so that it can be accessed on handheld devices. Hate groups have learned to harness the Internet to mask their "otherness" and assume positions as legitimate players in modern society.

Although it is startling to see the free-speech blue ribbons that adorn hate sites, they serve as reminders that the Constitution protects most speech, even speech that is offensive and debasing. Only speech that is libelous, threatens individuals, or persistently harasses specific persons is prohibited. Regulating the protected speech of racists would require regulating everyone's speech. In today's environment, this approach is neither technically feasible nor ethically desirable.

Especially for Teens: Music as Message
Music is so important in teenage life that its potential as a tool of persuasion warrants separate discussion. Although we do not (yet) see concrete

evidence that online hate speech has made significant strides in recruiting teens to extremist organizations, hate-based music might be another story. Music imprints our coming-of-age process with an indelible time stamp, differentiating each generation from the previous one. Those who understand this phenomenon have learned to manipulate it to their advantage. A National Public Radio story on the resurgence of hate crimes in Los Angeles reports that the relatively large number of skinheads in high schools may be based on the fact that kids are being recruited through music (Temple-Rastin 2008). Before the Internet, the white power music scene was an underground phenomenon, but now teens can simply play or download the music from the Web. Richard Eaton, who studies the white supremacist movement at the Museum of Tolerance in Los Angeles, describes the responses of young people who were asked about their impressions of the lyrics:

> "And they said, 'I only listen to it because I like the sound of the music,'"
> he says. "But when you are listening to this all the time and hear the lyrics, they stick with you." (Temple-Rastin 2008)

Indeed, the teen demographic makes up a substantial proportion of the white power music fan base. "Hatecore" artists perform in popular genres like punk, electronic, and rap. Marketing focuses on teens, who are thought to represent the future of the white power movement.

Because standard music outlets like retail stores and chains do not carry these products, they are sold online, where teenagers already hang out. The website of Resistance Records (www.resistance.com), the commercial music arm of the white supremacist organization National Alliance, has the usual bells and whistles that appeal to teens—a searchable database of artists and titles, music clips to download, and online ordering. But there is much more to be seen. Teens can order T-shirts, jewelry, and "Aryan-wear boots" from the merchandise area of the site. They can participate in a forum that includes an active Resistance Youth discussion area with topics ranging from music, media, and history to religion. The "Street and Internet Activism" topic exhorts participants to "Come in here for computer discussion and ideas for spreading racial awareness through the Internet; our last medium of free speech!"

PERSUASION TECHNIQUES

Grown-up white supremacists and their ilk recognize the Internet as an effective medium through which to advertise their mission, to persuade, and to recruit. The Internet is not the first medium to be used for propaganda purposes, nor are white supremacists the only group to discover the usefulness of various media types as tools of persuasion. Propaganda techniques apply to all modes of persuasive communication, not just the political. In fact, the same tactics are used by the good guys as well as the bad guys, from mainstream advertisers, nonprofit organizations, government agencies, and political campaigns to hatemongers and terrorist groups. Only the modes of delivery have changed over time, influenced by technology and cultural habit. Broadsides gave way to newspapers, radio, and television in turn. Now the arsenal includes websites, social networks, media-sharing sites, online forums, electronic mailing lists, and even spam.

Contemporary scholars began a serious study of the techniques of persuasion during the twentieth century, as new modes of mass communication blossomed and war in Europe loomed. From 1937 to 1942, the independent Institute for Propaganda Analysis published a series of books and newsletters to help Americans understand the tools of political propaganda. The journalists and social scientists who worked at the institute identified seven basic propaganda devices (*Propaganda Analysis* 1937), and their findings have since been adapted, expanded, and retooled for use in lectures, textbooks, and lessons on critical thinking and the mass media. I will add my own spin to theirs in describing several common tactics of persuasion. Though I illustrate these strategies with a variety of examples, I focus on hate groups as a case study simply because persuasion tactics are most obvious and egregious when used by extremists. This analysis is by no means comprehensive and is undoubtedly idiosyncratic. My goal is to provide an approach to understanding and deconstructing persuasive speech. This model and others like it can serve as a template for teaching students to conduct their own analyses.

Authority

The human psyche seems to crave outside authority, the secure feeling that someone else smarter or better is available as a guide in decision making. Knowing this human tendency, advertisers, propagandists, and others engaged in the business of persuasion often invoke images of authority. We are all familiar with the television commercials in which a figure dressed in a white lab coat refers to studies that prove the effectiveness of a household cleaner or a mouthwash or some other everyday product. The person in the lab coat is an actor, not a scientist, and the existence of bona fide, externally conducted research is doubtful. The elevated status of celebrities in modern society produces a similar aura of authority when the famous, and even the infamous, endorse product lines and political viewpoints for which they may have no particular claims to expertise.

Claims of authority may be misleading, misapplied, or outright false. For many years, Professor Arthur Butz of Northwestern University used his personal university web space for expressing his Holocaust revisionist views. Although he taught at a prestigious institution, his field was electrical engineering, not history. He capitalized on his title and the academic freedom afforded by Northwestern University to espouse beliefs that are based on prejudice and poor scholarship.

Another common strategy is to justify one's position by claiming it emanates from a higher authority, typically in the guise of government or religion. Detractors do not wish to appear as though they are arguing against God or country. The discourse of white supremacists often includes religious vocabulary and references. A search-engine query on the phrase "white Christian" brings up screen after screen of such examples. The implication, of course, is that a person cannot be a true Christian if he or she is either homosexual or nonwhite. Separatism has suddenly become a prescription from above. Some groups even claim authority from both religion and government, as in the Ku Klux Klan slogan "For God, Race, and Country."

The Christian patriot movement is an interesting case of the religion-and-government argument. Ironically, the movement's adherents are neither supporters of the contemporary U.S. government nor of mainstream Christianity. Sociologist James Aho (1990), who spent two years in northern Idaho studying the movement, noted that Christian patriots distinguish between Law and legality, Morality and legalese. They acknowledge only the "organic Constitution" (the original articles of the Constitution plus the Bill of Rights) and selected edicts from the first five books of the

Bible. Therefore, they feel no moral obligation to obey a secular law that is inconsistent with these texts. They get to have it both ways—the blessing of religion and government as well as the freedom to define each to suit a particular worldview. From the Christian patriot perspective, the present U.S. "Zionist Occupation Government" is biblically and constitutionally illegitimate, bent on promoting non-Christian religions, moral perversion, and equal rights for "unqualified" minorities. The Web provides an ideal platform from which to espouse these views.

Lies, Damned Lies, and Statistics

There are as many ways to misuse information as there are not to. We protect our children, our parents, and our friends by telling them the truth, but not always the full truth. Likewise, content providers learn to be selective with the information they report. They manipulate statistics and shape information through creative presentation. As long as there is a grain of truth in what is being said, the message sounds credible and authoritative. Statistics do not even have to be poorly conceived or manipulated to influence impressions. As noted earlier, the National Confectioner's Association tells me everything I want to hear about sweets, and not much of what I don't want to hear. Wholly different conclusions can be presented based on the same set of data. Cox Communications, in partnership with the National Center for Missing and Exploited Children, conducted a survey of teens on online and wireless safety issues (Cox 2009). The news articles that reported the results varied widely in their presentation of the data. The online *USA Today* article headline shouted "Survey: 1 in 5 teens 'sext' despite risks" (Leinwand 2009), in contrast to Internet safety expert Larry Magid's blog title, "Survey shows teens more safety savvy than thought" (2009a). Shaping a story is not new to the Web, but the Web magnifies and strengthens our ability to do so.

Consumers must also be aware of more sinister instances of the misuse of information. A lengthy essay titled "Who Rules America?" appears on the website of the National Alliance (www.natall.com/who-rules-america), a white power organization. This essay catalogs the ownership of the American mass media—from electronic news and entertainment media to print newspapers and magazines—and ties it to Jewish individuals or to those who have "sold out" to Jews or been "undermined" by Jews. Though dated, many of the facts in this story are indisputable. The names and companies mentioned are real. The historic role of Jews in Hollywood and the mass media is no secret, having been celebrated and documented in popular as well as scholarly writing.

But the National Alliance stacks the cards, using this information to draw conclusions that are not warranted by the facts. First, it asserts that the Jewish role amounts to conspiracy. "Despite a few prominent exceptions, the preponderance of Jews in the media is so overwhelming that we are obliged to assume that it is due to more than mere happenstance." Then a call to action is issued:

> But we must not remain silent on this most important of issues! The Jewish control of the American mass media is the single most important fact of life, not just in America, but in the whole world today. There is nothing—plague, famine, economic collapse, even nuclear war—more dangerous to the future of our people.

It is understood that "our people" are white Christians.

Looks Are Everything

The digital world is the ultimate makeover machine. The visual cues that help us categorize and otherwise process information may or may not be present online, or they may be packaged in such a way that vital associations either cannot be made or are misdirected. At first glance, the website of the Institute for Historical Review (www.ihr.org) presents an innocuous face, one that deflects attention from its mission as a Holocaust denial organization. The word *institute* in its name and the prominent link on its masthead to the *Journal of Historical Review* are designed to evoke scholarly associations. Never mind that the journal has been defunct since 2002 and that its contents were never indexed by reputable, scholarly databases. The "News and Comment" section, centrally placed, presents a stream of continuously updated article excerpts that link to the original sources. These sources represent all manner of mainstream news organizations, including Israeli newspapers and Jewish American publications. Their presence cannot help but leave an impression that the institute is endorsed by the likes of the *Los Angeles Times,* the *Jerusalem Post,* the *Economist,* and the *New York Times.* But the articles are selected to tell the story the institute wants to tell and are plucked, out of context, from sources that espouse the ideals of a free press and diversity of thought.

Co-opting Symbols and Traditions

A subtle way to evoke an aura of authority is to adopt the use of established symbols and traditions. Visual imagery and traditional practices are used to convey legitimacy, status, historical imprimatur, and other desirable qualities. For example, the logo of the National Recycling Coalition's "America Recycles Day" campaign is an American flag made from red, white, and blue plastic bottles and other recycled items. The image of the flag conjures patriotic associations in the minds of those who consider participating in the event, despite the fact that no government agency sponsors it. As adoptions of such symbols occur, original meanings may change or even be lost. Few of my students can trace the contemporary origins of the various "awareness ribbon" campaigns to the yellow ribbons that were used to welcome home long-lost loved ones, most notably the hostages held during the Iranian hostage crisis of 1979–1981. A simplified form of the yellow ribbon later came to signify support of military troops, and in other colors, the ribbons now represent awareness of causes from AIDS and heart disease (red) to breast cancer (pink) to drunk driving and child abuse (blue).

It is easy to find examples of symbols that have been adapted by hate groups. In some quarters, the yellow ribbon honoring members of the armed forces has been changed to read "Bring our troops home and put them on the Mexican border." American flags and patriotic color schemes adorn the websites of David Duke Online (www.duke.org) and the American Nationalist Union (www.anu.org). The National Socialist Movement (www.nsm88.com), which is the American Nazi Party, combines two iconic images—the American flag and the Nazi swastika (which, in turn, is an ancient symbol used by many cultures prior to the Nazis' adoption of it). For good measure, it also throws in a bald eagle superimposed on an American flag (see figure 6.2). Betsy Ross would be astonished to see what has happened to her flag design.

The Anti-Defamation League (ADL) maintains a large visual database of extremist symbols, logos, and tattoos (www.adl.org/hate_symbols/default.asp). Each item links to a table of information, which contains the type of group associated with the symbol (e.g., neo-Nazi, racist skinhead),

Figure 6.2
The National Socialist Movement combines imagery from the American flag, the bald eagle, and the Nazi-era swastika to portray the neo-Nazi perspective.

a physical description of the symbol, alternate names, its traditional use and origin, the name of the organization associated with the symbol, and that organization's background and history. Pagan symbols co-opted by extremist groups warrant their own section. Viking insignia and Norse mythological imagery now carry connotations their earlier users would never recognize or understand. Ironically, a number of swastika variants now exist because the traditional symbol, associated with the Nazis, has been banned in many countries.

The traditions that are co-opted can be as simple as the shared experiences of childhood or common habits of community and family. One of the websites my students find most disturbing is the children's section of the National Alliance online bookstore. Here they see treasured books from their own childhoods co-opted to represent "white values" and "white pride." The collection includes standard editions of *Blueberries for Sal, Anne of Green Gables, East o' the Sun and West o' the Moon, Little Men,* and many other familiar titles. My students feel squeamish for sharing the love of these books with people whose values they find reprehensible. They also experience associative culpability, a sense that words and thoughts have been put into their mouths without their permission.

Cloaking
Scholar Jessie Daniels defines two broad categories of white supremacy online: that which is *overt* and that which is *cloaked* (2008). Overt hate sites openly target their audience, showcase racist propaganda, or offer online community for white supremacists. Cloaked hate sites intentionally seek to deceive the casual web user. Daniels includes the Institute for Historical Review website in the cloaked category because of its polished

presentation and muted message. Its mission statement is "to promote peace, understanding and justice through greater public awareness of the past, and especially socially-politically relevant aspects of twentieth-century history." The website Martin Luther King Jr.: A True Historical Examination (www.martinlutherking.org) also uses a number of techniques to cloak its true intent. The first is its very official-looking domain name. Domain name deception occurs when someone grabs the rights to a domain name before the logical owner does. Pornography sites use similar trickery by buying domain names that are close enough to the real ones that unwitting users go to them in error. Martinlutherking.org is operated by the white supremacist organization Stormfront and has the professional look of a reputable site, with its rollovers and sleek layout. The site is designed to attract the attention of young readers. It sports a bright blue link across the top of the page that reads "Attention Students: Try Our MLK Pop Quiz," and an invitation at the bottom of the page to "Bring the Dream to life in your town! Download flyers to pass out at your school." One or two clicks into the site, however, and its actual messages of defamation and hate become apparent.

Cloaking is not a strategy that is exclusive to hate groups. It is also used to satirize, spark social commentary, or distract users from immediately detecting a website's agenda. The Citizens Commission on Human Rights (www.cchr.org) is not, as one might expect, devoted to the rights of political prisoners or oppressed groups. Rather, it is an advocacy site "dedicated to investigating and exposing psychiatric violations of human rights." Readers who delve further will learn that this organization is an arm of the Church of Scientology, which publicly opposes what it terms "the industry" of psychiatry. Clones R Us (www.d-b.net/dti), one of my favorite sites to use in teaching, pretends to be a commercial site where viewers can order a clone of themselves, a celebrity, or a beloved pet. The extensive price list, the FAQ page, the testimonials, the order forms, and the professional look make for a convincing commercial website experience. The purpose of the site is not to deceive but to stimulate critical thinking about cloning and the potential consequences of its legalization. Careful readers will eventually find the small-print disclaimer in the site. The hip-looking site Teenbreaks.com appears to be a teen health site, offering advice on topics like reproductive health, cutting, peer pressure, and self-esteem. In fact, its primary message is a pro-life one. The abortion section of the site is filled with testimonials from young women who regret having had abortions and from those who claim to be the surviving products of botched abortions.

Mainstreaming

A time-honored persuasion technique is the "plain-folks" approach, in which viewers see the faces of average citizens and read personal stories they can identify with. Advertisers make frequent use of the technique, showcasing before-and-after photographs of teens who use an acne-treatment product, or bald men who suddenly sprout luxurious shocks of hair. Advocacy group websites regularly feature personal stories and testimonials. America's Voice (www.americasvoiceonline.org), an organization that advocates for immigrant rights, also invites viewers to submit their own stories, adding their experiences to those "of the millions of hardworking immigrants trying to make lives for themselves in the United States." The website of the National Organization for Marriage (www.nationformarriage.org) employs a variant of the plain-folks technique. Because same-sex marriage is often portrayed as a threat to mainstream marriage, the "marriage talking points" page on the website instructs followers to frame the issue as one of common sense. When claims of bigotry are made, the suggested response is:

> Do you really believe people like me who believe mothers and fathers both matter to kids are like bigots and racists? I think that's pretty offensive, don't you? Particularly to the 60 percent of African-Americans who oppose same-sex marriage. Marriage as the union of husband and wife isn't new; it's not taking away anyone's rights. It's common sense.

Advocates are instructed to always come back to the main message, which is that "Gays and Lesbians have a right to live as they choose, they don't have the right to redefine marriage for all of us." The phrases "people like me" and "all of us" are designed to trigger the plain-folks response.

Hate groups have acquired more mainstream public faces by participating in a broader range of community activities. Many members of the Ku Klux Klan now wear regular street clothes to public functions rather than white robes, and the organization is welcoming more women to the ranks. Extremists have recoined the vocabulary that is associated with the discourse of white supremacy, sprinkling their websites with terms like *racialist* instead of *racist* and *separatism* rather than *supremacy*. Racialism is merely the practice of racial *integrity*. *Separatism* only signifies respect for the laws of nature, while the term *supremacy* implies control and subjugation—a goal Stormfront and other groups claim no interest in achieving. This tweaking of vocabulary turns the focus away from hate and places the emphasis on positive qualities like pride, heritage, and self-preservation. In most of this rhetoric, the tone is reasonable rather than strident, calm rather than defensive.

Antimainstreaming

The plain-folks tactic does not always attract teenagers, who, more often than not, want to distance themselves from mainstream society. They already feel different and would rather embrace their status than suffer for it. It does not take long for them to discover that the Internet is a generous host to anyone and anything that is antiestablishment. Anarchists, militia members, cult followers, and peace activists all find a voice in its nonjudgmental bosom. A student of mine went to a demonstration and heard this statement in a speech: "The Revolution may not be televised, but it will be uploaded!" In other words, mainstream media may not cover the underground, but social networks and media-sharing sites surely will. Online, the extreme right meets the extreme left. All manner of strange bedfellows reside side by side, giving alienated teens a huge smorgasbord from which to sample.

Many teens are particularly attracted to online resources that have the potential to give their lives a larger and deeper meaning. For example, those who are interested in animal rights can sign on with organizations devoted to the excoriation of fast-food chains (e.g., www.kentuckyfriedcruelty.com). Teens can gravitate to YouthNoise (www.youthnoise.com), a social network site for people under the age of twenty-seven "who like to connect based on deeper interests than Paris Hilton's wardrobe and want to get engaged within a cause." Participants can join or start a cause; blog, discuss, and debate its issues; participate in online activities; and organize projects. Some teen-cause sites are actually created and maintained by adults, a strategy that might be considered a form of cloaking. Teens for Life (www.teensforlife.com), subtitled Join the Revolution, is an outreach initiative of Indiana Right to Life, a state-level affiliate of the National Right to Life Committee. It maintains presences on sites like Facebook, MySpace, and Twitter. The "Speak Out" section of the website has no authorship tags for postings, so it is hard to tell if teens or adults are providing the updates, and it's equally difficult to assess the level of teen buy-in.

Despite their engagement in weighty moral issues, teens are still relatively powerless in our society. They reluctantly miss important concerts or protests or activist events because they cannot get permission to skip school or, even more frustrating, cannot arrange for transportation. They rail against world trade, capitalism, and other economic systems that, at some level of consciousness, they realize they benefit from. Activist teens cannot stop being their parents' children. They cannot suddenly become self-supporting, independent beings. Yet their parents' economic support provides them with the wherewithal to protest. They are not necessarily rebels without a cause, but their causes are undermined by their status.

Having antimainstream interests does not necessarily signify devotion to lofty humanitarian or political causes. The Internet provides teens with the means to engage in or document unconventional, underground, and even contraband activities. Teens find and exchange information related to rave culture, underground trance/dance clubs, "house" music, and popular DJs. There are online communities that exist solely for the purpose of sharing one's drinking or drug-using exploits. At the end of the day, teens are still teens and many are, well, adolescent and rebellious. They throw one another off invitation-only group blogs for infractions like "pissing off the mod" (moderator). They complain in online forums about being required to take standardized tests, being grounded, or being told to make their appearance more conventional. In short, they find sanctuary in the opportunities for expression and community that the Internet bestows.

The new information and communication technologies are here to stay. We would not have it otherwise. But their fallout is undeniable. We cannot afford to sit back and just watch change happen. Our services must adapt, and particularly in the school setting, it is our job to teach teens to meet the challenges of the new environment. Part 3 of this book addresses these next critical steps.

PART THREE

next steps

7

fishing poles, not fish: damage control

When all is said and done, schools and libraries face two basic types of ICT-generated areas of conflict: those that are related to student behavior and those that are related to students' access of inappropriate content. There is some question in my mind about which type actually presents greater difficulties for schools. In our school, behavioral issues—what students do to one another using communication technology—dominate ICT disciplinary cases. We have not struggled as much with inappropriate content issues. But in most schools, students simply have not had much access to communication technology until relatively recently. On the other hand, they *have* had access to information technology, which was the initial motivation for legislative bodies at all levels to regard Internet filtering software as the first line of defense in school and library Internet management. Now, though, information technology delivery systems typically come packaged with built-in communication tools and features, and filtering software is being employed to vet access to those as well.

Schools employ three basic approaches when dealing with ICT disciplinary issues: regulatory, technological, and pedagogical. The *regulatory* response consists of policies, rules, practices, usage agreements, and other mechanisms that clearly define the acceptable use of ICTs and the consequences for unacceptable use. The *technological* response involves building electronic security fences. These appear in the form of security protection against electronic intrusions and service disruptions, Internet content filters, software that allows teachers to view and interact with students' computers, and blocks on certain protocols like chat and instant messaging. The *pedagogical* response consists of the variety of methods used to teach students the responsible use of information and communication technologies.

How well do these approaches work? All have their place, and each fulfills an important role. Used alone, each method has weaknesses. The drawback of the regulatory approach is that students often forget what they have signed, do not understand it, or do not buy into it. Detection and enforcement are difficult, meaning the consequences may lack backbone. The technological approach is limited because technology fails, students find ways around it, and it requires significant resources to maintain. Its implementation can also create a false sense of security. For example, the installation of Internet filters sends the message to parents that there are easy, foolproof technological answers to their concerns. The pedagogical approach can also be problematic. Students excel in parroting what teachers want to hear, without necessarily possessing concomitant behaviors and beliefs. ICT ethics curricula are relatively new, untested, and potentially labor-intensive. In cases where education and personal responsibility have been emphasized, and rules and security measures minimized, schools have run the risk of losing the integrity of their technology systems (Van Buren 2001).

Some combination of all three strategies—regulatory, technological, and pedagogical—is the commonsense solution. Far from being mutually exclusive, the three approaches can be quite effective in concert. We already know how to implement regulatory and technological solutions. They were our initial lines of defense, so it is relatively easy to find information on policies and acceptable-use documents, on computer security and effective system administration, on filtering software issues, and on school discipline. My main interest lies in integrating the pedagogical approach, in learning how to give students the tools they need to make thoughtful choices and to achieve a deeper understanding of the issues.

Because teens use ICTs away from school, in unsupervised, unregulated environments, they need to learn to be their own filters, their own barometers of acceptable and intelligent use of the tools. The rest of this chapter will focus on the pedagogical approach, why it is important, and how it might be accomplished.

LEARNING HOW TO BE: BEHAVIOR

In the early days of the Internet, there were no teachers to tell users how they should behave online. Instead, an ethos developed organically, shaped and refined by the relatively small community of users. This ethos was characterized by self-regulation, the participants preferring internally agreed-upon norms and standards rather than externally imposed authority. Peer pressure was the favored method of encouraging compliance. Today's cybercommunities, much larger and less close-knit than they once were, still formulate informal codes of conduct and FAQs that prescribe acceptable behaviors. Tim O'Reilly even suggested a formal Blogger's Code of Conduct after serious threats were made to well-known blogger Kathy Sierra, causing her to exit from active participation in the online community (BBC News 2007). When his single-authored draft generated wide criticism, he opened it up for community editing on a wiki (http://blogging.wikia.com/wiki/Blogging_Wikia). Its modules address topics like taking responsibility for one's own words, managing anonymous or pseudonymous commenting, and connecting privately rather than publicly when appropriate.

When peer pressure fails, the self-regulation ethic can quickly turn aggressive. These are the instances in which enthusiastic netizens use their skills to thwart cybermiscreants who have committed crimes ranging in gravity from persistent flaming to serious destruction of computer resources. Most of this self-policing activity is fairly informal and spontaneous. For example, users who have misrepresented themselves on discussion boards may be blocked by the site administrator or simply shunned by other users. But some online community policing efforts are highly organized. CyberAngels (www.cyberangels.org), an offshoot of the community-based New York City subway-patrolling Guardian Angels, began by hunting pedophiles and software pirates and reporting them to

Internet service providers. The organization has now broadened its scope by offering a wide range of education and advocacy services.

The Home Setting

Middle-class teens generally receive their initial exposure and "training" in ICT behavior at home. Despite the stereotypes of clueless parents who don't themselves spend much time online, 87 percent of parents who have a child ages twelve to seventeen use the Internet—at least 17 percent more than average adults (Macgill 2007). These parents frequently check to see what websites their children view, know whether or not their kids have created profiles on social networking sites like MySpace or Facebook, and talk to them about privacy online. Clearly some kind of dialogue is occurring between parents and teens, but it is hard to get a clear picture of exactly how parents are speaking to teens about online behavior.

The current focus on online sexual predation may be having an unintended impact on the dialogue between teens and parents. The predator threat is heavily and continuously publicized through television shows like *To Catch a Predator* and in oversimplified media reports of research on Internet safety. Responsible parents find it difficult to dismiss presentations by representatives from law enforcement agencies who describe sting operations and tell stories of face-to-face meetings gone terribly wrong. As a consequence, many parents are likely to focus solely on the predator threat, without also engaging their children in discussion of other ethical issues about online life.

The reality of the situation is that teens are fairly savvy about managing advances from strangers. As noted in chapter 4, the evidence demonstrates that they do take measures to protect their privacy, that they (and their parents) report fewer unwanted contacts than popular fears and school policies seem to imply, and that teens are highly unlikely to respond to unwelcome solicitations (National School Boards Association 2007; Lenhart and Madden 2007). Unlike undercover law enforcement agents who engage the advances of would-be predators, real-life teens are sanguine about just saying no to them. Again, we also know that predators do not typically troll social networking sites to find victims, that they are instead more likely to use direct forms of contact such as e-mail or instant messaging, and that they are very clear about stating their intentions at the outset (Wolak et al. 2008). These comments from my students are typical in illustrating how teens summarily dismiss unwanted contacts:

> This guy wouldn't give up asking to meet me in real life (through a game site) so I blocked him.

> *

> There are always the random creepy friend requests from random guys with messages such as "I saw you and you're pretty attractive. Want to be friends with me" etc. I basically just usually ignore them.

> *

> If I'm feeling particularly reckless and pissed off, I might go and chew them out, but usually I just plain ignore them.

Comments like these reveal that parents and other adults need to view teens as *actors* in the online world, not merely as passive viewers or, in the worst cases, victims. Teens can affect this new world as much as it affects them. It therefore remains essential to avoid oversimplifying the issues. The predator panic, although still thriving in the public mind, has made room for the phenomenon of "sexting," in which kids use cell phones to send provocative pictures of themselves. Anne Collier, manager of NetFamilyNews.org, cautions against falling prey to another "technopanic," this time over sexting and bullying (Collier 2009). One of her concerns is that such panics cause fear, which interferes with parent-child communication because kids then go underground. She notes that when kids are in stealth mode, parents and other adults are then out of the equation, ultimately placing young people at greater risk.

A study commissioned by the Girl Scouts of the USA (Girl Scout Research Institute 2002) found that "most advice and rules girls receive about the Internet are in the form of prohibitive statements, rather than proactive advice about real-life situations that occur for them online" (11). Parental advice is very general, usually in the form of directives "not to" (not to give out personal information, not to go to inappropriate websites, and so on). The report urges adults to provide proactive rather than reactive advice. Girls are less likely to confide in their parents about bad things that happen online if they think they will get in trouble.

Similar advice could be given to parents about their children's online game playing. If parents take the time to become familiar with the games and with their children's involvement in them, their dictates will carry more weight. As with many safety issues, parents need to create an environment that is both realistic and protective.

The School Setting

When it became obvious that the Internet was in schools to stay, educators realized they needed to do something about managing its implementation. Kids had already found all sorts of ways to get into trouble online. Most had not benefited from the mentoring of Internet old-timers, who could have passed along their self-regulatory spirit and sense of obligation to the expanding community of web users. Some educators made the mistake of responding to these early problems by placing draconian limitations on in-school Internet use, rendering its presence fairly meaningless. A few schools learned hard lessons about what can happen in the absence of policies and programs delineating appropriate use. Throughout, schools have not been immune to the technopanics over online sexual predators, sexting, and the like.

Many schools sidestep behavior issues simply by tightly controlling the use of technology. For example, schools often choose to prohibit the use of social media sites like Facebook, YouTube, and Flickr. Had it passed, the Deleting Online Predators Act of 2006 (DOPA) would have mandated such restrictions by prohibiting access to commercial social network services and chat rooms in all public schools and libraries, exceeding the requirements of the existing Children's Internet Protection Act (CIPA). Under CIPA, schools and libraries that receive federal funding for Internet access from the E-rate program must have an Internet safety policy in place that includes technology protection measures to block or filter access to pictures that are obscene, constitute child pornography, or are harmful to minors. Although the language in CIPA only specifies visual content, filtering software is generally designed to identify and block text as well as images, URLs, and entire Internet protocols. Notably, CIPA does not prohibit social media services per se.

Because CIPA also requires school policies to address the safety and security of minors when using electronic mail, chat rooms, and other forms of direct electronic communications, schools often just block access to those services (or punish students who use them at school). The logic seems to be that if anything that might spell danger (or tempt misbehavior) is behind lock and key, no one will get into trouble—at least not on the school's watch. Another common approach to behavior and safety issues in schools is to create a "walled garden" by installing course management software or self-contained, locally hosted online tools. In these situations, students can experience some level of online, collaborative learning. But any connection to the real online world is very limited. The drawback to both the "block it" method and the walled-garden approach is that students will not have the opportunity to learn safe and responsible use of the tools in an educational context, with mentors and peers acting as coaches and safety nets.

We also now know that young people are not equally at risk in the online world. A report authored by Harvard University's Internet Safety Technical Task Force found that those teens who are most at risk engage in risky behaviors off-line as well as online, and they also experience difficulties in other parts of their lives (Berkman Center for Internet and Society 2008). The report notes that "the psychosocial makeup of and family dynamics surrounding particular minors are better predictors of risk than the use of specific media or technologies" (5). These findings represent one of the many pieces of evidence that are giving us a better picture of the online lives of young people, and they should help us target educational interventions more appropriately. Larry Magid notes that our improved understanding of the nature of youth risk online has led to "a whole new phase of Internet safety education focusing on such things as cyberbullying and urging youth to avoid posting material that could be embarrassing or get them into trouble with authorities and potential future employers" (2009b). Young people are likely to respond to such teaching efforts because they address the real problems teens face rather than the issues teens have been managing pretty well all along.

My concern about schools that adopt highly restrictive access policies is that they are effectively abdicating responsibility for teaching ethical and responsible online behavior. Technology writer Steven Levy (2003) believes that putting the kibosh on online activities is a recipe for disaster and that, in fact, computers and online access are essential tools for survival in today's society. Yes, kids need protection from the seedy side of technology. But they have a right to computers, web access, and "wise, wired teachers" who can keep in touch with students and parents online and who understand the difference between multimedia glitz and real learning opportunities (S. Levy 2003, E30). Schools are uniquely positioned and, in my mind, *obligated* to take on this charge.

Finally, young people respond to genuine demonstrations of respect and a consistent approach to technology management. They will be dismissive of preemptive security measures that appear punitive or patronizing, communicate mistrust, and leave no room for discussion or compromise. Key indicators of a respectful climate are the ways in which ethical online behavior is modeled by the school's teachers, any technology-related curriculum, and the school's policies and procedures. The litmus test of success lies in the balance that a school manages between maintaining network security and protecting students' online civil liberties.

Teaching Approaches: The Devil Is in the Details

How is ICT ethics training best accomplished? Though its particular application to digital technology is new, ethics education itself has a long history. Though labeled variously over time (e.g., citizenship training, character development, values education), it always attempts to influence moral growth and development through the formal education process.

As described in chapter 5, contemporary approaches to ethics education have been heavily influenced by the work of sociologist Émile Durkheim (1925/1961), psychologist Jean Piaget (1932), and, perhaps most important, psychologist Lawrence Kohlberg (1958, 1984). In Durkheim's view, the purpose of moral education is to teach adherence to societal norms via the transmission of traditions, using stories and examples and modeling desired behaviors. Through this behavioral psychology approach, students feel part of the larger society and have respect for its rules and symbols of authority. Piaget's position is that children should be placed in situations that require them to actively struggle with issues of fairness, ultimately choosing for themselves what is moral. Through this cognitive-psychology approach, learners develop a deep understanding of societal values and a sense of ownership in them. Kohlberg expanded Piaget's stages of moral development and created an assessment technique using fictional moral dilemmas. The influence of Piaget and Kohlberg is seen in contemporary dialogue-centered curricula.

Early on in the growth of the Internet, educators dipped into their tool kits and began to develop ICT ethics education programs that reflect the influence of these theoretical traditions. A very useful guide for schools was published in 1992 by the National Institute of Justice (Sivin and Bialo). Although 1992 is now considered ancient history in the life span of the Internet, the advice given in this slim monograph is still surprisingly fresh and relevant. Schools are counseled to take action on two fronts by (1) setting consistent school policies that model how students should behave, and (2) incorporating technology ethics education into the curriculum.

I believe that the choice of the term *model* is an important one in this context. The Durkheim perspective tells us that it is not enough for schools to simply dictate rules and regulations. School personnel must practice what they preach by purchasing legal copies of software, abiding by fair-use guidelines, using good netiquette, observing online privacy rights, and otherwise respecting community standards. If they do not, they will have created a "Do what I say, not what I do" milieu, which is a recipe for disaster where computer-savvy students are concerned. High standards of staff behavior are easy to mandate but tricky to realize. The teachers who are not comfortable with technology will not know enough about what they are doing to model appropriately or effectively. And the teachers who are ineffective role models in nontechnological matters are unlikely to take up the mantle when it comes to technology.

When it comes to the curriculum component, the 1992 guide suggests that information technology systems be presented as extensions and reflections of human society. ICTs are created by people and used by people. Therefore, like other human-engineered artifacts, they can be used in a variety of ways—productively or unproductively, to help or to hurt. Echoing Kohlbergian thinking, the guide's authors stress that behaving with moral responsibility, no matter what the context, is ultimately each student's individual choice to make. I would add that students do not come to their use of ICTs as blank slates, lacking either life experience or familiarity with technology. Their experiences inform their choices and should also inform the design of ethics education curricula. For example, most young people will tune out any curriculum that focuses solely on the "stranger-danger" phenomenon or other high-profile issues like sexting. For most teens, such a single-minded focus ignores the everyday realities of the ethics and safety issues they are much more likely to face. It renders the instructional effort irrelevant, even laughable. As Mitchell and Ybarra note, Internet safety messages may be most effective if they target the behavior first and the modality second, because the behaviors occur across platforms, and the platforms change (2009). At the same time, those students who do engage in risky behaviors because their personal lives are already compromised need to be identified and helped with appropriate interventions.

Since 1992, guides for teaching ICT ethical concepts have become widely available. For parents and the general public, books like Nancy Willard's *Cyber-Safe Kids, Cyber-Savvy Teens: Helping Young People Learn to Use the Internet Safely and Responsibly* (2007) and Anastasia Goodstein's *Totally Wired: What Teens and Tweens Are Really Doing Online* (2007) can be helpful. Larry Magid hosts SafeKids.com, a blog on Internet safety and civility, and Anne Collier is the author of NetFamilyNews.org, "kid-tech news for parents." Magid and Collier populate their sites with readable and intelligent entries suitable for a wide audience, including teens, parents, educators, and youth advocates. They also codirect a public forum space on a sister site, ConnectSafely.org.

For educators in school settings, the options are multifaceted, perhaps because attention to the issue has become increasingly pressing. Since the defeat of DOPA, legislative initiatives have continued to emerge. Congress seems to be shifting from reactive, restrictive measures like DOPA that emphasize filtering and monitoring to more proactive measures that emphasize public awareness and education (Essex 2009). Professional associations are updating their standards and guiding documents. "Ethical behavior in the use of information must be taught" is in the statement of common beliefs that prefaces the American Association of School Librarians *Standards for the 21st Century Learner* (2007). Standard 3 reads "Share knowledge and participate ethically and productively as members of our democratic society." Standard 4 ("Pursue personal and aesthetic growth") includes "Practice safe and ethical behaviors in personal electronic communication and interaction" (4.3.4). Of the six components that make up the *National Educational Technology Standards and Performance Indicators for Students* (International Society for Technology in Education 2007), one is devoted to digital citizenship. The Young Adult Library Services Association (YALSA) of the American Library Association offers the "Teens and Social Networking in School and Public Libraries" tool kit (Young Adult Library Services Association 2009), which "is designed to help librarians and library workers become more knowledgeable about online social networking tools, to give them ideas on how they can be used to provide library services, and to suggest ways that librarians and library workers can educate their community members about the positive uses of online social networking tools as well as provide them with Internet safety tips."

An ethics curriculum can be taught formally or informally. As a formal curriculum, ethics is the subject of explicit units of study. At this stage of the game, it is easier to find disparate resources than out-of-the-box curricula. Still, resources are emerging. The International Society for Technology in Education published *Digital Citizenship in Schools,* which advises educators on the creation of a "digital citizenship program" and contains lessons on topics ranging from digital etiquette to buying and selling items on online auction sites (Bailey and Ribble 2007). Many nonprofit educational organizations as well as for-profit groups are developing and posting (or selling) online ethics units and modules. Even school districts are getting into the act by developing their own guidelines and curricula.

An informal curriculum generally occurs more spontaneously, at points of need, when a teacher or librarian seizes a moment of relevance in the context of other activities or studies. An informal curriculum is also a by-product of the consistent cross-curricular implementation of policy, of modeling desired behaviors. For example, an implicit lesson is transmitted when teachers in multiple academic departments present the same expectations for citing online sources. Individual teachers may teach the different citation styles that are appropriate to their disciplines, but they speak in one voice when it comes to basic messages regarding plagiarism and the obligation to give credit where credit is due.

The jury is still out regarding students' responses to an overt ethics curriculum. Existing character education programs have met with mixed success. One of the best known of these is the Drug Abuse Resistance Education (DARE) program, which is still widely in use. However, long-term studies now show that DARE graduates are just as likely to use drugs as young people who have not been through the program (Kanof 2003; West and O'Neal 2004). Similar educational efforts to promote sexual abstinence before marriage appear to be equally ineffective. Title V, a program of the 1996 welfare reform act, mandated that considerable federal funds be used toward the implementation of such programs. More varied than the DARE curriculum, these programs are harder to evaluate as a whole. Many incorporate abstinence pledges, in which teens (usually in some sort of public ceremony) sign pledges that they will remain sexually abstinent until marriage. Researchers have found that two outcomes are likely: (1) teens alter their definition of sex to exclude anything but actual intercourse, believing that oral sex is not actually "having sex," and (2) when they do break their pledges, they are less likely to use protection such as condoms (Christian Century 2003). Rosenbaum (2009) found that five years after signing virginity pledges, 82 percent of the pledgers denied having done so. She recommends that clinicians provide birth control information to all adolescents, especially virginity pledgers.

The "just say no" approach of these values education programs reflects the Durkheim behaviorist tradition, in which the child is seen as an empty vessel waiting to be filled with the right kind of knowledge. But simply telling teens and preteens what is right and what is wrong has not proven effective in the long term, even with the attractive incentives that are built into programs like DARE. After all, the society at large models behavior that contradicts the messages of these programs. Kohlberg-influenced educators, on the other hand, have favored Socratic approaches infused with opportunities for dialogue. At my school, we use a dilemma-discussion approach that is similar to Socratic dialogue but sets the "moral of the story" in a context that is relevant to a teen's experience and, we hope, generates deeper engagement. Excerpts from some of these discussions appear in chapter 5. Most of the scenarios we use are based on real situations that have occurred at school. Here is one example:

> Jules has walked away from a lab computer without logging off. Trish
> sits down and, still logged in as Jules, sends inflammatory e-mail mes-
> sages out to a number of students and posts similar messages on the
> class web board.

The students first discuss this scenario in an online forum. The technology director and I then follow up with an in-class discussion, during which we tell the story of the real event (without using real names!) that inspired the scenario. In this example, a particularly hateful message was sent to the all-student mailing list, seemingly from one student, in which another student was spoken about in obscene terms. This instance of impersonation and slander caused the school to institute new procedures. Messages that are sent to the all-school e-mail lists now go to the technology director first, a practice that is now common knowledge. He screens them for such criteria as obscenity and defamation of character. During this class discussion, we clarify that regular (non–mailing list) e-mail messages are *not* routinely screened. In fact, students learn that the technology director is actually prohibited from reading personal mail unless the school principal suspects foul play and directs an investigation. Furthermore, we tell students that nothing prevents individuals from creating their own all-school mailing lists, which would then bypass the technology director.

Telling such tales in class serves several purposes. First, students learn that infractions of system rules can hurt real people and that access to ICTs is at once a powerful and a fragile privilege. Second, processes are demystified. As students come to understand the technology director's role and certain practical issues (e.g., the extremely high level of e-mail traffic—more than any human being could monitor), they realize their e-mail is relatively free from administrative snooping. Third, students learn that their school is not infallible and that the adults in charge have also had hard lessons to learn. What's more, their teachers trust them enough to confide these weaknesses and, even more astonishing, tell them how to get around the system if they wish. Finally, they learn that their teachers have students' best interests at heart.

It is extremely difficult, however, to evaluate the success of dialogue-based programs like ours. I have often wondered if our students are "nicer" as a result of our particular efforts. When I am inclined to think so, I have only to remember the student who, after he was caught in an act of transgression, wondered if he was going to be the subject of our next ethical scenario. He knew exactly what he had done wrong and why it was wrong. He even knew how his actions fit into our curriculum. But his awareness did not change his behavior. Speaking from a developmental neuroscience perspective, psychologist Laurence Steinberg (2007) observes that adolescents are hardwired for risky behavior because puberty pushes them toward thrill seeking at a time when their cognitive-control systems mature more slowly. Therefore, a more successful strategy than attempting to change how adolescents view risky behavior is to limit their opportunities for getting into trouble. For my part, I hearken back to the three-pronged regulatory, technological, and pedagogical approach. Yes, regulation is essential, as are technological safeguards. But because adolescents mature at different rates and in different ways, the education light has to be "on" and the conversations must be held.

LEARNING HOW TO SEE: CONTENT

In pre-Internet days, becoming a published author was something of a production. An outside entity—a book publisher, a magazine editor, an editorial board, some kind of organization—had to vet the content before it saw the light of day. Now, with minimal effort and resources, anyone can "publish" on the Web. Consumers of all ages need to be aware and to *beware,* recognizing that not everything they see online is what it appears to be. And much as we would like, there is no simple formula for discerning good web content from bad. At one time teachers rather routinely forbade .com resources on student bibliographies, a prohibition that now seems laughable. The theory was that any information that did not originate from a .edu site or, just possibly, a .org site was highly suspect. We have since learned that such coarse methods of content evaluation are not very meaningful. But some level of guidance must be provided to students if they are to make intelligent use of the Web.

I would like to think we are beyond the days when teens believed everything they read online. Technology guru Alan November (1998) once told the story of a fourteen-year-old boy who found Arthur Butz's Holocaust denial site and, because it was hosted by Northwestern University, assumed it contained credible, interesting new information. This boy not only was naive about the wide range of information that can be published on the Web but he also lacked the critical evaluation skills to properly interpret the information he saw. Today's fourteen-year-olds, who generally have had more exposure to questionable web content, are still unlikely to be very sophisticated about deconstructing it. There is much to be said for purposely taking students to a site such as Butz's and, as a collaborative activity, working through its pitfalls using standard media analysis criteria. This exposure serves as a kind of preemptive inoculation.

When I show my students the Martinlutherking.org site, they respond as one would expect. All of them are appalled and distressed that racism could be expressed in such an overt, public manner. Once the fact of the site is absorbed, though, there is (at least initially) not too much more to say except "How awful!" The real learning seems to occur a bit later when I display websites that *unwittingly* link to Martinlutherking.org. Unfortunately, such sites are not difficult to find. By using the "who's linking" features of various search engines, or by simply conducting a search on "Martin Luther King" and "Historical Examination," the sites are easy to pick out. Authors of the sites include teachers who are creating class websites on King, broadcast outlets commemorating the King holiday, students writing term papers, activist organizations providing information on King's life, and even public libraries posting resource pages on King. By not properly examining Martinlutherking.org before linking to it, each of these website authors is guilty of perpetuating its message. Their lack of care makes a great impression on my students because it is palpable proof of what happens in the absence of evaluation.

Local sensibilities must be respected when considering the use of sensitive materials. Otherwise, lessons may produce unintended, undesirable consequences. Fortunately (or unfortunately), the Web offers a wide range of examples to choose from in developing our lessons. A school librarian once told me that she could never present the National Alliance website's anti-Semitic rhetoric in class because it might simply reinforce existing stereotypes in her multiracial school population. In her situation, deconstruction lessons would probably have to begin with more neutral material, then progress to stronger examples as students' evaluation skills and sensitivities grew in sophistication. Conducting analyses away from computers might also be in order. Guided discussion could then focus on an uncluttered paragraph of text, without the distractions of keyboards and screens. No matter what the situation, the approach must be flexible: it must be sensitive to the local setting, the nature of the material, and, above all, the best interests of the students.

What Is the Object of Evaluation?

What exactly do we mean when we talk about teaching young people to evaluate online content? All online content? Or just some? Typical school evaluation rubrics emphasize academic criteria. Students are prompted to look for evidence of authority, currency, documentation, and bias. I would argue that evaluation criteria must also be flexible enough to accommodate a broad definition of information neighborhoods and a wide range of information providers, from hobbyists and geeks to nonprofit organizations and commercial interests. In one of my own evaluation exercises, I have added advocacy and enthusiasts' sites, as well as the all-forgiving category of "other," which allows students to simply explain what they see. Students are then better equipped to evaluate advocacy sites like the Republican National Committee (www.gop.org), the League of American Bicyclists (www.bikeleague.org), or even the International Federation of Competitive Eating (www.ifoce.com). They will know how to approach collaborative fiction-writing sites or movie-reviewing sites. There are vast qualitative differences among resources like these, yet the standard-issue academic evaluation rubrics do not fit them.

Not only is the distinction between academic and nonacademic content blurring, but *credible* and *authoritative* are becoming relative terms. How does one classify a news-and-commentary-style blog written by a public personality? Or the "news" as delivered by satirists Jon Stewart or Stephen Colbert? Even the *New York Times* posits that Jon Stewart, host of Comedy Central's fake news program *The Daily Show,* may be "the most trusted man in America" (Kakutani 2008). Is it ever appropriate to cite such sources for a school research paper? Teenager Qingshuo Wang (2003), who wrote an article for *Voice of Youth Advocates* on the journalistic function of blogs, posed some intriguing questions: "How do we find the blogs of the real September 11 witnesses? Which blogs are providing credible news? And which blogs are actually useful news as opposed to personal mumbling?" (28). He calls these sorts of blogs excellent complements to traditional journalism because they contain rich personal depictions of events and act as checks to the biases of mainstream media. Some can be regarded as authoritative; some cannot. The reader must evaluate them in terms of his or her own individual information needs and interests.

As educators, we need to ask ourselves about the scope of our lessons. There are increasingly compelling reasons to include quasi-academic and nonacademic web resources in evaluation lessons. Teaching kids "out-of-school" content promotes lifelong learning, which has long been a goal of mainstream education. Indeed, it would be shortsighted not to include the sorts of citizen-journalism resources just described, considering their growing predominance in our mediated culture. Perhaps the most compelling rationale for broadening our scope is that with some 93 percent of youth online (Macgill 2007), out-of-school use undoubtedly comprises a huge portion of their information intake. At home, teens undergo less supervision and are typically limited by fewer restrictions. Most of all, kids hang out online, so it makes sense to meet them on their own terms, or at least in their own territory, with lessons that will help them stay safe and put them in control rather than under control. As a society, it is in our best interests to make sure school lessons encompass a wide range of information neighborhoods. Here are some examples of the way such lessons could look:

- Students follow the same news story as it is covered by different media outlets, including blogs and Twitter.
- Students critique and compare music-reviewing sites. They look for evidence of professionalism and conflict of interest.
- Students compare and contrast different online financial services, tracking the stock market advice given by each. Or students evaluate differences in how these services profile individual companies, then compare this information to the companies' own online promotional material.
- Students analyze the differences between sites like eBay and Craigslist. They conduct price and service comparisons across sites as well as with standard online retail outlets.
- Students compare the information on a disease in different types of sources: consumer-oriented websites, websites designed for medical professionals, and postings on web forums.

Developing Critical Evaluation Skills

When it comes to being able to deal with questionable Internet content, information evaluation skills are the first line of defense. After the initial shock of exposure to sites such as Martinlutherking.org, the next step is to systematize the viewing with analytical techniques like discourse analysis. As noted in chapter 6, basic persuasion techniques are time-honored and well-worn, yet their deconstruction must be relearned by each new generation. Even young teens are capable of conducting such exercises. As long ago as 1938, the Institute for Propaganda Analysis was developing instructional materials for schools. Consider the following exercises, excerpted from the institute's *Propaganda: How to Recognize It and Deal with It,* in terms of their relevancy to analyzing material found on the Web:

> Find examples of lack of precision in speech, such as "This is the greatest nation in the world," or "The Japanese are an inferior race." Ask: What do these statements mean? What are these particular claims asserting?
>
> Test authorities cited in commercial and political propagandas by asking: (1) Is the authority scientific in his methods; that is, does he begin with hypotheses which he holds only as hypotheses until they are documented by research—facts, figures, statistics; (2) Does the authority have any important self-interest at stake? (3) Are you accepting the authority simply because he is a fashionable authority; if so why is he fashionable? Does the reason in any way impair his authoritativeness?
>
> Make a scrapbook list of popular beliefs based on lack of evidence. These beliefs may be economic, social, or racial. Make a corresponding list of superstitions which still exist, of superstitions which existed a century ago—for example, the New England belief in witchcraft. (*Propaganda* 1938, 54–55)

Some basic questions must be asked when evaluating information found on the Web. What is the purpose of the website? What is its authorship? What clues—visual, technical, and otherwise—reveal this information? And what devices are being used to persuade readers, or even deceive them?

Purpose

There are really two facets to the notion of purpose—in any information context, not just on the Web. First, there is the purpose of the website itself, and second, there is the user's purpose in seeking the information. The user's purpose will dictate which information neighborhood should be visited. For example, a student who is assigned to write a science paper will need to be able to distinguish between popular science writing and peer-reviewed research literature. There are markers that identify each of these neighborhoods, which can be found both online and in print. If the scholarly literature proves incomprehensible, the student will need to reevaluate her purpose and look for something simpler or possibly some basic science reference sources to help her decipher the literature.

In assessing the purpose of a website, there are some important questions to ask and cues to look for. Is there an "About Us" section? Do the statements there seem to fit what the viewer sees? Who is the site's intended audience? Is the information original to the site or taken from elsewhere? Is there value-added material? The teen looking for samples of an artist's work might appreciate a site that offers both the art and some explanatory material. Is Information-with-a-capital-*I* even the point of the site? It may be a discussion area, a collaborative poetry-writing community, or a site that provides services rather than information per se. Students need to cast their evaluation of a site in terms of their own interest in it. Perhaps a student should look for an advocacy site precisely because such a site will articulate a specific point of view. A blog may be useful as a primary source when a student needs the perspective of someone who has witnessed important events or represents a certain perspective.

Authorship

Another critical key to understanding the purpose of a website lies in clarifying its authorship. Once authorship is clear, purpose tends to become evident. In the online world, standard identifiers, like a book's title page or an article byline, either may not exist or may appear in unexpected places and guises. The search process itself can mask authorship. For example, keyword searches in an online catalog produce bibliographic records that prominently display title and author fields. By contrast, keyword searches in a search engine can land the searcher smack in the middle of a website, without clear reference to its "front" page. This result is like having a catalog search send the user directly to page 157 of a book, with no direct reference to title, author, or table of contents.

Certain problems of authorship, such as conflict of interest and bias, are perennial concerns. For example, through deceptive reporting practices, William Randolph Hearst's newspapers were able to stir up public sentiment to such a degree that they actually helped start the Spanish-American War of 1898—all for the purpose of selling more newspapers. In pre-Internet days, students were taught to spot editorial perspective and analyze argumentation techniques. Such lessons continue to be relevant, regardless of the format of publication. In the context of the Web, many of the telltale signs of conflict of interest can be taught. Who is the author affiliated with? Does the author benefit in some way from the information on the website? Is something for sale?

At the smoking cessation site My Time to Quit (www.mytimetoquit.com), readers will find information about nicotine addiction, a doctor discussion checklist, a health benefits time line, and an animation that demonstrates the path of nicotine in the brain. They will also find an external link to a site with a "prescription treatment option." Both sites are owned by Pfizer, a pharmaceutical company that markets the prescription treatment. The information about smoking cessation may be valuable, but it must be weighed in the context of an inherent conflict of interest. Some conflicts of interest are harder to detect. The Federal Trade Commission is investigating the practice in which bloggers receive perks or payments in exchange for reviewing or plugging products on their blogs (Yao 2009). Unless such posts are clearly identified as commercial messages, they may be out of compliance with the disclosure rules under truth-in-advertising guidelines. Praise of a product on (what appears to be) a noncommercial gamers blog may carry more weight than a banner ad for the same product.

Influences that affect authorship are not always easy to identify or categorize. The Body (www.thebody.com), an HIV/AIDS information and support resource, is "a service of Body Health Resources Corporation." Although the site is technically a company, its purpose is more akin to that of a nonprofit organization. When I ask my students to look at this page in class, they are initially put off by its flashy appearance and the prominent display of the logos of the pharmaceutical companies that are its sponsors. They are confused by the links to further information that look very much like the links to advertisements, except for the small "advertisement" label that accompanies the latter and not the former. I wonder how many viewers take the trouble to find and read this portion of the site's advertising policy:

To preserve the integrity of The Body as a neutral forum for the presentation of information, it is our policy that the editorial content of the site be maintained strictly independent from and outside the influence of our advertisers. Consistent with this advertising policy, users of The Body will be made aware of the difference between consumer advertising and the materials provided by organizations that publish on The Body.

At the end of the day, The Body is a reputable and authoritative source of information about HIV/AIDS, despite the potential for conflict of interest and, in my view, the likelihood that readers will misinterpret its visual design elements.

Deconstruction Techniques

The predominant model for teaching students to judge what they see online has been the website evaluation checklist, which focuses on criteria including accuracy, authority, objectivity, currency, and coverage (Metzger 2007). Students examine websites with teacher- or librarian-assigned checklists in hand, looking for evidence of each element. Though the checklists are well suited to academic research and imposed query situations, a few problems are associated with their use. In practice, students tend not to use the checklists unless they are required to. When checklists are not required, most forget the evaluation "rules" and fall back on personal credibility assessment criteria such as design and presentation elements (Fogg et al. 2003; Agosto 2002). Even users who are skeptical of web-based information often fail to verify questionable information they find online (Flanagin and Metzger 2007).

If checklists are the sole evaluative rubric used, the criteria can even be misleading. Noncredible sites can meet the technical requirements of checklists, while credible sites can fall short (sometimes in the face of common sense). The Body is an example of a site that might "fail" the checklist test because of the potential for conflict of interest with its corporate sponsors. Finally, checklists tend to force students into yes or no responses, when more qualified answers might be the better option. It almost goes without saying that checklists are not helpful in everyday life information seeking tasks because the criteria typically are not relevant in evaluating nonacademic information. Yet even nonacademic sites vary widely in quality and should be subject to some form of evaluation by consumers.

Rather than forcing all web content to match up to a prescribed checklist form, we should consider more open-ended alternatives. One approach is to employ a compare-and-corroborate strategy that stimulates critical thinking (Meola 2004). Students begin with one website, which serves as a reference point for the next. As more websites are examined, new ones rise to the top and are made to serve as reference points. The exercise encourages students' ability to assess bias, controversy, similarities, and differences. This type of corroboration is a time-honored journalistic technique and helps readers verify information that might be questionable. Miller-Cochran and Rodrigo (2008) propose a resource matrix for categorizing resources on a scale of static, syndicated, and dynamic. These elements are cross-referenced with a scale that includes edited, peer-reviewed, and self-published criteria. By asking questions about the status of a resource (fixed in time, released over time, or continually changeable) and the nature of its level of review, students and teachers can better assess the credibility of resources in a way that matches the task at hand. Metzger (2007) suggests a "sliding scale" approach that matches the learner's motivation and purpose in information seeking. She observes that students who are not very motivated or who have an information need that is less academically rigorous can be taught some simple heuristics that will enable them to assess credibility in a way that they will be more likely to use, both inside and outside of the classroom.

The checklist model need not be thrown out entirely. Rather, it can be re-created as an activity that is more open-ended and expansive. The 21st Century Information Fluency Project, which provides professional development and resources to help educators and students improve their understanding of digital information, offers an online evaluation tool (http://21cif.com/tools/evaluate) that poses "who, what, where, and why" questions rather than demanding "yes" or "no" checkbox answers. It even allows the user to choose the evaluation criteria for each website. My own version of the checklist primarily consists of a list of open-ended questions and concludes with the most open-ended of all: "After thinking about the above questions, explain why this Web site would be truly useful to your project. How would you use the information it provides?"

Even the simple process of creating a bibliographic citation can help students understand what they are looking at. Bibliography-generation software like NoodleBib (www.noodletools.com) enhances learning because it prompts the user with questions for each entry, first about the source type, and then about each bibliographic element within the source. Another strategy is to create "Whodunit" assignments, in which students determine the authorship and purpose of various websites. My (ever-changing) version of this activity can be found at www.uni.illinois .edu/library/computerlit/sourcing.html. I like to include sites like the blog BoingBoing, which summarizes stories found elsewhere on the Web. Students need to parse out the difference between a blog entry author, the person or source from whom the blog author learned about the story, and the author (and source) of the original story. Librarians can also teach simple technical tricks that help students determine authorship. One time-honored technique is to simply shorten the URL of a site when there is no built-in navigation to its true home. When authorship proves more elusive, a visit to one of the many registrars of domain names is the next step. In this manner I was able to discover who was behind the Martinlutherking.org site before the link to the hate group Stormfront was added to the site.

Fortunately, educators do not have to reinvent the wheel when it comes to teaching students how to spot the rhetorical tricks described in chapter 6. Most "point of view" websites can still be evaluated in terms of the seven devices identified by the Institute for Propaganda Analysis (*Propaganda Analysis* 1937): name calling, glittering generality, transfer, testimonial, plain folks, card stacking, and bandwagon. The first two, name-calling and glittering generality, occur when words are used to link people or ideas to either negative or positive associations. These are loaded terms like *family values, tax-and-spend liberal, redneck, patriot, terrorist, freedom fighter*—and so on. The second two devices, transfer and testimonial, imply false or unwarranted connections to persons, ideas, or symbols that, again, carry certain associations. We see this in the depiction of American flags by hate groups, in first-person testimonials on political party websites, and in celebrity endorsements of consumer products. The plain-folks device occurs when speakers claim that they are "just like everyone else." Card stacking is the technique of piling up arguments, evidence, statistics, and information (or misinformation) to slant an argument—particularly for the purposes of inciting fear. Conspiracy theorists are especially adept at employing this tool. Finally, the bandwagon device lures us with the argument that "everyone else is buying/believing/doing this, so you should be too." The Canadian-based Media Awareness Network (n.d.) brings this type of analysis to bear on the persuasion strategies of hate groups—the use of pseudoscience and intellectualism, historical revisionism, patriotism, misinformation, nationalism, hate symbols, and claims of "racialism" rather than racism. Lesson plans and classroom activities are also available on this website.

Deconstruction techniques can also be taken home. I have found it productive to have students analyze a set of particularly challenging websites for their parents after we have finished our in-class practice. (See figure 7.1.) This assignment requires that students not only understand what they have seen online but understand it at a deep enough level to be able to articulate their knowledge to others. It brings parents into the fold, keeping them informed as well as involving them in the learning process. Students have a chance to model what they know and to display their competence. Finally, the activity gives the family a set of information evaluation tools to use in the future.

What comes next? We know from educational research and our own experience that such learning is most successful when it is built into activities that occur over time, across the curriculum, collaboratively, and in the context of application. It makes a great deal of sense to put students more directly in the driver's seat. Applying evaluation principles to genuine information needs will give meaning to students' abstract knowledge. Students can be asked to develop evaluation rubrics to suit their own individual tasks and projects. They, rather than their librarians or teachers, can use a variety of Web 2.0 tools to create research pathfinders or annotated bibliographies that are meaningful to the context in which they are working. Outside school, they will be prepared to develop criteria that are appropriate to more personal information needs. The goal is to make thinking about evaluation automatic, a habit of mind that is deeply ingrained into the process of information use in any context.

Figure 7.1

Evaluating Websites: Sharing the Fun

Take your parent(s)/guardian(s) on a tour of the websites you visited at www.uni.illinois.edu/library/computerlit/evaluatingsites.html. Show them the high points and the low points. See if they can spot the tricks!

If you don't have Web access at home, see me and we'll figure out an alternative.

To get full credit, signed forms (below) are due by _____.

Dear parents/guardians,

As a parent myself, I know how difficult it can be to get students to share their school day experiences. In the case of this particular assignment, I have a special interest in involving you. First, I'd like you to know what is happening in this Computer Literacy 1 unit on web searching and website evaluation. As you know, the Internet—although a valuable resource for learning—also contains a good deal of unvetted material. We want our students to learn to be critical consumers. Second, I feel strongly that parents and teachers are in this effort together. Your involvement is key to helping students understand the importance of being informed users of online (and paper!) information sources.

Please be aware that one site on this list is highly offensive. It is included so students learn to read carefully and look beyond surface appearances. If you have any questions or concerns, please do not hesitate to contact me.

Thanks very much,

Frances Jacobson Harris
University Laboratory High School Librarian

My son/daughter _____ took me on a tour of the websites found at www.uni.illinois.edu/library/computerlit/evaluatingsites.html. He/she helped me understand how to evaluate the sites for accuracy, objectivity, authority, and appropriateness of use for different purposes.

Parent/Guardian signature _____ Date _____

Comments (optional):

8

putting it all together

As the new generation flocks to the Internet without a backward glance, libraries may begin to look like relics from another age. At the same time, librarians are becoming deeply aware of how much their services are needed. The important teaching and learning processes discussed in the previous chapter do not happen by magic. Librarians have learned that though most young Americans are well versed in the use of digital technologies, many are novices when it comes to searching, selecting, and assessing the meaning and value of the information they find online (Valenza 2006; Educational Testing Service 2006; Rowlands et al. 2008). The fact that teens think they know all they need to know is an important factor in how we plan our services and programs.

INFORMATION STRUCTURES
AND INFORMATION MEANINGS

"Format agnostic" is the label Abram and Luther (2004) ascribe to the younger generation. Because web search results can include anything from websites and blogs to encyclopedia and magazine articles, teenagers do not think in terms of source type:

> Information is information, and NextGens see little difference in credibility or entertainment value between print and media formats. Their opinions can be modified and influenced by an information ocean that does not differentiate between journals and books, network or cable television, or blogs or web sites. (Abram and Luther 2004, 34)

The library world is on its way to accommodating this mind-set with federated and broadcast search tools that comb multiple databases and catalogs from a single query. Even when searching within an individual proprietary database like EBSCO's MAS Ultra School Edition, a teen can find journal articles, images, primary sources, pamphlets, and reference sources.

At the present time, however, there is no genuinely universal search tool, no bona fide one-stop shopping. Technical limitations prevent web search engines from achieving total saturation of the free Web. They can neither continually crawl every web server that is online nor penetrate the free resources that are hidden behind database walls, such as many library catalogs and digital archives. One good example of the latter is the Library of Congress's American Memory service (http://memory.loc.gov), which includes nine million primary-source documents scattered across more than a hundred thematic collections. For best results, each collection really needs to be queried individually. Access to digital collections like these is improving with developments in metadata harvesting and is realized in initiatives (like some at the Library of Congress) that now provide open-to-the-Web item-level metadata for some of their collections. It is possible, for example, to use Google to find a panoramic photograph of attendees at the Anti-Saloon League, held in Washington, D.C., December 8, 1921, or three different versions of the traditional folk tune "Frosty Morning," played by fiddler Henry Reed—all physically housed at the Library of Congress. But most resources in archives like these are still well hidden from search-engine view. Finally, it goes without saying that Google and its competitors cannot yet deliver the bulk of content from proprietary information resources. Teens (and probably most other searchers) have little awareness of this lack of universality in searching different types of sources.

As educators, we need to ensure that teens have a sense of the actual breadth and depth of the information landscape, the importance of that vastness, and the steps required to uncover what hides behind formal and informal information-retrieval systems. As they search for information, teens must be cognizant of the differences between the free Web and the deep—or invisible—Web. Additionally, they need to appreciate the enormity of the nondigitized information world. When it comes to selecting and evaluating information, we have an opportunity to capitalize on teens' format agnosticism and to validate their instinctive belief that format is a superficial attribute. It is *not* terribly important if an article appears on a website or in a print journal. It *is* important to consider the nature of the article's authorship. Who wrote it? Why was it written? Who authorized and sponsored its publication? Questions like these keep teens' eyes on the prize, on the nature of authorship and intent, and therefore on the true value of the source.

FORMAL AND INFORMAL REVISITED

Here, at the frontier of format agnosticism, is where the conversation comes back to the issues discussed in the first two chapters of this book: the tensions between formal and informal information systems, the library and the Internet, the off-line and the online worlds. The distinctions among these worlds are becoming less clear (and less meaningful) every day. Perhaps the time is ripe for us to make the tensions both irrelevant and instructive by exploring ways we can use them to enlighten and inform.

When "Easy" Does Not Mean "Transparent"

As arcane as formal library search systems may seem, students need to be aware that the inner workings of commercial web search engines are also shrouded in mystery, but of a more suspect type. Search-engine relevance criteria are protected trade secrets. As noted in chapter 2, the search-engine community has no membership-based cataloging and classification committees to propose and debate standards in a public forum, no Library of Congress to establish consistency and uniformity in descriptive practice and terminology. Instead, search-engine algorithms constantly shift in response to technical developments and marketplace factors. Services like searchenginewatch.com are useful for keeping up-to-date with some of these changes, but staying current requires continual monitoring on the part of the user.

Still, users can generally count on certain commonly employed relevance-determination principles, such as the occurrence of key terms in metadata and text, the high incidence of links to a site, and more frequent crawling of sites that are updated often. None of these factors is a guarantor of credibility. The high placement of Martinlutherking.org on any search of "Martin Luther King" is mainly caused by the large number of sites that link to it—most created by librarians who link to the site in their lessons on website evaluation! When significant changes occur in the web environment, they can wreak havoc with these established protocols. For example, once blogs began to proliferate, particularly as they started being syndicated, the frequency of self-referencing and cross-linking in them skewed the results of search-engine relevance criteria. Blogs began to dominate search-engine results lists. Google quietly developed strategies for identifying blogs and assigning them lower rankings.

The shady factor in search-engine results lists arises when rankings have less to do with relevance than they do with revenue generation for search-engine companies and their clients. Commercial website owners employ search-engine optimization techniques, modifying content and HTML coding so keywords are more likely to be retrieved by the indexing algorithms of search engines. Some search engines allow clients to pay for high placement of their sites on lists of results. Advertisers can also "lease" keywords. Every time a user types in those words, the advertiser's links appear as sponsored links alongside the list of search results. I have asked my students to imagine publishers or authors inserting sponsored bibliographic records alongside catalog search results, or paid placement citations edging out other citations at the top of their database search results lists. This prospect highlights how accustomed we have all become to the commercial nature of the "free" Web.

Demystifying the Process

For a long time, I was probably the only librarian in America who still taught teens how to use the print version of the *Readers' Guide to Periodical Literature*. Why did I persist? Besides some purely pragmatic issues (e.g., the lack of enough computers for a class of students to access online databases in my library), one reason was the portrayal of the venerable index in an old video called *How to Use the Readers' Guide* (1987). In a pivotal scene, an indexer at the H. W. Wilson Company is shown examining an article and assigning subject headings to it. After watching (and laughing at) this portrayal of ancient library times, the students in my classes enjoyed identifying the elements that had changed since its production, from hairstyles to computer hardware. But an essential ingredient remained (and still remains) the same—the use of human indexers who personally index every article that is cited in each of the company's print and electronic database products. Even the most naive among my students realized that automated search-engine processing could not come close to the quality and judgment of the human brain for this task.

The fact that I used this old video, or even the *Readers' Guide,* to teach this lesson is not so important. Other search tools and different teaching hooks would have worked just as well, as long as they illuminated a couple of important points. One of these points is that the inner workings of some long-standing library-world finding tools are quite transparent in their construction (even if confusing to use), in contrast to the secretive world of search-engine protocols. Another point is that lessons like these can help students develop very useful mental models about indexes and databases. When I sorted a stack of our library's periodicals into those that were indexed by the *Readers' Guide* and those that were not, the students saw physical evidence of its scope. I could also show which titles were indexed by other database services, helping students begin to have a sense of databases as a whole new and diverse world. And when we talked about the chances of finding the articles that are in these periodicals through a Google search, they began to understand the profound differences between the free Web and the deep Web. The point of this type of instruction is to lay bare the infrastructure and focus of search tools, enabling students to select and use them intelligently.

INTEGRATION

Just how we accomplish our instruction varies considerably, in part because the territory is so variable. One of the unanticipated consequences of today's rich information landscape is the necessity of working in so many different search environments. We are past the days when all we had to think about were the card catalog, a couple of periodical indexes, and our reference collection. Nowadays, the tools are innumerable and overlapping, with most containing both formal and informal structural elements. Many are hybrid creations, featuring both bibliographic data and full-text and multimedia content. At least non-federated information services still come with labels or instructions that reflect their attributes. The *Readers' Guide to Periodical Literature* is, as it says, an index to periodical literature. But with most search tools (including *Readers' Guide*) now being served by the Web, they assume a superficial similarity to the point that users can lose track of what they are searching. This environment, an ironic mix of uniformity and complexity, creates special considerations for acquiring searching and content evaluation skills.

Searching

For all the reasons covered in chapter 2, searching effectively for information in any environment remains a skill that requires much analytical thought. The strategy used to search a bibliographic index like *Readers' Guide* produces different results when applied to its full-text online counterpart, and different results yet again when applied to the open-ended free Web. Students who are accustomed to searching the Web with standard search engines tend to carry over the same strategies when using other search tools. In practice, this means they clutter their searches with the extremely specific terminology that works so well in Google. A web search for "causes of earthquakes in California" yields a plethora of results, but it falls flat when applied to a bibliographic database. For the latter, searchers need to move to a higher level of abstraction, removing adjectival terms like *causes* or *effects* and including only those nounlike terms the system is likely to recognize. And this strategy has not yet even taken the prospect of controlled vocabulary into consideration.

Teaching with concrete examples can help establish the mental models that searchers need as they move from one search environment to another. When I teach catalog use, I hand a library book to each student in the class and ask them to open it at random and read a sentence from it. Could they find the book in the library's catalog by looking under the words in that sentence? No. They immediately recognize the futility of that particular strategy. I direct them to look at the Cataloging in Publication (CIP) data on the back of the title page (calling it the "secret librarian handshake"). The bibliographic record they see there contains the only searchable terms they can use to find the book. This concrete illustration helps them understand they have to think in terms of what the whole book is about, abstract its subject to two or three key terms or phrases, and then look in the catalog under those terms.

What about the web environment? Could my students find their book by searching Google for the words in that sentence? With the digitization of millions of titles on the Google Books project, it becomes more likely every day. But it is still more unlikely than not. As students realize that their book's entire contents may not yet be digitized (and are therefore not searchable on the Web), they begin to understand that neither are the majority of the books in the library—or the bookstore, or on the shelves at home. Even as Google and other Internet search providers collaborate with research libraries and publishers to digitize books, it will be a long time before the balance of print book material, whether in or out of copyright, is available in digital form in the same proportion as it is available in print form.

Computer and information scientists, as well as web content providers, are working feverishly to make natural language and full-text searching more feasible. A search in Google Books (http://books.google.com) on "Alicia Svigals," one of today's foremost klezmer-style violinists, seems almost magical. Because Svigals has not (yet) been the subject of a book-length biography or written a book herself, all the hits that appear indicate places where she is mentioned within the contents of other books—whether her name appears in the acknowledgments, a list of recordings, or the text itself. These books are, for the most part, general titles about modern klezmer or world music. Each entry includes an excerpt that mentions her, citing the page number on which it appears, and a link to the digitized image of that full page.

One of the titles on this results list is a book called *Jewish Mothers: Strength, Wisdom, and Compassion* (Wolfson and Wolf 2000), which profiles fifty American Jewish women, from the first woman rabbi hired by a major Conservative congregation to the puppeteer Shari Lewis. That Alicia Svigals is one of these women is no surprise, but a searcher could only discover this by using a search tool like Google Books. A library catalog would not suffice, because the five very general Library of Congress subject headings assigned to the book are along the lines of "Mothers -- United States -- Interviews" and "Jewish Women -- United States -- Social conditions -- 20th century." Clearly, full-text searching of books is a boon to anyone doing research on Svigals. On the other hand, the lack of vocabulary control in such full-text searches can produce extremely imprecise results. The Google Books search on Svigals also retrieves the first edition of *this* book (the one you are currently reading) and a book called *Wild Fermentation: The Flavor, Nutrition, and Craft of Live-Culture Foods,* for which Svigals is thanked by the author for "Yiddish consultations." Still, many searchers, including teens, are willing to put up with a certain number of false hits as a price worth paying for the ability to find so much other previously hidden content. Interestingly, a Google Books search on my earlier example—the causes of earthquakes in California—retrieves hits from early twentieth-century volumes of the *Readers' Guide to Periodical Literature,* bringing the search back full circle to the retrieval of bibliographic citations.

Focusing the Scope

An important key to successful searching in today's complex environment is to focus the scope of the search by subdividing it into manageable chunks. Specialized search tools, such as search directories and website "collections," are a chief means by which this has been accomplished. These website collections resemble traditional libraries in that items are intentionally chosen in much the same way as books in a library are chosen. The sites that are selected fit within a defined collection scope and meet certain standards of quality. Searchers need not be concerned about hidden factors like paid placement that might influence qualitative rankings.

Some directory services are nonprofit efforts, like ipl2: Information You Can Trust (http://ipl2.org), which contains approximately 20,000 websites in its database, and the archives of the Internet Scout Project Report (http://scout.wisc.edu/Reports/ScoutReport/Current), a little larger at about 25,000 websites. Their annotations are written by outside reviewers, librarians, and subject-matter specialists, and neither service accepts advertising. Other directory services are, like Wikipedia, creations of the web community itself. The Open Directory Project (www.dmoz .org) is edited and maintained by a large community of volunteers. The search industry also markets website directories, such as Thinkronize's K–12 netTrekker product (www.nettrekker.com), for which the annotated resources are aligned to state standards and organized by grade and reading level. In these cases, subscription fees eliminate the need for outside advertising. Even with 300,000 digital resources in the netTrekker database, its search universe is considerably smaller than the free Web, and value is ostensibly added by its being targeted to the school audience and vetted by teacher-selectors.

There is an important side note to add here about searching, a problem briefly referred to in chapter 2. Although web directories connect searchers to web content, users are actually searching bibliographic databases rather than full-content websites. But web directories look like search engines, with their search window prominently displayed, and users often expect them to behave like search engines. Users will experience the same type of level-of-specificity problems described earlier if their searches are constructed too narrowly. For example, when I search for "macadamia nut turkey stuffing" in ipl2, of the first ten results, five are about Turkey (the country); four are about cooking turkeys (the bird); and one is about the turkey vulture. The term "macadamia" does not appear in the bibliographic information of these entries, regardless of whether the websites themselves contain stuffing recipes that use these nuts. A user is better off choosing broader search terms (e.g., "turkey," "Thanksgiving," "recipes") that better convey the context of the desired information.

Searchers can also use databases of various types to focus the search universe. In addition to ensuring some level of quality, databases use other focusing criteria such as subject (e.g., subject-specialized databases); audience (e.g., scholars, the K–12 market, the business community, etc.); and publication type (e.g., journal articles rather than websites). Quality control is not guaranteed. Students may not realize that there are significant qualitative differences between a free database site like findarticles

.com and a subscription database like OCLC FirstSearch's Wilson Select Plus. Both purport to index a wide variety of periodical resources. But the findarticles.com database is filled with trade journals and public relations releases, and its indexing schedule lags significantly. The "premium articles" it offers for a fee may already be available at no charge to users of libraries' databases. In contrast, Wilson Select Plus is updated weekly and includes important periodical titles ranging from *Time* magazine to the *Journal of Atmospheric and Oceanic Technology*.

Google Scholar (http://scholar.google.com) is Google's very successful attempt to create access to information that heretofore has only been accessible via the proprietary databases that search the invisible Web. Its coverage is very broad, which can reduce the necessity to repeat a search in different databases. My search on earthquakes in California yields articles from scholarly journals, government websites, conference proceedings, and books. When users click through to items that are not available on the free Web, they are typically given purchasing or subscribing options. Many libraries offer widgets or online tools that link Google Scholar results to library database holdings, completing the circuit to desired resources.

Some databases are hybrid types, their content encompassing bibliographic periodical records as well as full-text websites. For example, Elsevier's science database Scirus (www.scirus.com) consists of websites as well as journal articles, and it also includes non-Elsevier content, such as portions of the National Library of Medicine's PubMed database. Access to Scirus is free, though access to the full text of the articles from its Science Direct component and from other science information business partners is fee-based, which makes Scirus an interesting case of a database that, like Google Scholar, indexes both the free Web and the invisible Web. The company's likely business model is that profits from the full-text service subsidize free access to the bibliographic information.

Librarians also help their clientele focus the information universe by providing them with online pathfinders, research guides, and other traditional tools of the trade. Today, library websites have an especially important role in supporting the user's search experience. Well-designed sites can be customized to meet the needs, interests, and cultural backgrounds of the community. The website of the Homer Township Public Library (www.homerlibrary.org), of Homer Glen, Illinois, features RSS feeds to local news, the director's blog, and upcoming teen events, each with links to translation services for Arabic, Polish, and Spanish. Library websites eliminate the clutter of commercial web portals and contain links to value-added services that only a library can offer, such as their proprietary databases. At the Public Library of Charlotte and Mecklenburg County (North Carolina), users can actually create a personalized version of the library's website to suit their own needs. This service, called brarydog (www.brarydog.net), allows users to add their favorite links to an already structured set of free and subscription-based resources and even to alter the look of the page by selecting background image and color. The page is available to them wherever they have Internet access.

Students can learn techniques that will help them focus the search process for themselves. Social bookmarking is a method of saving, organizing, and sharing bookmarks of websites. Users tag their bookmarks by keyword, making them searchable. Searching for links on social bookmarking sites like Delicious or Diigo is a way of tapping into the wisdom of the crowd, a rough method of filtering web results to sites that are recommended by others. Many libraries now use social bookmarking to maintain their lists of recommended websites, which automatically allows users to subscribe to updates. Another useful strategy, mentioned briefly at the close of the previous chapter, is to require students to develop their own pathfinders, either as precursors to research projects, as ends in themselves, or as guides for others. Though the pathfinder process is a focusing exercise, it also pushes students into using a wider variety of sources than they otherwise might, particularly if a template or model is provided for them to emulate.

Buffy Hamilton, library media specialist at Creekview High School in Canton, Georgia, uses a range of Web 2.0 tools to help students and teachers focus their search experience. Her extensive Pageflakes "pagecasts" (www.pageflakes.com/theunquietlibrary) provide access to news and information feeds on topics as varied as environmental science, a peanut butter salmonella scare, and veterans' issues. One of her pagecasts is a sample student information portal containing widgets for a variety of research tools, including a Google Books search, database searches, Delicious bookmarks, embedded presentations on VoiceThread and SlideShare, a Meebo link for instant messaging the librarian, and several news feeds (see figure 8.1). Using this model, students can create their own portals for their own research-based projects or for personal use. Making deliberate choices among different resource types as they create and use these portals most certainly helps improve searching and evaluation skills.

"I Found It on the Internet"—Selection and Evaluation

As alluded to earlier in this chapter, the attribute of "youth" in and of itself does not equate with expertise in all things technological. Although today's young people possess unprecedented levels of exposure to information and communication technologies (ICTs), their actual abilities and individual backgrounds vary widely. Researchers at CIBER (School of Library, Archive and Information Studies, University College London) conducted a longitudinal study of the impact of the digital world on the information behavior of the "Google generation" in hopes of informing effective development of future library and information services (Rowlands et al. 2008). Some of their findings speak directly to selection and evaluation concerns:

> The information literacy of young people has not improved with the widening access to technology: in fact, their apparent facility with computers disguises some worrying problems.
>
> Internet research shows that the speed of young people's web searching means that little time is spent in evaluating information, either for relevance, accuracy or authority.
>
> Young people have a poor understanding of their information needs and thus find it difficult to develop effective search strategies. (Rowlands et al. 2008, 295)

The researchers conclude that the ubiquitous presence of technology in young people's lives has not resulted in improved information-retrieval, information-seeking, or evaluation skills. They note, however, that young people are not unique in possessing these deficits. All of us have changed our information behavior, and in many ways, we can all be considered members of the Google generation. At the same time, it must be acknowledged that the cognitive development of young people is in flux and matures at different rates. We need to take into account how this

Figure 8.1

This partial view of the Creekview High School sample student information Pageflakes portal shows feeds for Delicious and Diigo bookmarks, a Google Books search, spaces for student VoiceThread and SlideShare presentations, and a window for live chats with the librarian.

variability in development influences perceptions of credibility (Eastin 2008).

The complexities of selecting and evaluating information will only increase as information technologies continue to diversify and grow. The current ubiquity of community-built information paints a whole different picture of expertise and requires us all to develop new credibility measures when using the Web. Howard Rheingold (2009) is blunt in his assessment of the current state of affairs: "Unless a great many people learn the basics of online crap detection and begin applying their critical faculties en masse and very soon, I fear for the future of the Internet as a useful source of credible news, medical advice, financial information, educational resources, scholarly and scientific research." Writing from a perspective that "the issue of information literacy could be even more important than the health or education of some individuals," he suggests some excellent twenty-first-century strategies for assessing credibility. Have others linked to a site under review, and if so, who are they? Have others bookmarked the site in Delicious or Diigo? Can the information be corroborated in other sources? He discusses adapting the detective profession's technique of triangulation by trying to find three different ways to test a source's credibility. Many "cyberforensic" tools are now available for doing so, such as hoax-debunking sites like Snopes.com and Factcheck.org, which checks out claims made by political factions.

Authority has traditionally been thought of as hierarchical and centralized, manifested in the form of a single entity or set of entities. We are seeing a shift from this authority-based approach to credibility to a "reliability approach," which depends on access to a multiplicity of sources and an amassed set of results that are dependable and consistent in quality (Lankes 2008). Rheingold recommends that consumers learn how to use online filters like "hashtags," community-generated terms used to identify and retrieve information on the same topic or event. When a critical mass of citizen-reporters posts online, such filters improve opportunities for corroboration of information. He quotes Clay Shirky, who observes that the order of information dissemination in online communities is "publish, then filter," rather than the journalism model of filter (i.e., submit for editorial review), then publish (Shirky 2002). The blog *Twitter Journalism* offers a list of eight ways to verify a tweet, such as checking a tweeter's biography (both on Twitter and Google), reading for further context in the person's Twitter stream, and looking for related tweets (Kanalley 2009). Rheingold points to organizations like NewsTrust.net that cultivate select communities for crowdsourcing duty. NewsTrust's bipartisan virtual community members evaluate news stories from both mainstream and alternative news sources using a set of review tools that ask questions based on core principles of journalism, such as fairness, accuracy, context, and sourcing. Not all reviewers in the community are considered equal, which prevents malicious or amateur efforts from rising to the top.

FORGING NEW PATHWAYS

So far in this chapter, I have focused on the information world, emphasizing its marvelous richness and its confounding complexity. But information technology is only half of the ICT puzzle, and as discussed in earlier chapters, communication technology is the key to the contemporary teenager's heart. For many teens, "communication technology" is not a noun but a verb; it is a fundamental means of interaction with their world. Yet teens encounter many obstacles to the use of communication technologies at school and in public institutions, places in which they spend a considerable proportion of their lives. It is time to assemble a more integrated ICT library environment for them. Doing so means imagining libraries in a new light and facing change in proactive ways.

Before plunging ahead, I believe it is important to address an issue that is an ICT deal-breaker for many libraries, particularly school libraries. As mentioned earlier, schools typically prohibit student access to "inappropriate" online material and activities. *Inappropriateness* tends to be defined in two ways. First, some content is labeled inappropriate because it is considered harmful to children. Filtering software is the legislated response to this concern. But as discussed in chapter 7, filters are often set to block material and activities in ways that go well beyond the child protection requirements of CIPA. For example, social media tools—teens' favored form of communication technology—are often blocked *as a class.* Second, the "inappropriate" label also often includes any online content, activity, or interaction that is not directly related to what is going on in the classroom. In such settings, computing resources are only to be used for narrowly defined categories of educational activities. In chapter 6, I discussed this issue as it relates to student access to recreational or personal-interest types of information.

Sometimes the latter view of appropriateness is implemented through prescriptive methods rather than restrictive methods. Though in these cases the emphasis is on what students *can* do rather than what they *can't* do, the range of options is extremely limited. We see this phenomenon when teachers or librarians restrict students to searching preselected sets of websites, proprietary databases, or web portals that only index a discrete set of vetted websites. Educators may choose this strategy as a way to scaffold learning, a step to take before moving students into more open-ended and self-directed searching and evaluation tasks. But by the secondary school level, such efforts should only be considered temporary, the training wheels students need for learning to critically evaluate information for themselves. We need to take the training wheels off while students are still in our care and can continue to benefit from some level of teaching and guidance. Some of us use well-intentioned lures to promote database use that can, in some ways, work at the expense of teaching web evaluation skills. For example, students might be required to fill out web evaluation forms for sources found using web search engines but not for articles found using databases. The lack of scrutiny of database content implies that *all* information found in magazines, journals, newspapers, and other "traditional" sources is credible and of equal merit (Harris 2009). Until the impact of these types of prohibitions is understood and mitigated, change toward a more integrated ICT library environment will be difficult to achieve.

Changing Roles for Libraries and Librarians

In the Web 2.0 world, libraries play an important yet somewhat invisible role. In describing library users' lack of appreciation of their seamless access to expensive databases, Rowlands et al. note that: "Libraries are increasingly between a rock and a hard place: the publisher or search engine gets the credit; they just pick up the tab" (2008, 298). The stakes are high. An effective ICT role for libraries can ensure that teens, because they are comfortable in today's libraries, will become tomorrow's library users and supporters. But the impact of changing ICTs on the roles of librarians and libraries cannot be discounted either. Librarians need to assume leadership roles in managing that change if they and their institutions are to remain viable.

The *New York Times* profile of school librarian Stephanie Rosalia was a bit of a media breakthrough for the profession (Rich 2009). Rosalia is described as "part of a growing cadre of 21st-century multimedia specialists who help guide students through the digital ocean of information that confronts them on a daily basis." She is portrayed as representative of today's librarians, who believe that literacy includes, but also exceeds, books. Yet in her New York City district, only about one-third of the city's public schools have certified librarians. Even so, Rosalia reflects the spirit of the many librarians serving young adults today who are defining new pathways for their profession. Another exemplar of this spirit is high school librarian Buffy Hamilton, mentioned earlier in this chapter. Hamilton employs a "participatory librarianship" approach that positions librarians as agents of change in their learning communities (2009). As such, they create information-rich environments using new media tools (in combination with welcoming physical spaces) that support participation, conversation, inquiry, reflection, and knowledge construction.

Way back in 2002, blogger Jenny Levine developed the "shifted librarian" model as a much-needed response to fundamental changes in young people's information needs and expectations:

> To my mind, *the biggest difference is that they expect information to come to them, whether it's via the Web, e-mail, cell phone, online chat, whatever.* And given the tip of the iceberg of technology we're seeing, *it's going to have a big impact on how they expect to receive library services,* which means librarians have to start adjusting now. I call that adjustment "shifting" because I think you have to start meeting these kids' information needs *in their world,* not yours. *The library has to become more portable or "shifted."* [author's emphases] (Levine 2002)

In Levine's vision, books and other traditional services still occupy center stage, but they are given a boost from new modes of communication and service delivery. This expanded repertoire comes in many guises—in social tools that support user interests and needs, in personalized electronic services like the brarydog service of the Public Library of Charlotte and Mecklenburg County, and in school libraries like Buffy Hamilton's where young people actively participate in and contribute to their library experience.

Give 'Em What They Want

Does the "shifted librarian" model mean turning the library into a mall or an arcade? The concern about sacrificing quality to meet popular demand is an old one, hearkening back to the development of early public libraries as places for self-improvement rather than as places to exchange dime novels. In the more recent 1980s, Charles Robinson and the staff of the Baltimore County Public Library (BCPL) raised the hackles of the library profession when they launched the notorious "Give 'em what they want!" campaign (Rawlinson 1981). The gist of the model was that public money should be spent on what the public wants, not on what librarians think the public ought to have. The epicenter of the controversy was collection development, with the BCPL committing a substantial proportion of its dollars to purchasing the types of materials that would generate high circulation. Critics decried what they saw as a "McLibrary" approach, in which centralized selection and catering to the (perceived) lowest common denominator threatened to eradicate the personalized services, specialized skills, and pedagogical role that had been the pride of the profession.

Judging by this debate, it is an easy stretch to imagine a worst-case "shifted library" scenario, in which a library offers only the ICT services the public appears to want. Its young adult space would be populated with zombielike teens sitting at computers, glued to their social network services, blasting music, playing raucous video games, and downloading pornographic images, with nary a book nor a librarian in sight. However, "shifted" does not have to mean the abandonment, or even a compromise, of principles. It is important to remember that technology itself is value-neutral. Even its use can be neutral, depending on the situational and contextual factors that surround it. But if technology is inherently neither good nor bad, it does require careful management. The shifted library can therefore be a hard sell at administrative levels, but the potential for reward is great.

For most practitioners, what does it actually mean to become "shifted"? First, librarians need to become knowledgeable about ICTs, to know which ones are being used by area teens and how they are being used. Next, dabble a bit and test the waters. Having personal experience with a new ICT makes it much easier to understand those who are avid users of it. Start small and pick a tool to learn that will provide immediate personal benefit. In the days before cell-phone texting was common, I used instant messaging for quick communication with my husband and grown kids. I decided to take it to the next step by making my screen name public at school, and then watched as my "coolness" stock rose considerably. I was surprised by the number of students who felt comfortable using IM to ask me for help outside school hours. Any initial awkwardness I felt with the technology was soon eclipsed by the benefits it brought me, both personally and professionally.

The learning curve for such ventures doesn't have to be steep. Many "Library 2.0" mavens have created wonderful do-it-yourself guides to the tools. Among the most comprehensive is Donna Baumbach's WebTools4U2Use (http://webtools4u2use.wikispaces.com), which covers everything from wikis and RSS to mapping tools and podcasting. Newbies can pick one tool from her list and develop some comfort with it at their own speed before deciding whether it makes sense for their libraries. It's a win-win when a new tool replaces an old one and even improves or streamlines practice. I felt this way when I learned about using the Google Docs forms function to develop surveys. The forms are fully featured and easy to create and share online. The results populate a spreadsheet and can be displayed in graphical format. Not only is the survey process simplified but the value as a library marketing tool is hard to beat.

The next step is to allow teens their tools in libraries in ways that are feasible and useful to them. For example, libraries need to provide room for both multitasking and nonmultitasking behaviors, solo work and group work, while establishing parameters that make sense for all users of the library, including staff. Librarians working with teens are in a position to educate their colleagues about why multitasking and collaborative behaviors in the library should be supported and what policies can be implemented to make them work (Braun 2004). Huge changes are not required. Merely allowing a teen to plug headphones into a sound-capable computer is one inexpensive, low-impact example. Those who wish to listen to music while working can do so; those who would rather not can skip it. At the same time, it is just as important, as Jennifer Burek Pierce notes, to encourage young people to read as "a necessary counterpoint to facilitating their ready use of ICTs" (2008, 55–56). Shifted librarians can find abundant resources for help achieving these kinds of transformations. Resources like Kimberly Bolan's *Teen Spaces: The Step-by-Step Library Makeover* (2009) and the "YA Spaces of Your Dreams" column in each issue of the *Voice of Youth Advocates* address physical changes in the library. Librarians looking to invigorate their services can also tap into any number of online professional learning networks (e.g., the Teacher Librarian Ning, at http://teacherlibrarian.ning.com) to find real-life examples of Web 2.0 implementations and to seek targeted advice about particular issues—including helping kids understand how to practice safe and responsible ICT use.

Gaming is another domain that may not be seen as "library-friendly." But if libraries are in the business of supporting literacy, librarians may well want to take another look at how playing video games can support teen literacy. Braun (2007) points to the inherent storytelling features of video games. Not only do gamers immerse themselves in the stories but they also read (and possibly write) text in the form of online guides and books about characters and game worlds, online discussions about the game, and fan fiction devoted to the game. Recent research on the topic makes it clear that gaming is not passive entertainment and that it can play a major role in helping youth develop personal identity, learn to organize and execute plans, and interact effectively with others in a highly social environment (Braun 2007; Gee 2008). Gaming scholar James Paul Gee distinguishes between what he calls "game" with a small "g" and "Game" with a big "G."

> The "game" is the software in the box and all the elements of in-game design. The "Game" is the social setting into which the game is placed, all the interactions that go on around the game. (2008, 24)

He concludes that the big "G" Game and the little "g" game become tightly knit together, as the two become a learning, knowledge-building, design community.

Some libraries have found that games also become a gateway activity for kids who are typically not library users, which has a huge payoff for everyone (Gorman 2002). Playing games on the Internet helps these teens feel comfortable with the computer and within the library environment. They gradually sign up for activities like computer classes and begin to use other software for schoolwork and for fun. As with the headphones-and-music solution, libraries still need to find ways to integrate these nontraditional services in ways that do not impede core library activities. Those seeking guidance will find it in ALA's "The Librarian's Guide to Gaming: An Online Toolkit for Building Gaming @ your library" (http://librarygamingtoolkit.org), which includes supportive evidence, resources, tips, and links to best practices at public and school libraries.

It's Not All Candy: Adapting Traditional Services

Despite what critics had to say about the "Give 'em what they want!" campaign at the Baltimore County Public Library, the classics always maintained a strong presence on the shelves there. The same thing can be said for service "classics" in the shifted library. In fact, ICTs have always been used to enhance core library services, from the first online union catalogs to today's online delivery of interlibrary loan articles. Of course, the road to change is not always a smooth one. Virtual reference service is an interesting example of a somewhat rocky adaptation of a traditional service. In this case, one service is actually catching up with another—remote users are now getting help with the remote resources that have already been made available to them. The pacing and lingo of virtual interactions can be challenging for those who are not accustomed to communicating online, in real time. The librarians who were early adopters of the service felt compelled to answer immediately, as they did for in-person or telephone reference transactions.

Providing access to physical as well as electronic collections will always remain an essential core service. Fortunately, NextGen catalogs and databases are making access more transparent than ever. For example, many commercial databases now provide downloadable widgets that facilitate visual recognition and portability. Libraries can install these widgets on their web portals and, better yet, help their users install them on their personal portals—be they social networking sites, iGoogle, or smart phones. Some libraries are using homegrown software solutions to improve access and to make traditional library searching a more socially engaging process. School library system coordinator Christopher Harris developed the Fish4Info project (http://fish4info.org), a library portal that accommodates book reviews, forums, comments, and tags. Students have a voice in the library's interface and can connect with peers there as well.

Adaptations to core teaching activities are also needed in ICT-enhanced environments. As discussed earlier, we are beginning to acknowledge that digital literacy does not result in information literacy and that the "Google generation's" facility with technology may not result in expert searching (Rowlands et al. 2008). Unfortunately, the complex efforts of searching, selecting, and evaluating information are generally not rewarded by teachers and often are not even acknowledged. Instead, they are discounted as the amorphous-but-necessary library research stage that is merely a precursor to the "real" work to be done by students. But if students are expected to demonstrate good judgment in selecting and synthesizing sources, the search process must be given its due. This goal can be accomplished by constructing rubrics that credit detection and analysis work, assigning students to maintain research journals or blogs to promote reflective thinking, and otherwise making the process as important as the product. The goal is to develop thoughtful habits of mind that serve the user throughout adulthood.

Many Web 2.0 tools seem tailor-made for libraries and classrooms. Tools like wikis, blogs, microblogging services, photo-sharing sites, and RSS have great potential for enhancing traditional services. Software providers have made these tools easy to set up and maintain, inexpensive to run (if not actually free), and inviting for target audiences. RSS can be an unobtrusive way to keep content fresh and to allow users to stay tuned by following the library in ways that are most convenient for them. Some school and public library websites are even built on blog or wiki software. Student products have evolved as well. Instead of traditional term papers and reports, students are often asked to use a blend of technology-based multimedia and communication tools to synthesize and present information. All these formats can "bump up" traditional library services in ways that are recognizable and welcoming to online teens. All offer controls for privacy and access. Successful education-related technology implementations are on the rise, as evidenced by growth in Web 2.0 tools that are designed with safety concerns in mind. Sites like Edublogs, for blogging, Gaggle, for student e-mail, and TeacherTube, for video sharing, offer the same learning opportunities as their mainstream counterparts, without being quite so open to the entire web world, and are (one hopes) less likely to be blocked in schools.

Assessment techniques also need to be modified. It takes a different skill set to grade Web 2.0 products than it does to grade term papers. Class discussions must be handled differently in the online environment than they are in the classroom. During in-class discussions, students can see one another's facial expressions, and the teacher can control the flow of conversation by calling on individuals. Online class discussion may have to be more structured to produce desired learning outcomes. Students need to learn to quote one another appropriately to provide their peers with sufficient context for new comments. Without being directed to summarize one another's responses and provide specific feedback, students tend to simply exchange speeches. In other words, "listening" online requires just as much effort, if not more, than does listening in face-to-face interactions. Again, the potential payoff of the new environment is high. Students who do not ordinarily speak out in class may do so online. Online discussions have fewer time restrictions; no bells are going to ring.

On their own (and whether we like it or not), students use all manner of online tools to support their formal learning experiences—querying friends on social networking sites, using "Ask an Expert" services, consulting literature summary and analysis sites like Sparknotes.com, and relying on Wikipedia. This year, a group of students at my school created a study wiki for their U.S. history class. They made the choice to check with the teacher first and invited him to view it and even add to it. I know of similar efforts in the past that involved blogs, e-mail, and instant messaging. Though teachers have been concerned that a few students were doing the work for many, most felt that the diversity and quantity of their classroom assessments overshadowed any long-term negative effects of this student "collaboration." On the positive side, out-of-school group engagement with the content can also have very beneficial learning outcomes.

Finally, new tools present all sorts of opportunities for librarians to collaborate with teachers. One of our English teachers uses a blog for class announcements and homework assignments. Parents as well as students always have access to it. The library contributes to the interactive wiki she uses for projects, embedding the resources and links students need for their research. On the poetry explication area of her wiki, students write an analysis of a poem, upload images, create internal links to their vocabulary definitions, and provide a brief history of the poem and the poet. They also access databases and other information sources and create bibliographic citations for their references. In a sense, the library is in her wiki, and her wiki is in the library. This "link love" is a product of old-fashioned collaboration between teacher and librarian, accompanied by traditional face-to-face instruction and coaching by both teacher and librarian.

Ethics "R" Now-More-Than-Ever Us

Librarians are still the information specialists. But if librarians are *only* information specialists, particularly if they work with teens, they are not fulfilling their charge. It is also the librarian's job to teach the responsible use of information, which these days encompasses both information and communication technologies. Although librarians have a long history of teaching ethics, its scope has typically been limited to the traditional confines of plagiarism and copyright lessons. Now, even our professional standards tell us to take those lessons further. As noted in chapter 7, the American Association of School Librarians *Standards for the 21st Century Learner* indicate that students will be taught to "Practice safe and ethical behaviors in personal electronic communication and interaction" (2007, 4.3.4). Likewise, the International Society for Technology in Education standards include a component devoted to digital citizenship (2007). Together, these standards expand the scope of our traditional territory and make ethics education a core responsibility of librarians.

There are compelling reasons why librarians should take a lead role in teaching ICT ethics. In both school and public libraries, librarians are in a position to see the whole ICT picture and the relationship teens have to it. Content, behavior, and management issues are all part of the librarian's purview. It would therefore be counterproductive not to assist teens in understanding the complications and consequences of the ICT environment. In the public library setting, who else will take care of this if not the librarian? At school, other stakeholders have their own interests to pursue. The science teacher is likely to teach science ICT applications and resources, the French teacher is likely to teach French ICT applications and resources, and so on. Even the computer teacher is likely to focus on technical skills and, if technology ethics are taught at all, may neglect the information ethics component. Only the school librarian's priorities are, by definition, focused on the big picture.

In chapter 7 I described how schools and libraries employ three basic strategies in managing ICT disciplinary issues: regulatory, technological, and pedagogical. For the most part, and possibly in self-defense, we seem to regard the first two as being well within our domain. No one questions whether librarians should be involved in setting policies for acceptable Internet use or making decisions about security and filtering software. But the pedagogical role is one that librarians have seemed hesitant to assume. I find this reluctance puzzling. Perhaps it exists because librarians have a professional Library Bill of Rights (American Library Association, Library Bill of Rights), which instills a kind of hands-off attitude; respecting users' rights to privacy and promoting open access to information are sacred trusts. But upholding those principles does not mean that librarians do not also have a responsibility to introduce ethics concepts to their users. In fact, in today's complex world, information skills are so closely associated with moral principles that one is hard to teach without the other. Librarians have a new sacred trust, which is to teach teens to become responsible as well as intelligent citizens in the virtual and physical worlds.

As I see it, we have an overarching professional obligation to engage in conversation about ethics with young people. First, we need to engage with students on these topics because teen access to ICTs is fundamentally an intellectual freedom issue (Adams 2008). The Library Bill of Rights includes the following interpretation: "The rights of minors to retrieve, interact with, and create information posted on the Internet in schools and libraries are extensions of their First Amendment rights" (American Library Association, Minors and Internet Activity). When problems do arise, we are advised that instances of inappropriate use of the digital tools should be addressed as individual behavior issues, "not as justification for restricting or banning access to interactive technology." In other words, the common practice of simply prohibiting adolescents' use of online social tools misses the target, because so many information, production, and educational tools now have the attributes of social tools. Instead, we should do our best to understand how the tools work and the context of the actual dangers. We can even use social tools to convey our messages, provided we respect teens' privacy. In their assessment of adolescent behaviors and social networking sites, Mitchell and Ybarra (2009) advise pediatric health professionals to find a balance between the risks and benefits of social network sites and other online tools. Their advice surely applies to librarians and teachers as well. Part of achieving the balance is teaching teens to engage in responsible and ethical online behavior.

If we are going to teach ethics, we must also engage in ethical behavior ourselves. We need to take care in how we connect with young people outside of school and the library. Again, being careful does not mean prohibiting any kind of contact. In my relatively small community, I see students all over town, as do the teachers I work with. These out-of-school contacts are anything but suspect and often result in useful conversations. Scholar danah boyd (2009) notes that much of the fear about online teacher-student interactions may be unwarranted. She urges that we focus on people, roles, relationships, and expectations, noting that a teacher's role in relation to a student should not end at the classroom door and never has. "To say that teachers shouldn't respond when a student asks for their help simply because of the technology is to do damage to students and society more broadly." She observes that being a friend with a young person on a social network site is not automatically problematic or equivalent to trying to be a young person's friend in real life. When it comes to social network sites, she advises that teachers not invade a student's space by initiating the contact. If a student invites a teacher to be a friend, the adult should enter the relationship as a teacher, mentor, and guide—not a peer.

SUGGESTIONS FOR EFFECTIVE LIBRARIANS

Librarians have always been involved in literacy efforts, and ICT literacy is no exception. In her overview of recent literacy movements, June Pullen Weis (2004) comments on the growing mainstreaming of ICT literacy. Unlike previous literacy initiatives, including librarians' own information-literacy bandwagon, "ICT literacy is recognized by a wide range of global stakeholders, including K–12 education, postsecondary education, and business and government leaders" (14). She feels the time is right for the key players to collaboratively articulate common definitions and implement shared goals. The National Council of Teachers of English is addressing the ICT literacy issue head-on. In a special report on teaching writing in the twenty-first century, former NCTE president Kathleen Blake Yancey notes that "we have moved beyond a pyramid-like, sequential model of literacy development in which print literacy comes first and digital literacy comes second and networked literacy practices, if they come at all, come third and last" (2009, 6). She views ours as an "Age of Composition," a period where writers learn to write just as much through "extracurricular social co-apprenticeship" as they do through formal instruction. If there are any lingering doubts about the changing face of literacy, findings from the Digital Youth Project indicate that in some quarters (e.g., the gaming world) adult leadership is central in how standards for expertise and literacy are being defined in digital media environments (Ito et al. 2009). All adults, not just educators, can function as role models and more experienced peers in assisting young people's interest-driven use of ICT tools. To stay relevant in the twenty-first century, educators not only need to keep pace with the rapid changes introduced by digital media but also need to take a proactive role in enlisting the help of others in supporting young people's learning.

Publications like these from the Digital Youth Project are good news for librarians, who have an important opportunity to influence the development of ICT education. But first, librarians must themselves understand the changes wrought by ICTs and shape them into a force that promotes the core values of librarianship. Those core values continue to be important. Principals, legislators, students, teachers, and anyone who has an opinion on the subject have been known to pose the question: "Why do we need a library or a librarian when we have the Internet?" We all have our "elevator speeches" for responding to this question: "The Internet is like a library with all its books dumped on the floor." "Librarians are still needed because 'everything' is not on the Internet and because librarians are trained to find the most appropriate information, regardless of format." And so on. Stephen Abram (2008) tells the story of being sick and scaring himself silly after searching the Web and databases like Medline to learn about his illness and treatment options. He could not rest easily until consulting his local consumer health information professional, who provided him with the appropriate amount and kind of information that suited his level of information literacy in that domain. Here is his answer to why we continue to need librarians:

> Although it might change, at this point search engines and electronic information do a very poor job of sensing the end user's specific context. Google cannot tell the difference between a youngster in ninth grade searching STDs for his health project and a worried adult needing a support group. It's just a big stupid empty search box. Personal service easily senses the difference. The lesson: information has context and so do end users. (Abram 2008, 33)

Librarians do much more than just help people find information. We teach, we bring the magic of discovery to small (and large) children, we help people connect to one another, and we provide a sense of place in our facilities. Today, librarians have the power to make the merger of information and communication technologies work for people in ways that are humane and enriching. Teenagers are our partners in this endeavor. They are the innovators whose imaginations we must value. We will not succeed without their vision and energy, and they will not become library users without our skill and passion. It's a marriage made in heaven.

REFERENCES

Abbas, June. 2005. Out of the mouths of middle school children: I. Developing user-defined controlled vocabularies for subject access in a digital library. *Journal of the American Society for Information Science and Technology* 56 (14): 1512–24.

Abram, Stephen. 2008. Finding our voices in an Internet world. *Information Outlook* 12 (12): 32–33.

Abram, Stephen, and Judy Luther. 2004. Born with the chip. *Library Journal* 129 (8): 34–37.

Adams, Helen R. 2008. *Ensuring intellectual freedom and access to information in the school library media program.* Westport, Conn.: Libraries Unlimited.

Agosto, Denise E. 2002. Bounded rationality and satisficing in young people's web-based decision making. *Journal of the American Society for Information Science* 53 (1): 16–27.

Aho, James A. 1990. *The politics of righteousness: Idaho Christian patriotism.* Seattle: University of Washington Press.

American Association of School Librarians. 2007. *Standards for the 21st century learner.* Chicago: American Library Association.

American Library Association. Library Bill of Rights. www.ala.org/ala/ issuesadvocacy/intfreedom/librarybill.

———. Minors and Internet Interactivity: An Interpretation of the Library Bill of Rights. www.ala.org/ala/issuesadvocacy/intfreedom/librarybill/ interpretations/minorsinternetinteractivity.cfm.

Anderson, James D., and Melissa A. Hofmann. 2006. A fully faceted syntax for Library of Congress Subject Headings. *Cataloging and Classification Quarterly* 43 (1): 7–32.

Association for Library Collections and Technical Services. 2003. Final report of the Subcommittee on Subject Reference Structures in Automated Systems. www.ala.org/ala/mgrps/divs/alcts/mgrps/ccs/cmtes/sac/inact/subjref/ RefStructuresFinal.doc.

———. n.d. SAC Task Force on Library of Congress Subject Heading Revisions Relating to the Poor People's Policy. Report on proposed headings. www .ala.org/ala/mgrps/divs/alcts/mgrps/ccs/cmtes/sac/lctf/ppp.pdf.

Aulls, Mark W., and Bruce M. Shore. 2008. *Inquiry in education, volume 1: The conceptual foundations for research as a curricular imperative.* New York: Lawrence Erlbaum Associates.

Bailey, Gerald, and Mike Ribble. 2007. *Digital citizenship in schools.* Eugene, OR: International Society for Technology in Education.

BBC News. 2007. Call for blogging code of conduct, 28 March. http://news.bbc .co.uk/2/hi/technology/6502643.stm.

Bennett, Jessica. 2008. The flip side of Internet fame: In an age of Google and YouTube, public shaming can turn anyone into a celebrity—or a fool. *Newsweek* (International edition) 151 (9) n.p.

Berkman Center for Internet and Society. 2008. *Enhancing child safety and online technologies: Final report of the Internet Safety Technical Task Force.* Cambridge, MA: Harvard University.

Berman, Sanford. 1984. C'mon guys, lighten up! *Technicalities* 4 (12): 9. Also published in Berman, Sanford. 1988. *Worth noting: Editorials, letters, essays, an interview, and bibliography.* Jefferson, NC: McFarland.

———. 1987. The terrible truth about teenlit cataloging. *Top of the News* 43 (3): 311–20. Also published in Berman, Sanford. 1988. *Worth noting: Editorials, letters, essays, an interview, and bibliography.* Jefferson, NC: McFarland.

———. 1993. *Prejudices and antipathies: A tract on the LC subject heads concerning people.* Jefferson, NC: McFarland.

Blood, Rebecca. 2002. *The Weblog handbook: Practical advice on creating and maintaining your blog.* Cambridge, MA: Perseus.

Bolan, Kimberly. 2009. *Teen spaces: The step-by-step library makeover.* 2nd edition. Chicago: American Library Association.

Borgman, Christine L., et al. 1995. Children's searching behavior on browsing and keyword online catalogs: The Science Library Catalog Project. *Journal of the American Society for Information Science* 46 (9): 663–84.

boyd, danah. 2008a. Taken out of context: American teen sociality in networked publics. PhD diss., University of California–Berkeley, School of Information. www.danah.org/papers/TakenOutOfContext.pdf.

———. 2008b. Why youth heart social network sites: The role of networked publics in teenage social life. In *Youth, identity, and digital media,* ed. David Buckingham. Cambridge, MA: MIT Press, 119–42.

———. 2009. When teachers and students connect outside school. *Apophenia* (blog). 27 May. www.zephoria.org/thoughts/archives/2009/05/27/when_teachers_a.html.

boyd, danah, and Nicole Ellison. 2007. Social network sites: Definition, history, and scholarship. *Journal of Computer-Mediated Communication* 13 (1), article 11. http://jcmc.indiana.edu/vol13/issue1/boyd.ellison.html.

Branch, Jennifer. 2002. Helping students become better electronic searchers. *Teacher Librarian* 30 (1): 14–18.

Braun, Linda W. 2004. Multitasking in the library. *Voice of Youth Advocates* 27 (2): 111.

———. 2007. *Teens, technology, and literacy; or, Why bad grammar isn't always bad.* Westport, CT: Libraries Unlimited.

Bruce, Harry. 2002. *The user's view of the Internet.* Lanham, MD: Scarecrow.

Budd, John. 1996. The complexity of information retrieval: A hypothetical example. *Journal of Academic Librarianship* 22 (March): 111–17.

Burek Pierce, Jennifer. 2007. Research directions for understanding and responding to young adult sexual and reproductive health information needs. In *Youth information-seeking behavior II,* ed. Mary K. Chelton and Colleen Cool. Lanham, MD: Scarecrow Press, 63–91.

———. 2008. *Sex, brains, and video games: A librarian's guide to teens in the twenty-first century.* Chicago: American Library Association.

Busey, Paula, and Tom Doerr. 1993. Kid's Catalog: An information retrieval system for children. *Journal of Youth Services in Libraries* 7 (1): 77–84.

Callahan, David. 2004. *The cheating culture: Why more Americans are doing wrong to get ahead.* Orlando, FL: Harcourt.

Case, Donald O. 2002. *Looking for information: A survey of research on information seeking, needs, and behavior.* San Diego: Academic Press.

Center for Social Media. 2008. Recut, reframe, recycle: Quoting copyrighted material in user-generated video. Washington, DC: American University. www.centerforsocialmedia.org/sites/default/files/CSM_Recut_Reframe_Recycle_report.pdf

Chelton, Mary K. 1999. Behavior of librarians in school and public libraries with adolescents: Implications for practice and LIS education. *Journal of Education in Library and Information Science* 40 (2): 99–111.

———. 2001. Young adults as problems: How the social construction of a marginalized user category occurs. *Journal of Education in Library and Information Science* 42 (1): 4–11.

———. 2002. The "problem patron" public libraries created. *Reference Librarian* nos. 75–76: 23–32.

Christenbury, Leila. 2009. It's not as simple as it seems: Doing honest academic work in an age of point and click. *Knowledge Quest* 37 (3): 16–23.

The Christian Century. 2003. Teens break no-sex vows, study suggests: Some say oral sex not sex, 27 December, 14.

Cochrane, Pauline A. 1986. *Improving LCSH for use in online catalogs.* Littleton, CO: Libraries Unlimited.

Collier, Anne. 2009. Why technopanics are bad. *NetFamilyNews.org,* 23 April. www.netfamilynews.org/2009/04/why-technopanics-are-bad.html.

Cox Communications, in partnership with the National Center for Missing and Exploited Children. 2009. *Teen online and wireless safety survey: Cyberbullying, sexting, and parental controls.* Atlanta: Cox Communications.

Cutter, Charles A. 1876. Library catalogues. In *Public libraries in the United States of America: Their history, condition, and management.* Special report, Department of the Interior, Bureau of Education. Part 1. Washington, DC: U.S. Government Printing Office, 526–622.

Daniels, Jessie. 2008. Race, civil rights, and hate speech in the digital era. In *Learning, race and ethnicity: Youth and digital media,* ed. Anna Everett. John D. and Catherine T. MacArthur Foundation Series on Digital Media and Learning. Cambridge, MA: MIT Press, 129–54.

Dervin, Brenda. 1976. Strategies for dealing with human information needs: Information or communication? *Journal of Broadcasting* 20 (3): 324–33.

Dewey, John. 1902. *The child and the curriculum.* Chicago: University of Chicago Press.

———. 1915. *The school and society.* Chicago: University of Chicago Press.

Dewey, Melvil. 1876. Catalogues and cataloguing, Part 1. In *Public libraries in the United States of America: Their history, condition, and management.* Special report, Department of the Interior, Bureau of Education. Part 1. Washington, DC: U.S. Government Printing Office, 623–48.

Dickerson, Chad. 2004. When games are more than child's play. *InfoWorld,* 16 January. www.infoworld.com/d/developer-world/when-games-are-more-childs-play-117.

Drabenstott, Karen M., Schelle Simcox, and Eileen G. Fenton. 1999. End-user understanding of subject headings in library catalogs. *Library Resources and Technical Services* 43 (3): 140–60.

Dresang, Eliza T. 1999. More research needed: Informal information-seeking behavior of youth on the Internet. *Journal of the American Society for Information Science* 50 (12): 1123–24.

———. 2005. The information-seeking behavior of youth in a digital environment. *Library Trends* 54 (2): 178–96.

Durkheim, Émile. 1925/1961. *Moral educations.* New York: Free Press.

Eastin, Matthew S. 2008. Toward a cognitive developmental approach to youth perceptions of credibility. In *Digital media, youth, and credibility,* ed. Miriam J. Metzger and Andrew J. Flanagin. John D. and Catherine T. MacArthur Foundation Series on Digital Media and Learning. Cambridge, MA: MIT Press, 29–47.

Economist. 2008. And the winners were . . . 6 December, 13.

Educational Testing Service. 2006. *ICT literacy assessment: Preliminary findings.* www.ets.org/Media/Products/ICT_Literacy/pdf/2006_Preliminary_Findings.pdf.

Essex, Don. 2009. From deleting online predators to educating Internet users: Congress and Internet safety; A legislative analysis. *Young Adult Library Services* 7 (3): 36–45.

Estabrook, Leigh, Evans Witt, and Lee Rainie. 2007. Information searches that solve problems. Pew Internet and American Life Project. www.pewinternet.org/Reports/2007/Information-Searches-That-Solve-Problems.aspx.

Fidel, Raya, et al. 1999. A visit to the information mall: Web searching behavior of high school students. *Journal of the American Society for Information Science* 50 (1): 24–37.

Fisher, Karen E., Elizabeth Marcoux, Eric Meyers, and Carol F. Landry. 2007. Tweens and everyday life information behavior: Preliminary findings from Seattle. In *Youth information-seeking behavior II,* ed. Mary K. Chelton and Colleen Cool. Lanham, MD: Scarecrow Press, 1–25.

Flanagin, Andrew J., and Miriam J. Metzger. 2007. The role of site features, user attributes, and information verification behaviors on the perceived credibility of web-based information. *New Media and Society* 9 (2): 319–42.

———. 2008. Digital media and youth: Unparalleled opportunity and unprecedented responsibility. In *Digital media, youth, and credibility,* ed. Miriam J. Metzger and Andrew J. Flanagin. John D. and Catherine T. MacArthur Foundation Series on Digital Media and Learning. Cambridge, MA: MIT Press, 5–27.

Foehr, Ulla G. 2006. *Media multitasking among American youth: Prevalence, predictors, and pairings.* Menlo Park, CA: Henry J. Kaiser Family Foundation.

Fogg, B. J., Cathy Soohoo, David R. Danielson, Leslie Marable, Julianne Stanford, and Ellen R. Tauber. 2003. How do users evaluate the credibility of web sites? A study with over 2,500 participants. *Proceedings of the 2003 conference on Designing for User Experiences.* New York: Association for Computing Machinery, 1–15.

Gee, James Paul. 2008. Learning and games. In *The ecology of games: Connecting youth, games, and learning,* ed. Katie Salen. John D. and Catherine T. MacArthur Foundation Series on Digital Media and Learning. Cambridge, MA: MIT Press, 21–40.

Girl Scout Research Institute. 2002. *The net effect: Girls and the new media.* Executive summary. New York: Girl Scouts of the USA.

Goodstein, Anastasia. 2007. *Totally wired: What teens and tweens are really doing online.* New York: St. Martin's.

Gorman, Michele. 2002. Wiring teens to the library. *Library Journal NetConnect,* Summer, 18–20.

Grinter, Rebecca E., and Leysia Palen. 2002. Instant messaging in teen life. In *Proceedings of the ACM Conference on Computer Supported Cooperative Work,* New Orleans, LA.

Gross, Melissa. 2006. *Studying children's questions: Imposed and self-generated information seeking at school.* Lanham, MD: Scarecrow Press.

Hagerty, Barbara Bradley. 2004. Teen-age Wiccans. *All Things Considered.* National Public Radio, 13 May.

Hamelink, Cees J. 2000. *The ethics of cyberspace.* London: Sage.

Hamilton, Buffy. 2009. Transforming information literacy for nowgen students. *Knowledge Quest* 37 (5): 48–53.

Hargittai, Eszter. 2007. Whose space? Differences among users and non-users of social network sites. *Journal of Computer-Mediated Communication* 13 (1), article 14. http://jcmc.indiana.edu/vol13/issue1/hargittai.html.

Harris, Frances Jacobson. 2008. Challenges to teaching credibility assessment in contemporary schooling. In *Digital media, youth, and credibility,* ed. Miriam J. Metzger and Andrew J. Flanagin. John D. and Catherine T. MacArthur Foundation Series on Digital Media and Learning. Cambridge, MA: MIT Press, 155–79.

———. 2009. Challenges to teaching evaluation of online information: A view from LM_NET. *School Library Media Research,* 12. www.ala.org/ala/mgrps/divs/aasl/aaslpubsandjournals/slmrb/slmrcontents/volume12/harris.cfm.

Harris Interactive and Teenage Research Unlimited. 2003. Born to be wired: The role of new media for a digital generation. Study commissioned by Yahoo! and Carat Interactive. http://docs.yahoo.com/docs/pr/release1107.html.

Hirsh, Sandra G. 1999. Children's relevance criteria and information seeking on electronic resources. *Journal of the American Society for Information Science* 50 (14): 1265–83.

Holson, Laura M. 2008. Text generation gap: U R 2 Old (JK). *New York Times,* 9 March, BU01.

Holthouse, David. 2009. The year in hate, 2008. *Intelligence Report,* no. 133 (Spring). www.splcenter.org/intel/intelreport/article.jsp?aid=1027.

Holtzman, Alexander. 2009. Original misunderstanding. *Knowledge Quest* 37 (3): 62–64.

How to use the Readers' Guide. 1987. Directed by Richard S. Blofson. 18 min. Produced by Visual Education for the H. W. Wilson Company. Videocassette.

Hughes-Hassell, Sandra, and Denise E. Agosto. 2007. Modeling the everyday life information needs of urban teenagers. In *Youth information-seeking behavior II,* ed. Mary K. Chelton and Colleen Cool. Lanham, MD: Scarecrow Press, 27–61.

Hunt, Karen. 2006. Faceted browsing: Breaking the tyranny of keyword searching. *Feliciter* 52 (1): 36–37.

International Society for Technology in Education. 2007. *National Educational Technology Standards and Performance Indicators for Students.* Eugene, OR: ISTE.

Ito, Mizuko, et al. 2009. *Living and learning with new media: Summary of findings from the Digital Youth Project.* Cambridge, MA: MIT Press. http://mitpress.mit.edu/books/chapters/Living_and_Learning.pdf.

————. 2010. *Hanging out, messing around, and geeking out: Kids living and learning with new media.* Cambridge, MA: MIT Press.

James, Carrie. 2009. *Young people, ethics, and the new digital media: Summary of findings from the Good Play Project.* Cambridge, MA: MIT Press.

Jin, Qiang. 2008. Is FAST the right direction for a new system of subject cataloging and metadata? *Cataloging and Classification Quarterly* 45 (3): 91–110.

Johnson, Doug. 2003. *Learning right from wrong in the digital age: An ethics guide for parents, teachers, librarians, and others who care about computer-using young people.* Worthington, OH: Linworth.

Joinson, Adam N. 2003. *Understanding the psychology of Internet behaviour: Virtual worlds, real lives.* Basingstoke, UK: Palgrave Macmillan.

Jones, Steve. 2002. The Internet goes to college: How students are living in the future with today's technology. Pew Internet and American Life Project. www.pewinternet.org/Reports/2002/The-Internet-Goes-to-College.aspx.

Jones, Sydney, and Susanna Fox. 2009. Generations online in 2009. Pew Internet and American Life Project. http://pewinternet.org/Reports/2009/Generations-Online-in-2009.aspx.

Kakutani, Michiko. 2008. The most trusted man in America? *New York Times,* 17 August, AR1.

Kanalley, Craig. 2009. How to verify a tweet. *Twitter Journalism* (blog). 25 June. www.twitterjournalism.com/2009/06/25/how-to-verify-a-tweet.

Kanof, Marjorie. 2003. *Youth illicit drug use prevention: DARE long-term evaluations and federal efforts to identify effective programs.* Washington, DC: General Accounting Office. Also available at www.gao.gov/new.items/d03172r.pdf.

Keen, Andrew. 2007. *The cult of the amateur.* New York: Doubleday.

Kelley, Tina. 2007. Lock the library! Rowdy students are taking over. *New York Times,* 2 January, A01.

Kohlberg, Lawrence. 1958. The development of modes of moral thinking and choice in the years ten to sixteen. PhD diss., University of Chicago.

————. 1984. *The psychology of moral development: The nature and validity of moral stages.* Vol. 2, *Essays on moral development.* San Francisco: Harper and Row.

Krebs, Brian. 2005. Sony's fix for CDs has security problems of its own. *Washington Post,* 17 November, D01.

Kuhlthau, Carol C. 1997. Learning in digital libraries: An information search process. *Library Trends* 45 (4): 708–24.

———. 2004. *Seeking meaning: A process approach to library and information services.* 2nd ed. Westport, CT: Libraries Unlimited.

Landau, Elaine. 1986. *Different drummer: Homosexuality in America.* New York: Messner.

Lankes, R. David. 2008. Trusting the Internet: New approaches to credibility tools. In *Digital media, youth, and credibility,* ed. Miriam J. Metzger and Andrew J. Flanagin. John D. and Catherine T. MacArthur Foundation Series on Digital Media and Learning. Cambridge, MA: MIT Press, 101–21.

Leadership Conference on Civil Rights Education Fund. 2009. *Confronting the new faces of hate: Hate crimes in America 2009.* www.civilrights.org/publications/hatecrimes.

Leinwand, Donna. 2009. Survey: 1 in 5 teens "sext" despite risks. *USA Today,* 25 June, 3A. www.usatoday.com/tech/news/2009-06-23-onlinekids_N.htm.

Lenhart, Amanda L. 2007. Cyberbullying. Pew Internet and American Life Project. www.pewinternet.org/Reports/2007/Cyberbullying.aspx.

———. 2009. Teens and social media: An overview. Pew Internet and American Life Project. www.pewinternet.org/Presentations/2009/17-Teens-and-Social-Media-An-Overview.aspx.

Lenhart, Amanda L., and Mary Madden. 2007. Teens, privacy, and online social networks. Pew Internet and American Life Project. www.pewinternet.org/Reports/2007/Teens-Privacy-and-Online-Social-Networks.aspx.

Lenhart, Amanda L., Joseph Kahne, Ellen Middaugh, Alexandra Rankin Macgill, Chris Evans, and Jessica Vitak. 2008. Teens, video games, and civics. Pew Internet and American Life Project. www.pewinternet.org/Reports/2008/Teens-Video-Games-and-Civics.aspx.

Lenhart, Amanda L., Lee Rainie, and Oliver Lewis. 2001. Teenage life online: The rise of the instant-message generation and the Internet's impact on friendships and family relationships. Pew Internet and American Life Project. www.pewinternet.org/Reports/2001/Teenage-Life-Online.aspx.

Lenhart, Amanda L., Mary Madden, Aaron Smith, and Alexandra Rankin Macgill. 2007. Teens and social media. Pew Internet and American Life Project. www.pewinternet.org/Reports/2007/Teens-and-Social-Media.aspx.

Levine, Jenny. 2002. What is a shifted librarian? *The Shifted Librarian,* January 19. http://theshiftedlibrarian.com/stories/2002/01/19/whatIsAShiftedLibrarian.html.

Levy, David M. 2001. *Scrolling forward: Making sense of documents in the digital age.* New York: Arcade.

Levy, Steven. 2003. A geek bill of rights. *Newsweek,* 8 September, E30.

Lewis, Cynthia, and Bettina Fabos. 2000. But will it work in the heartland? A response and illustration. *Journal of Adolescent and Adult Literacy* 43 (5): 462–69.

———. 2005. Instant messaging, literacies, and social identities. *Reading Research Quarterly* 40 (4): 470–501.

Lih, Andrew. 2009. *The Wikipedia revolution: How a bunch of nobodies created the world's greatest encyclopedia.* New York: Hyperion.

Loertscher, David V., and Blanche Woolls. 2002. Teenage users of libraries: A brief overview of the research. *Knowledge Quest* 30 (5): 31–36.

Luke, Allan. 2003. Foreword to *Literacy in the information age: Inquiries into meaning making with new technologies,* ed. Bertram C. Bruce. Newark, DE: International Reading Association, viii–xi.

Macgill, Alexandra Rankin. 2007. Parent and teen Internet use. Pew Internet and American Life Project. www.pewinternet.org/Reports/2007/Parent-and -Teen-Internet-Use.aspx.

Madden, Mary. 2009. The state of music online: Ten years after Napster. Pew Internet and American Life Project. http://pewinternet.org/Reports/2009/ 9-The-State-of-Music-Online-Ten-Years-After-Napster.aspx.

Madden, Mary, and Lee Rainie. 2005. Music and video downloading moves beyond P2P. Pew Internet and American Life Project. www.pewinternet .org/Reports/2005/Music-and-Video-Downloading.aspx.

Magid, Larry. 2009a. Survey shows teens more safety savvy than thought. *LarrysWorld.com,* 24 June. www.pcanswer.com/2009/06/24/survey-shows -teens-more-safety-savvy-than-thought.

———. 2009b. Teen online safety mostly about behavior. *LarrysWorld.com,* 16 June. www.safeteens.com/2009/06/16/teen-online-safety-mostly-about -behavior.

Mann, Thomas. 2003. Why LC subject headings are more important than ever. *American Libraries* 34 (9): 52–54.

Marwick, Alice E. 2008. To catch a predator? The MySpace moral panic. *First Monday,* 2 June, 13 (6). www.uic.edu/htbin/cgiwrap/bin/ojs/index.php/ fm/article/view/2152/1966.

McQuade, Samuel C. 2008. *Survey of Internet and at-risk behaviors (undertaken by school districts of Monroe County New York).* Rochester, NY: Cyber Safety and Ethics Initiative. www.rrcsei.org/RIT%20Cyber%20Survey%20Final%20 Report.pdf.

Media Awareness Network. n.d. Deconstructing hate sites. www.media -awareness.ca/english/issues/online_hate/deconst_online_hate.cfm.

Mehra, Bharat, and Donna Braquet. 2007. Process of information seeking during "queer" youth coming-out experiences. In *Youth information-seeking behavior II,* ed. Mary K. Chelton and Colleen Cool. Lanham, MD: Scarecrow Press, 93–131.

Meola, Marc. 2004. Chucking the checklist: A contextual approach to teaching undergraduates website evaluation. *portal: Libraries and the Academy* 4 (3): 331–44.

Metzger, Miriam. 2007. Making sense of credibility on the Web: Models for evaluating online information and recommendations for future research. *Journal of the American Society for Information Science and Technology* 58 (13): 2078–91.

Miller-Cochran, Susan, and Rochelle Rodrigo. 2008. Use Wikipedia and YouTube in research! Debunking the library vs. Internet research dichotomy. Paper presented at Rock the Academy: Radical Teaching, Unbounded Learning. New Media Consortium 2008 Fall Virtual Conference.

Mitchell, Kimberly J., and Michelle Ybarra. 2009. Social networking sites: Finding a balance between their risks and their benefits. *Archives of Pediatric and Adolescent Medicine* 163 (1): 87–89.

MLA Handbook for Writers of Research Papers, 2nd ed. 2009. New York: Modern Language Association.

Moore, Penelope A., and Alison St. George. 1991. Children as information seekers: The cognitive demands of books and library systems. *School Library Media Quarterly* 19 (3): 161–68.

Moreno, Megan A., Malcolm R. Parks, Frederick J. Zimmerman, Tara E. Brito, and Dimitri A. Christakis. 2009a. Display of health risk behaviors on MySpace by adolescents. *Archives of Pediatric and Adolescent Medicine* 163 (1): 27–34.

Moreno, Megan A., Ann VanderStoep, Malcolm R. Parks, Frederick J. Zimmerman, Ann Kurth, and Dimitri A. Christakis. 2009b. Reducing at-risk adolescents' display of risk behavior on a social networking web site. *Archives of Pediatric and Adolescent Medicine* 163 (1): 35–41.

Nardi, Bonnie A., and Vicki L. O'Day. 1999. *Information ecologies: Using technology with heart.* Cambridge, MA: MIT Press.

National School Boards Association. 2007. Creating and connecting: Research and guidelines on online social—and educational—networking. Alexandria, VA: NSBA. www.nsba.org/site/docs/41400/41340.pdf.

Neuman, Delia. 2003. Research in school library media for the next decade: Polishing the diamond. *Library Trends* 51 (4): 503–24.

November, Alan C. 1998. Teaching students to fish: Proper use of the Net. *High School Magazine* 6 (1): 22–24.

NPD Group. 2009. Always a bellwether for the music industry, teens are changing how they interact with music. www.npd.com/press/releases/press_090331a.html.

Nussbaum, Emily. 2004. My so-called blog. *New York Times,* 11 January, 33.

O'Connor, Maureen. 2008. Make it new: Queens Library for teens. *School Library Journal* 54 (7): 38–39.

Oder, Norman. 2007. Dropping Dewey in Maricopa. *Library Journal* 132 (12): 14.

———. 2008. BiblioCommons emerges: "Revolutionary"; Social discovery system for libraries. *Library Journal.* www.libraryjournal.com/article/CA6579748.html.

Oei, Ting-Yi. 2009. My students. My cellphone. My ordeal. *Washington Post,* 19 April, B01.

Olson, Tod A. 2007. Utility of a faceted catalog for scholarly research. *Library Hi Tech* 25 (4): 550–61.

Palfrey, John, and Urs Gasser. 2008. *Born digital: Understanding the first generation of digital natives.* New York: Basic Books.

Pew Internet and American Life Project. 2009. Daily Internet activities, 2000–2009. http://pewinternet.org/Static-Pages/Trend-Data/Daily-Internet-Activities-20002009.aspx.

Piaget, Jean. 1932. *The moral judgment of the child.* New York: Free Press.

Pressler, Margaret Webb. 2007. For texting teens, an OMG moment when the phone bill arrives. *Washington Post,* 20 May, A01.

Propaganda Analysis. 1937. How to detect propaganda. 1 (2): 1–4.

Propaganda: How to recognize it and deal with it. Experimental unit of study materials in propaganda analysis for use in junior and senior high schools. 1938. New York: Institute for Propaganda Analysis.

Quintarelli, Emanuele, Andrea Resmini, and Luca Rosati. 2007. FaceTag: Integrating bottom-up and top-down classification in a social tagging system. *Bulletin of the American Society for Information Science and Technology* 33 (5): 10–15.

Raaijmakers, Jeroen, and Richard M. Schiffrin. 1992. Models for recall and recognition. In *Annual Review of Psychology,* 43. Palo Alto, CA: Annual Reviews, 205–34.

Rawlinson, Nora. 1981. Give 'em what they want! *Library Journal* 106 (20): 2188–90.

Rheingold, Howard. 2009. Crap detection 101. *City Brights* (blog). SFGate. *San Francisco Chronicle,* 30 June. www.sfgate.com/cgi-bin/blogs/rheingold/detail?entry_id=42805.

Rich, Motoko. 2009. In web age, library job gets update. *New York Times,* 16 February, A1.

Rosenbaum, Janet Elise. 2009. Patient teenagers? A comparison of the sexual behavior of virginity pledgers and matched nonpledgers. *Pediatrics* 123 (1): e110–e120.

Rowlands, Ian, David Nicholas, Peter Williams, Paul Huntington, Maggie Fieldhouse, Barrie Gunter, Richard Withey, Hamid R. Jamali, Tom Dobrowolski, and Carol Tenopir. 2008. The Google generation: The information behaviour of the researcher of the future. *Aslib Proceedings: New Information Perspectives* 60 (4): 290–310.

Savolainen, Reijo. 1995. Everyday life information seeking: Approaching information seeking in the context of "way of life." *Library and Information Science Research* 17 (3): 259–94.

Search Institute. 1997, 2007. 40 developmental assets for adolescents. www.search-institute.org/content/40-developmental-assets-adolescents-ages-12-18.

Seigenthaler, John. 2005. A false Wikipedia "biography." *USA Today,* 30 November, 11A.

Shell, Lambert. 2008. Flipping it: How Queens Library is turning "gangs" of teens into its biggest success story. *Voice of Youth Advocates* 31 (2): 116–17.

Shirky, Clay. 2002. Broadcast institutions, community values. *Clay Shirky's Writings about the Internet* (blog). 9 September. www.shirky.com/writings/broadcast_and_community.html.

Simmons, Rachel. 2002. *Odd girl out: The hidden culture of aggression in girls.* Orlando, FL: Harcourt.

———. 2003. Cliques, clicks, bullies and blogs. *Washington Post,* 28 September, B01.

Simon, Herbert A. 1979. *Models of thought.* New Haven, CT: Yale University Press.

Sivin, Jay P., and Ellen R. Bialo. 1992. *Ethical use of information technologies in education: Important issues for America's schools.* Washington, DC: National Institute of Justice, U.S. Department of Justice.

Solomon, Paul. 1993. Children's information retrieval behavior: A case analysis of an OPAC. *Journal of the American Society for Information Science* 44 (5): 245–64.

———. 1994. Children, technology, and instruction: A case study of elementary school children using an online public access catalog (OPAC). *School Library Media Quarterly* 23 (1): 43–51.

Spalding, Tim. 2008. Build the Open Shelves Classification. *Thing-ology Blog.* 8 July. www.librarything.com/thingology/2008/07/build-open-shelves -classification.php.

Spink, Amanda, and Charles Cole. 2001. Introduction to the special issue: Everyday life information-seeking research. *Library and Information Science Research* 23 (4): 301–4.

St. George, Donna. 2009. Sending of explicit photos can land teens in legal fix. *Washington Post,* 7 May, A01.

Steinberg, Laurence. 2007. Risk taking in adolescence: New perspectives from brain and behavioral science. *Current Directions in Psychological Science* 16 (2): 55–59.

Stripling, Barbara K. 2003. Inquiry-based learning. In *Curriculum connections through the library,* ed. Barbara K. Stripling and Sandra Hughes-Hassell. Westport, CT: Libraries Unlimited, 3–39.

Subrahmanyam, Kaveri, Patricia M. Greenfield, Robert Kraut, and Elisheva Gross. 2002. The impact of computer use on children's and adolescents' development. In *Children in the digital age: Influences of electronic media on development.* Westport, CT: Praeger, 3–33. Also published in *Applied Developmental Psychology* 22 (1): 7–30.

Sydell, Laura. 2009. Iranians still connect to social-networking sites. *Morning Edition.* National Public Radio, 18 June.

Tedeschi, Bob. 2008. How to give your child an allowance, the mobile way. *New York Times,* 31 July, C05.

Temple-Rastin, Dina. 2008. Experts aim to explain hike in L.A. hate crimes. *All Things Considered.* National Public Radio, 24 November.

Vaidhyanathan, Siva. 2008. Generational myth: Not all young people are tech-savvy. *Chronicle of Higher Education,* 19 September, B7.

Valenza, Joyce Kasman. 2006. They might be gurus: Teen information-seeking behavior. *Voice of Youth Advocates* 29 (1): eVOYA feature. www.voya.com.

Van Buren, Cassandra. 2001. Teaching hackers: School computing culture and the future of cyber-rights. *Journal of Information Ethics* 10 (1): 51–72.

Van Der Hoven, Jeroen. 2000. The Internet and varieties of moral wrongdoing. In *Internet Ethics,* ed. Duncan Langford. New York: St. Martin's, 127–57.

Viadero, Debra. 2008. Project probes digital media's effect on ethics: Howard Gardner leads team studying youths' web norms. *Education Week,* 19 November, 1, 12.

Wallace, Carol M. 1983. *Should you shut your eyes when you kiss? or, How to survive "The best years of your life."* Boston: Little, Brown.

Walter, Virginia A. 2003. Public library service to children and teens: A research agenda. *Library Trends* 51 (4): 571–89.

Walter, Virginia A., and Christine L. Borgman. 1991. The Science Library Catalog: A prototype information retrieval system for children. *Journal of Youth Services in Libraries* 4 (2): 159–66.

Walter, Virginia A., and Elaine Meyers. 2003. *Teens and libraries: Getting it right.* Chicago: American Library Association.

Wang, Qingshuo. 2003. Beware of the blog: The possibilities of journalism of the masses. *Voice of Youth Advocates* 26 (1): 28.

Wayne, Teddy. 2009. Drilling down: Social networks eclipse e-mail. *New York Times,* 18 May, B3.

Weis, June Pullen. 2004. Contemporary literacy skills: Global initiatives converge. *Knowledge Quest* 32 (4): 12–15.

West, Steven L., and Keri K. O'Neal. 2004. Project D.A.R.E. outcome effectiveness revisited. *American Journal of Public Health* 94 (6): 1027–29.

Willard, Nancy E. 1998. Moral development in the information age. In *Proceedings of the Families, Technology, and Education Conference, Chicago.* Also available as ERIC document ED 425 016.

———. 2007. *Cyber-safe kids, cyber-savvy teens: Helping young people learn to use the Internet safely and responsibly.* San Francisco: Jossey-Bass.

Williams, Robin. 1990. *The Mac is not a typewriter.* Berkeley, CA: Peachpit.

Wolak, Janis, David Finkelhor, Kimberly J. Mitchell, and Michelle L. Ybarra. 2008. Online "predators" and their victims: Myths, realities, and implications for prevention and treatment. *American Psychologist* 63 (2): 111–28.

Wolak, Janis, Kimberly J. Mitchell, and David Finkelhor. 2007. Unwanted and wanted exposure to online pornography in a national sample of youth Internet users. *Pediatrics* 119 (2): 247–57.

Wolfson, Paula E., and Lloyd Wolf. 2000. *Jewish mothers: Strength, wisdom, and compassion.* San Francisco: Chronicle Books.

Yancey, Kathleen Blake. 2009. *Writing in the 21st century: A report from the National Council of Teachers of English.* Urbana, Ill.: National Council of Teachers of English.

Yao, Deborah. 2009. FTC plans to monitor blogs for claims, payments. Associated Press Online. 21 June.

Young Adult Library Services Association. 2009. Teens and social networking in school and public libraries: A toolkit for librarians and library workers. Chicago: American Library Association. www.ala.org/ala/mgrps/divs/yalsa/profdev/socialnetworkingtool.pdf.

INDEX

You may also be interested in

Young Adults Deserve the Best: The first book to thoroughly expand on YALSA's "Young Adults Deserve the Best: Competencies for Librarians Serving Youth," this useful resource includes anecdotes and success stories from the field, guidelines which can be used to create evaluation instruments, determine staffing needs, and develop job descriptions, and additional professional resources following each chapter that will help librarians turn theory into practice.

Young Adult Literature: From Romance to Realism: This survey helps YA librarians who want to freshen up their readers' advisory skills, teachers who use novels in the classroom, and adult services librarians who increasingly find themselves addressing the queries of teen patrons by covering the reading habits of today's teens, influence of new technologies and formats, and new YA lit awards.

Urban Teens in the Library: Research and Practice: From a team of experts who have researched the information habits and preferences of urban teens to build better and more effective school and public library programs, this book will show readers the importance of moving beyond stereotypes and revamping library services, the value of street lit and social networking, and how a library website can meet the information needs of teens.

A Year of Programs for Teens 2: This volume offers several new themed book lists and read-alikes as well as appendices with reproducible handouts for the various programs. Also included is a section of introductory material that includes general programming advice, information on teen clubs, and marketing ideas, and more than 30 programs cleverly organized around a calendar year, including several that focus on technology, with many other ideas that can adapted year-round as needed.

Order today at www.alastore.ala.org or 866-746-7252!

ALA Store purchases fund advocacy, awareness, and accreditation programs for library professionals worldwide.